KING GEORGE V

JOHN GORE, C.V.O.

KING GEORGE V

A Personal Memoir

PUBLISHED BY AUTHORITY OF
HIS MAJESTY THE KING

JOHN MURRAY
ALBEMARLE STREET, LONDON

FIRST EDITION . . . *March* 1941
REPRINTED . . . *April* 1941
ALBEMARLE LIBRARY . . . 1949

Awarded James Tait Black
Memorial Prize
1941

PRINTED AND BOUND IN ENGLAND BY
HAZELL WATSON & VINEY Ltd
AYLESBURY AND LONDON

CONTENTS

v

CONTENTS

ILLUSTRATIONS

Between pages 2 and 3

PREFACE

THIS memoir of King George V was undertaken at the request of Their Majesties, the King and Queen Mary. Its scope was clearly defined. It was to be a personal memoir and not a study of the official aspects of the reign. His Majesty realised that some years must still elapse before the fires of political controversy, which rose high in his father's day, can be expected to die down and the confusing smoke to clear off. It is still too early to consider with a calm and right judgment the events of that tremendous and troubled epoch, or to set each in its place in history in just proportion and right relation to the whole. At the same time His Majesty realised that, with the passing of the years, much useful evidence and valuable sidelights on the late King's character might be lost beyond recall, if efforts were not soon made to collect some of the memories and impressions of his family and intimate friends and of others who served King George V, or were in close contact with him, in various spheres of his activity. In deciding to authorise the writing of a character-study His Majesty had these considerations in mind; and, in accordance with his instructions, I set out to collect and arrange evidence and information from such sources, my design being to make use of all the material so collected which might prove suitable for present publication and relevant to the purpose of this book, and to leave what remained on record and available for the use of some future biographer with another aim in view.

Obviously no character-study of the late King could be written without reference to the many and grave political events which continuously troubled his reign. Early in it he created and established a new conception of the meaning of Constitutional Monarchy, and none can fail to realise how greatly he influenced the events of his reign and contributed to the welfare of his peoples by his qualities of leadership, by his character and personality, by his restraint and good sense and by the example of his personal integrity and his selfless devotion to duty. Politics and political events must play a chief part in any biography of any sovereign, and particularly so in the case and age of King George V. But I have tried— having regard to the scope of this particular study—to translate them into the simplest language, to introduce them as a necessary background in a personal study of a sovereign, and to examine them rather to discover the part they played in the development of the King's character than to assess the effect of his influence upon them. Some future biographer will examine them one by one with the meticulous care and impartiality required of an important contribution to history, and with a judgment cooler and more accurate than is possible to-day.

The existence of King George's diary and the definition of the scope of the memoir decided the method of writing it. It was not without anxious thought that I finally adopted a biographical form which seemed best to serve the ends in view and to satisfy the conditions present and imposed. A narrative in strict chronological order has certain disadvantages; among them, it is a form which does not lend itself to detached and inclusive summaries of various spheres of King George's activities. But it affords to the average reader in the Empire, for whom the book is written, the advantage of greater clarity. The character of every man is to a great extent formed by the experience of his life, and, even if he come to wear a crown, much of that experience is comparatively trivial. He is a part of all that he has seen, and when he looks back over his life, even if that life be a part of history, the film of his memory is a mosaic of events, important and trivial, often unrelated and always difficult to date. It is the sum rather than the quality of his experience which forms a man's character, and it may be that use and familiarity in playing a leading part in historic events reduce the effect which such major experiences may have on the characters of princes.

King George's youth was—for a man in his position—exceptionally free from such major experiences. For half his

life he lived in a privacy and with a lack of constitutional responsibility which seem remarkable to-day. It was not until
the death of Queen Victoria in 1901, when he was in his
thirty-sixth year, that he began, under the best masters,
seriously to prepare himself for kingship and regularly to
assume public responsibilities of importance. Thus, when he
came to the throne he came as an unknown and untried man,
and one not very completely trained. Therein lay the greatness of his achievement as King, and a measure of his handicaps. For whatever the public and some of his biographers
may declare, it is very doubtful if at any time in his reign he
himself would have endorsed the view that his training solely
as a professional sailor until his twenty-sixth year was the best,
or even a good, education for what proved to be his destiny.

His own journals lay ready to my hand, a simple narrative,
restrained, unadorned and accurate. I have adopted them as
the basis of this memoir and as an indication of the style in
which it should be dressed. I have tried to keep out features
of royal biographies and Court memoirs which he disliked
and distrusted, adulation, gossip, indiscretions, exaggeration
and dramatisation. I have tried to show him as the frank,
simple, honest and good man he was, and to leave him to
speak for himself in words and actions. I have carried the
reader with me through the whole course of his life, keeping
the proportion of the years rather than of the periods of chief
historical importance, constantly preferring the personal to
the political aspect, always accepting the relevance of any
evidence throwing light on the development of his character
or on his personal traits, using, wherever possible, his own
words to describe events and to voice his opinions, and leaving
it to the readers to form their own conclusions and judgment
from the mass of evidence (some of which is " trivial " and
some of which has been deliberately stressed by repetition)
collected from very many sources. And it seems to me beyond
question that a character-study in this form will best serve
his future biographers. Somewhere in his critical writings
Mr. Desmond MacCarthy wrote or quoted this judgment:
" A genuine biography is a ' book with a hero '; one in which
politics are translated as far as possible into terms of personal

living, while the history necessary to make the subject's views and actions intelligible is clear and interesting." In this character-study of King George V, I have tried to keep that model before me.

. . . . .

I have made no attempt to deal with Queen Mary's part in the achievements of the reign or with the many activities and interests of her life. King George's life and reign were triumphs of a partnership. He never failed to record in his diary, with his reference to each important event, how great had been Queen Mary's share in its success and how deep was his gratitude for the help she constantly gave him. The few references by him, out of many in such terms, printed in this memoir suffice to give the most authoritative and clear esti-mate possible of her worth as wife and as Queen.

. . . . .

It remains to add one more note by way of preface. This book was in part written and wholly revised for press under the shadow of a world war more terrible and an international crisis more dangerous than those through which King George V lived. I have made no attempt to readjust opinions I had expressed which, commonly held up to May 1940, may thence-forth seem out-of-date, nor have I in biographical or other notes attempted to complete beyond May 1940 the careers and records of persons and institutions mentioned in the memoir.

JOHN GORE.

ROGATE,
   Oct. 1938–Oct. 1940.

NOTE ON THE PRESENT EDITION

THE original edition of *King George V—a Personal Memoir* comprised not far short of 190,000 words.

It was authorised by H.M. King George VI in the form of a personal character-study, and for that reason it was designed (as explained in the preface) to carry the reader through the whole course of the King's life, keeping the proportion of the years rather than of the periods of chief historical importance. In that design, the book was divided into three fairly equal parts, the King's youth and education as a sailor 1865–92, his education for kingship 1892–1910, and his reign 1910–36.

Since the publication of the memoir in 1941, many requests have been preferred that it should be made available in a cheaper edition to a wider public. That object is now attained by its inclusion in the Albemarle Library publications, but the great length of the original forbade its publication *in extenso*, required indeed reduction so considerable as to necessitate the sacrifice of design and balance. Obviously, the major cut had to fall on the first section; for, while admitting that nursery and home influences, education and professional training, play a very important part in the character and affect the career of every notable person—and to an unusual degree in the case of King George V—those years of novitiate do not compare in importance with the years of maturity, and in King George's case his youth was passed in an era of less importance in world politics than were those which followed his emergence as heir to the Throne. Accordingly, nothing remains of the first section of the memoir but a brief résumé. It has not been necessary to deal so severely with the two other sections. Both have, indeed, been rigidly and repeatedly pruned, but neither has been truncated. They retain in essentials their original design.

In the original editions I acknowledge incompletely the extent of my indebtedness to all who helped me in collecting material and in every subsequent stage up to publication. That acknowledgment and a list of printed authorities consulted are perforce omitted from the present edition.

J. G.

1948

CHAPTER I

The Education of a Sailor. 1865-92 [1]

KING GEORGE V, second son of Edward, Prince of Wales, afterwards King Edward VII, was born prematurely at Marlborough House on 3rd June, 1865. His mother, Princess Alexandra, the eldest daughter of Prince Christian of Glücksborg, afterwards King Christian IX of Denmark, was 21 at the time of his birth. The child was christened George Frederick Ernest Albert.

His was a notably affectionate and self-sufficient family; his childhood was colourful and gay, his upbringing sensible. He was devoted to his mother, who inculcated in him a simple religion and unquestioning loyalty, and all his life he admired his father " next idolatry." He was the close companion of his elder brother, the Duke of Clarence, during the latter's short life, and remained in constant sympathy with his sister, Princess Victoria.

In 1877 the Princes entered the *Britannia*, and in 1880 made prolonged World and Empire voyages in H.M.S. *Bacchante*. Early influences importantly shaped Prince George's character. His childhood at Sandringham and the loving influence exercised by his mother bound him to the traditions of his youth and gave him a lifelong devotion to his home in Norfolk. His admiration for his father, tinged as it was with awe, produced in him a certain diffidence. His first governor, John Dalton, afterwards Canon of Windsor, inculcated a high moral, and perhaps a democratic, tone, though he was not so successful in his efforts at general education. One of his first captains, Henry Stephenson, helped materially to give him his devotion to the Service and to the sea. His service in the Navy was continuous and practical. He rose, largely by merit, to the command of ships, and served in the normal course on the Atlantic and Mediterranean Stations. Soon

[1] Brief résumé of Part I (pp. 1–99 in the original).

after the Duke of Clarence's death in 1892, he left the Service on becoming heir to the Throne, a thoroughly efficient naval officer, but with the very minimum of training and experience in affairs of State and with all too little store of general education.

But his character was forming satisfactorily; he was forthright, cheerful and breezy, but steady and thoroughly dependable, and his good sense had been recognised by the Queen, his grandmother, who had distinguished him with her confidence to an almost prophetic degree. When he became heir to the Throne, he had already gained a personal knowledge of the Empire which exceeded that of a majority of British statesmen. But he was little known to public men, and outside the Service and his family circle had made remarkably few intimate friends.

The tragic death of his elder brother, on 9th January, 1892 (only a month after the announcement of his engagement to Princess Mary of Teck), for a time affected his own health.

King George returning from a Review

Prince George of Wales, 1875

The Duke of York, 1899

King George and Queen Mary in their Coronation robes,
22nd June, 1911

*King George, with Marshal Joffre, Monsieur Poincaré, Marshal Foch
and Sir Douglas Haig, Valvion, 19th August, 1916*

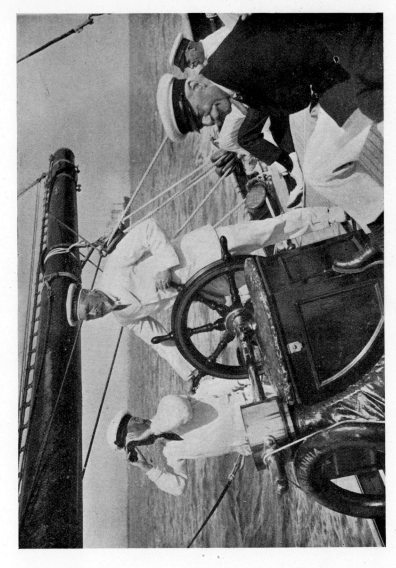

King George on board the Britannia, 1924

King George and his family, after the wedding of the Duke of York, 26th April, 1923

Queen Mary

King George and Princess Elizabeth
From a snapshot by the Duke of York

King George riding in Hyde Park, 1932

King George broadcasting at Sandringham, 1934

King George's tomb in St. George's Chapel, Windsor, with the effigy
l . . . *St . . . W . . . R . . . D . . . I . . . R . . . f . .*

Marriage.   1892-94

§ 1

PRINCE GEORGE'S health improved very rapidly in the Spring of 1892. Prince Eddy's death had hit him hard at a time when he was ill-prepared to face a shock. Indeed, for days afterwards his nights were troubled, and the services of a nurse who had attended him during his own illness had been called upon again. Dissimilar in character as the Princes were, they had been devotedly attached to each other. For most of Prince Eddy's short life they had been always together, inseparable companions. They had kept no secrets the one from the other, sharing good fortune and ill, hopes and anxieties, as Prince Eddy's letters to his brother clearly show. Nearly all of these were written between 1883 and 1891. Before then, there was no need of writing. For many years poignant memories of his brother constantly reminded Prince George of what he had lost, and all his life he cherished his memory and kept it alive by many acts of loyalty. (It was, for example, Prince Eddy's pen which he used for most of his writing.) But, as his health improved, the resilience of youth came to his assistance, and he took up his life again with a gradual recovery of interest and zest.

Soon after their return from the South of France, the family went to Denmark for the grandparents' Golden Wedding celebrations on the 23rd May. It was while he was in Denmark that the Birthday Honours List was published, with the item of chief interest in the forefront.

" The Queen has been graciously pleased to confer the dignity of a Peerage of the United Kingdom upon His Royal Highness Prince George of Wales, K.G.,[1] by the name, style

---

[1] He had been nominated K.G. in 1884.

and title of Duke of York,[1] Earl of Inverness and Baron Killarney." Telegrams of congratulation flowed across to him. On the 17th June he took his seat in the Upper House, supported by his father and his uncle, the Duke of Connaught. Though he was now heir to the Throne, he did not instantly abandon his naval career; nor indeed for some time to come did he assume in full measure the duties and responsibilities of his new position. The question of a Personal Household and of Establishments came now to be considered. Plans were put in hand for preparing the Cottage at Sandringham and certain historic rooms at St. James's Palace for the Duke's use. Both these homes in due course were called after his new title. His first Household was appointed. Major-General Sir Francis de Winton became his Comptroller, Lieutenant Sir Charles Cust his Equerry. Soon afterwards, Mr. Derek Keppel joined his Staff.[2] The arrangements already in existence for continuing his naval career were allowed to stand.

After the briefest holiday he was despatched to Heidelberg for a few weeks, to improve his German under the instruction of Professor Ihne.[3] But it is to be feared that the amenities were lost on the Duke and that he made little progress with the language.

§ 2

The Duke was home in November and the family started shooting again. Indeed, for weeks on end his diary is a

[1] Queen Victoria disliked the title Duke of York. On a memorandum dated the 5th March, 1890, from her Secretary setting out a list of titles suitable for the Prince of Wales' sons, she had endorsed: " The Queen does not at all wish to revive the title of York, or she would have done so for her own son Alfred." Before being persuaded to approve the title Duke of York for Prince George, she proposed that of Duke of London. King George V gave this information to his present Majesty.

[2] Younger son of the 7th Earl of Albemarle, he became Master of the Household in 1913. He married a daughter of the 5th Lord Suffield.

[3] Wilhelm Ihne, Professor of History at Heidelberg University, was a notable historian of ancient Rome. The Prince of Wales had met him some time before and had made friends with him. The Professor was often at Sandringham (where for a time he helped to coach Prince Eddy) and at Balmoral. He was very proud of his connection with the English Royal Family.

record of great days of sport at Sandringham and Castle Rising and other famous shoots which he visited. In December he paid a visit to the Queen at Windsor, and she spoke to him at great length about his future, about marriage, and of what was in her heart concerning him.

Something may appropriately be said here of Queen Victoria's relations with her grandson as revealed in her letters to him. These letters are contained in two bound volumes and cover the years 1873 to 1900, from his eighth birthday until almost the end of her life. She seldom failed to write to him on his birthday, and they always exchanged letters at Christmas and the New Year. Always difficult to read, her handwriting towards the end of her life, when her eyesight grew worse and worse, is barely decipherable, but her letters to him serve to correct some misapprehensions about her character and his. Those written to him when a child are as gay and affectionate, as free from moral precepts and sermons, as a healthy boy could wish to receive. She gave him news of old friends and pets at Balmoral or Windsor and accounts of picnics and balls, and always she displayed a lively interest in his doings and plans. There is a greater freedom of reference to matters of State than may always be found in her letters to the Prince of Wales, and it is to be observed also that in family or social references she introduces an occasional note of mild cynicism anent the motives or actions of some of their relations, which lends sparkle to the correspondence. They are, in short, the letters of a woman of the world to a man of the world. Those which she wrote to him between the time of Prince Eddy's death and his own marriage are marked by a rare sympathy, breadth of mind and understanding, and by all her usual good sense besides. And her interest in the welfare and progress of his children continued vivid to the end of her life.

The Duke contributed to the correspondence two or three letters to every one of hers, but her contribution leaves in no doubt the devoted affection she felt for him, her admiration of his character, her appreciation of his vivid sympathy, her faith in his unchanging dependability and innate soundness and sense, and her confidence in his future—good opinions, all of which she extended to cover the Duchess very soon after his marriage. "You have," she wrote in 1894, "always been so dear and affectionate to me and I am sure you will ever be a loving son and husband, and grandchild to me, and a blessing to your country." In short, it is clear from first to last that the Queen and her grandson each shrewdly appreciated the great qualities of the other, and valued them above all for their importance, present or yet to be revealed, to the Empire; and that a rare bond of sympathy and understanding united them.

§ 3

On the 3rd January, 1893, the Duke was promoted Post-Captain. But the new year opened sadly enough for him. Oliver Montagu was dying abroad. "We are all in despair about it," he wrote; "he is my oldest and best friend." There is preserved in the diary a very touching telegram from Montagu in response to one from the Duke: "Humanly speaking, we shall not meet again. God bless you. OLIVER." "Alas," he commented when the news of Montagu's death came, "why do all one's greatest and best friends go first?" He went with his father to Hinchingbrooke for the funeral.

They were in London again in February, and the Duke attended debates in the House of Commons more than once. On the 13th February: "Heard Gladstone bring in the Home Rule Bill. He made a beautiful speech and spoke for $2\frac{1}{4}$ hours which was wonderful for a man of 83. The House was crammed." He was in the Commons again a day or two later and came in for an "Irish row. It was very amusing. Heard Redmound [sic], Sexton, Dillon and O'Brien speak. Then Randolph Churchill spoke against the Home Rule Bill. He was very nervous at first. . . ." He records, too, seeing *King Lear*, "but did not care about it." Indeed, all his life the more serious and philosophic of Shakespeare's plays were "sad stuff" to him. As was natural, he saw at this time a good deal of the Duke and Duchess of Teck, and their family, and attended many more public banquets and private dinner-parties.

6

Still at this time, as his diary shows, he found difficulty in spelling correctly the names of persons he met, even those most notable in the society of the day or in politics. Indeed, his spelling had improved very little since *Britannia* days, and such schoolboy obstacles as " business," " mausoleum," " academy " and so on brought him down constantly.[1] He continued to read a great deal, Thackeray and other classic novelists occupying him at this time. In London the family kept late hours, often breakfasting as late as eleven o'clock, and one of his abiding pleasures was to read to his mother while she had her hair done. He took infinite pleasure in playing with Princess Louise's [2] " sweet baby."

On the 4th March, he left with the Princess for Genoa to join the R.Y. *Osborne*. The Princesses Victoria and Maud were of the party, with Miss Knollys, Sir Arthur Ellis and Sir Charles Cust in attendance. They cruised in leisurely fashion and made many land expeditions, visiting Porto Fino and Spezia and seeing the sights of Pisa, Florence and Elba. In Rome, the Duke heard the wonders of Edison's phonograph, and the Royal Family had an interesting conversation with Pope Leo XIII. They went on to Naples and Sicily and Corfu, where the Empress of Austria showed them her new house. Thence they sailed for Greece. After a few days with the Vivians at the Embassy in Rome, where he represented Queen Victoria at the silver wedding celebrations of the King and Queen of Italy, the Duke returned to London on the 30th April.

§ 4

He went down almost immediately to stay with his sister and the Duke of Fife at East Sheen Lodge, and there in the garden on Wednesday, the 3rd May, he proposed to Princess May of Teck. " The darling girl consented to be my wife. I am so happy."

The announcement was made next day in the Press, and was read with great satisfaction. The Duke went down to

[1] Let it be made clear that, by persistence, he made good in later years many of the deficiencies of his education.
[2] Duchess of Fife.

Windsor to receive from the Queen her warm and heartfelt approval. She wrote in her diary:

I found dear Georgie had arrived, and he had much to tell me. He seemed quite pleased and contented, and was going to see his father to-morrow. Poor Alix sent me a sad telegram, though she is really pleased at the same time. . . .[1]

The royal couple were now seen by the London public daily, driving in the Park or at the Opera, and the nation's approval of the match constantly increased in warmth.

The 6th July, the wedding-day, dawned hot and wonderfully fine:

All went in state to Buckingham Palace. At 11.45 drove with Papa and Uncle Alfred (supporters) to St. James's Palace by Piccadilly and St. James's St. . . . decorations quite lovely. . . . At 12.30 darling May and I were married in the Chapel Royal by the Archbishop: I am indeed lucky to have got such a darling and charming wife.

The Queen gave her version of the ceremony in her journal:

The Queen of Denmark came in with her grandson the Cesarewitch, and dear Alix (looking very pale) with her father. The Bridegroom's procession followed rapidly, being supported by his father and Uncle Affie, all in naval uniform. They had to wait a very short time, when the Bride appeared, followed by her ten dear bridesmaids, Victoria, Maud, Ducky, Sandra, Baby B., Thora, Daisy, Patsy, Alice Battenberg and Ena,[2] the four little ones looking very sweet. . . .
Georgie gave his answers very distinctly, while May, though quite self-possessed, spoke very low. . . .
I could not but remember that *I* had stood, where May did, fifty-three years ago, and dear Vicky thirty-five years ago, and that the dear ones, who stood where Georgie did, were gone from us! May these dear children's happiness last longer!

[1] Queen Victoria had set her heart on the marriage during the past year. It was not to be expected that the Princess or the Prince would at this time receive the news with the same degree of enthusiasm, nor did they. A very short time sufficed to convince them of the Queen's right judgment.

[2] Princesses Victoria and Maud of Wales; Victoria, Alexandra and Beatrice of Edinburgh; Helena Victoria (daughter of Princess Christian); Margaret and Patricia of Connaught; Ena of Battenberg.

There followed the reception and the ordeal of photography.

At 4.30 we said good-bye to everyone and drove away alone together in plain clothes in an open carriage with Blues escort to Liverpool St. . . . magnificent reception the whole way.

They drove from Wolferton Station to York Cottage [1] in their new carriage with an escort of the Loyal Suffolk Hussars. Only one member of the Duke's Household was chosen for duty during the honeymoon, Mr. (afterwards Sir) Derek Keppel. He found accommodation at Appleton with the Stanley Clarkes, [2] and came over to the Cottage daily to cope with the enormous piles of correspondence. Sir Derek recalled that drive from Wolferton. The Duchess was in white, the Duke in a black frock-coat. The dust rose in dense clouds under the feet of the horses. When the happy pair reached the Cottage, the Duchess appeared to be dressed in black, the Duke in white. At that moment, thanks to the heat and the fatigues of the long day, they were both almost too tired to appreciate the humours of their condition.

§ 5

York Cottage was to be his home for more than thirty years, including the greater part of his reign. Here all his children, save the eldest son, were born. Something has been said about it. Because King George and Queen Mary lived in it so long, it requires a fuller reference. The Cottage, tucked away at an angle of the deer park, lies lower than the big house and it is less familiar to sight-seers. A small garden surrounds it and melts imperceptibly into the larger parkland; the lower waters of the lake or pond system border the little lawn in front of the house. The water is the haunt of duck of many varieties, and is musical day and night with the cries of wildfowl. Of many styles—none very meritorious—it is an amalgam of architectural fancies. There are patches

---

[1] As the Bachelors' Cottage, in its restored form, was henceforth named.
[2] Major-Gen. Sir Stanley Clarke became Paymaster of the Household to King Edward VII. Appleton, a mile or two from Sandringham, later became the English home of Princess Maud, afterwards Queen of Norway.

of pseudo-black-and-white, some features of the attractive local stone-layering, of rough-cast and of Victorian Gothic. The last important alterations attempted not very happily to harmonise the whole. In the first year of marriage it was perfectly adequate. Further alterations were made when a nursery became necessary, but, for the purposes for which it was in later years used, it remained altogether too small and rather inconvenient.

The exterior, no doubt, concealed its cubic content, which was by no means insignificant. The larger drawing-room was a pleasant room, though filled to capacity by the Family and Household, who invariably sat in it for tea and after dinner. A smaller drawing-room was used as a reception-room for callers. The Household had a small office, with bedrooms opening out of it. There was a fair-sized billiard-room and dining-room. Upstairs, when the family was in need of it, there was a schoolroom, and rooms for the Lady-in-Waiting,[1] the tutor and the governess. There remained a few rooms usually occupied in the shooting season by " guns," seldom more than three at a time. It was very rarely that a lady visitor was entertained. Some of the private rooms were small and dark, very few indeed seemed to enjoy to the full such natural amenities of light and air as existed, and King George's own sitting-room was particularly small and sunless. As for the Staff, it had largely to be boarded out, and King George was more than once heard to remark in later days that he supposed his servants slept in the trees. But it is a recognised fact that the house is not everything. An ugly, even an inconvenient, house may be a house beloved by those who live in it, and there was much in the surroundings of York Cottage to inspire affection and to lend charm, in winter and in summer. As Prince and King, King George was happy and contented there, and in the early days of his marriage the Duchess of York and the Royal Family all expressed satisfaction with it.

[1] Lady Eva Greville received the first appointment to the Duchess in 1893. Only daughter of the 4th Earl of Warwick, she married Col. F. Dugdale in 1895. The next lady to be appointed to the Duchess's Household was Lady Mary Lygon in 1895. Daughter of the 6th Earl Beauchamp, she married in 1905 the Hon. Henry Trefusis, son of the 20th Lord Clinton.

§ 6

The weather continued very hot during the first days of the honeymoon. The Duke and Duchess usually breakfasted and dined out of doors in the summer-house, where Mr. Keppel would sometimes join them. They arranged furniture and hung pictures and walked and drove about. The Duke was fond of reading aloud, and at this time read some of the Greville Memoirs to the Duchess. On the 16th July he wrote to his old friend Bryan Godfrey-Faussett, then Flag-Lieutenant to Vice-Admiral Stephenson on the Pacific Station:

I can hardly yet realise that I am a married man, although I have been so for the last 10 days. All I can say is that I am intensely happy, far happier than I ever thought I could be with anybody. I can't say more than that. We are spending our honeymoon here in this charming little cottage which my father has given me & it is most comfortable & the peace and rest after all we went through in London is indeed heavenly. . . .

You will have read the many accounts of our wedding in the papers, so I shall not tell you anything about it. It is a day that I shall never forget as long as I live, they say it was almost the largest crowd that has ever been in the streets of London. . . .

Did you ever hear of a more awful calamity than the loss of the *Victoria* with poor Tryon & nearly 400 officers and men, it is one of the most terrible catastrophes that has befallen our Service & the country for many years. Poor Bourke, I do so feel for him, his C.M. begins tomorrow at Malta.[1]

Give my love to all old friends & believe me always, Yr very sincere old friend, GEORGE.

They returned to London at last on the 26th February, 1894, and spent a good deal of time arranging York House to their satisfaction. They gave two or three formal dinner-parties. The Duke now began to turn his attention to

[1] Sir George Tryon, C.-in-C. Mediterranean Squadron, was drowned with more than half the crew when his Flagship collided with the *Camperdown* on 22nd June during manœuvres off Tripoli. Capt. Bourke commanded the Flagship. He was cleared, the blame for the disaster falling on the Admiral.

educating himself for his new destiny. Mr. Tanner[1] came to give him instruction in Constitutional history, and laid down a course of reading, which the Duke spasmodically pursued.[2] He took up, too, at this time the game of (real) tennis,[3] having lessons from Latham at Prince's. And he sometimes played in the Duke of Fife's court at Sheen. The chief functions which fell to him were a couple of engagements at Worcester and Newcastle and the dinner of the Trinity House, at which, as Master, he took the chair and entertained his father and his Uncle Alfred, making a short speech.

The birth of their first child was expected towards the end of June, and the Duchess was living at White Lodge. On the 23rd June, the Duke wrote in his diary:

WHITE LODGE, 23rd June.—At 10.0 a sweet little boy was born and weighed 8 lb. . . . Mr. Asquith [Home Secretary] came to see him.

The christening was performed at White Lodge on the 16th July, and the Royal Family attended in force. The child, who had twelve sponsors, behaved very well, and received the names of Edward Albert Christian George Andrew Patrick David. He was to be known as David in his family circle. After the ceremony the " four generations " posed for photographs, which became immensely popular. Soon afterwards the Duke hurried to Sandringham to inspect the new alterations to the Cottage, which had become necessary. Letters of congratulation from the wide circle of his relations throughout Europe and from his friends poured in on him, and he was kept busy answering them.

§ 7

The letters written to him over many years by relations of various nationalities throw a revealing light on his family

[1] Mr. J. R. Tanner, of St. John's College, Cambridge, a Pepysian authority and historian.

[2] Years afterwards Lord Stamfordham was heard ruefully to remark that of the Sovereigns he had known, only Queen Victoria understood the meaning of the British Constitution.

[3] After his accession he sometimes played the Indian and Canadian variety of the game in the court (now a swimming-pool) at Buckingham Palace.

life. On both sides of his family, display of affection was a characteristic. The Courts of Europe constantly exchanged letters breathing goodwill and sympathy expressed in terms of devotion. The Duke was obviously a great favourite with all his aunts and uncles and cousins in England, Scandinavia, Greece, Russia and Germany. His relations with the Duchess's family were particularly happy. The Duchess of Teck loved him as a son and reposed in him the utmost confidence, as did his uncle, the Duke of Cambridge[1]; and his brothers-in-law wrote constantly to him with obvious affection during their periods of service with their regiments in India or Africa. He deserved to be loved. He never failed to sympathise with each and all in their joys and in their tragedies and sorrows, and clearly possessed the rare gift of showing in simple and convincing language the genuineness of his feelings. He constantly responded in punctual and practical form to their requests or needs, and when in due course he himself became head of a wide family, he carried out that trust with unswerving generosity and with constant devotion. With his own and the preceding generations he lived on terms of the warmest affection and of mutual sympathy.

It is a fact which has significance when his relations with his own children in later life come to be considered. From childhood's earliest days, in his family life the banner over him was love. He had rarely seen the other side, had been nurtured in family affection, so warmly expressed on all occasions as to suggest to the cynical or less fortunate a mutual-admiration society. And when he grew to man's estate, that sympathy, those easy, loving relations, continued unchanged. His father's confidence, love and respect constantly encouraged him in his preparation for the great destiny which was to be his. There was every reason in the world why these relations should have continued for another generation, under the ægis of one in whom loyalty to the past was a religion and memory a strong tower.

[1] He was a first cousin of Queen Victoria and the Duke's uncle by marriage, being brother of the Duchess of Teck.

CHAPTER III

First Years of Marriage. Retirement from the Navy. 1894-97

§ 1

THE early years of his married life, the years covering the births of his elder children, may be briefly dealt with. He settled down in 1894 to an existence which, for many months every year, was as ordered, as regular, as placid and as little disturbed by business and duties as that of the most favoured country squire. The evidence of his own writings is convincing that he attained during these quiet years the height of happiness, that he constantly blessed his good fortune in marriage, and asked nothing better than to enjoy it and the simple pleasures of domestic life at the Cottage. He was very much a family man, immensely proud of his first baby, was assiduous in his attendance at the ceremony of the evening bath, in which, with a sailor's efficiency, he soon won the right to assume the chief executive part. " I made," he said with pride to one of the Queen's ladies, " a very good lap."

Outside the Cottage, on the estate, he extended his responsibilities in whatever direction the Prince might suggest. He was constantly in consultation with Jackson, the head keeper, concerning the shooting, the arrangement of the shooting weeks, the planning of new drives and stands. He took in hand a small farm, and the running of it occupied some of his time. He soon gained in experience of farming and stockbreeding, under the guidance, among others, of George Brereton.

His life at Sandringham was exactly ordered. One day told another. Throughout the shooting season he rarely missed a day's sport. When the Duchess was laid up, he would give her her breakfast at nine o'clock, eat his own at half-past nine, and be off by ten.   After tea he did whatever business was called for with his Comptroller, when he would pay his evening visit to the nursery, read to the Duchess, dine, and read to her again.   And then, after a game of billiards with the Equerry-in-Waiting, he went early to bed.   Between the births of the children in those years the Duchess sometimes went abroad with her mother, and life at the Cottage then continued on a bachelor footing.   It was his invariable custom on Sunday afternoons, with any guest who might be staying with him, to join his father and the visitors at Sandringham on the stroke of three o'clock in the Gardens, when followed a regular tour of inspection of the glasshouses, racing stables and kennels; and a visit was usually paid to the Princess's model dairy.   He became keen on various aspects of gardening; of flowers and shrubs he never attained to much knowledge, but he was interested in garden trees.   He was very careful in those years to keep himself in the background.   He would never allow any demands to be made from the Cottage on the garden produce and fruit beyond what was usually supplied.   If his tastes sometimes differed from his father's, he was careful to suppress them.

.   .   .   .   .   .

So the Summer and Autumn of 1894 passed quickly away. When the Duchess went to St. Moritz at the end of July, the Duke went to Cowes for the Regatta[1] and passed the rest of the

---

[1] The following incident may be set down as an example of his love of sport and his sense of duty.   One afternoon, while on a visit to Her Majesty at Osborne in August 1894, the Duke of York was to take command of his battalion of Isle of Wight Volunteers (of which he was Hon. Colonel) at Queen Victoria's inspection of the battalion in the park at Osborne.

He was also on the same day to race with the Prince of Wales (King Edward VII), in the R.Y.S. Regatta in the Solent.   In order not to miss a race, and at the same time to make sure of being in time for the inspection —which was timed for 6 p.m.—arrangements were made for one of R.Y. *Osborne's* steam pinnaces to lay off near the finishing line when the *Britannia* was to cross it at the end of the first round.   The Duke of York and his Equerry (Mr. Keppel) were then to jump overboard from the *Britannia* and swim to the pinnace, and be put ashore at Trinity Pier, East Cowes, where a Royal Carriage was to drive them up to Osborne House in time for them to change and get on their horses for the parade.

To the great disappointment of all on board the *Britannia*, they were deprived of this sporting little entertainment by the Sailing Committee of R.Y.S. stopping the race after the first round, on account of weather conditions.

time at York Cottage. They met again in London on the last day of August, and in September paid a couple of ceremonial visits to Birmingham and Liverpool, receiving addresses of congratulation. There was an official visit to Leeds in October, with an " incident " which might have been more serious than it was. As they drove through the streets, a madman jumped on the carriage step. The Duke tried to dislodge him, and soon enough Prince Adolphus of Teck, in command of the 17th Lancers escort, with the help of his sergeant, got the man down.

§ 2

The news of the death of his uncle, Tzar Alexander (he had married Queen Alexandra's sister) brought into their lives a note of deep sorrow. He died on the 1st November, the day after the Prince and Princess of Wales had set out to join the Tzaritza.

It is [the Duke wrote in his diary] a terrible calamity for the whole world, a more honest, generous and kind-hearted man never lived. Poor darling Toria's grief is very great. She worshipped him. I tried my best to comfort my sweet angel of a sister. . . . God help and protect darling Aunt Minny, dear Nicky and Cousins in their sorrow.

On the 12th November, the Duke had to tear himself away from Sandringham and to set out, with Lord Carrington and Mr. Keppel in attendance, for St. Petersburg, to be present at the late Tzar's funeral and the marriage of his successor. There followed a long and very interesting visit to Russia, in the course of which the Duke's informal methods of sightseeing astonished the Court and greatly embarrassed the police who had charge of his safety.

The Prince of Wales, the new Tzar and all the Grand Dukes welcomed him on arrival, and he lodged at the Anichkov Palace with his own and the Russian royal families. The funeral was not until the 19th, the intervening days being passed in official calls and daily services in the Chapel of SS. Peter and Paul. A thousand people were crowded into the

Fortress Chapel when the late Tzar's funeral at last took place.

Another week passed in visits and sight-seeing, and on the 26th (" Nicky and Alicky's ² wedding day ") the new Tzar Nicholas was married in the Chapel of the Winter Palace. After the wedding the Duke visited Tzarkoë Selo and on the 2nd December left for Berlin with his father to stay with his Aunt, the Empress Frederick, at the Kaiser Friedrich Palace. On the 6th December they were at Windsor, reporting to the Queen. For the rest of the year there were no events of any importance which disturbed the quiet life at the Cottage.

§ 3

The year 1895 brought the great frost, which set in in earnest at the end of January. Every day was devoted to skating and ice-hockey, and the fun continued fast and furious by torchlight. The ladies took advantage of the chance. The Princess was often on the ice, and the Duchess showed marked improvement before they went to London. Then the lake at Buckingham Palace was in constant use, and day after day friends brought picked teams to the Palace, to do battle with the Prince and Duke and their Households. In March the Duke went down with a sharp attack of influenza, and his recovery was slow. He recuperated in April at Sandringham, taking up clay-pigeon shooting very assiduously. The Summer of 1895 brought him rather more in the way of ceremonial duty. In May he and the Duchess visited Sheffield, staying with the Duke of Norfolk, and the Duke made a speech in the City of London on the occasion of his receiving the Freedom of a City Company. He saw Lord Rosebery win the Derby for the second successive year in his Premiership, and the Jockey Club dinner at Marlborough House was an historic occasion. In June he sailed *Britannia* to victory over *Ailsa* at the Cinque Ports Regatta, and soon after left in the R.Y. *Osborne* for an important function, the opening of the Kiel Canal. On the 20th June the yacht reached the Canal, and the Duke dined with the Kaiser on board the *Hohenzollern*.

¹ Princess Alexandra of Hesse. Both bridegroom and bride were the Duke's first cousins.

His diary expressed appreciation of the scene and spoke warmly enough of his host.[1]

Goodwood, Cowes, Balmoral, Dunrobin[2] and Sandringham claimed him in turn, and he was shooting constantly until the end of October. He was now gaining a great reputation as a shot, and his diary modestly records many occasions when he " topped the score " in very crack company.

On the 14th December, the Duke wrote in his journal:

. . . a little boy [3] was born weighing nearly 8 lb. at 3.40 (S.T.),[4] everything most satisfactory, both doing very well. Sent a great number of telegrams, had something to eat. Went to bed at 6.45 very tired.

Opposite this entry, he pasted in a cutting from the *Globe* of that day, which had an unforeseen interest for posterity:

Under any circumstances the birth of a second son to H.R.H. the Duke of York would be of significance as insuring to all appearance for many years to come the devolution of the Crown in the direct male line, but the auspicious news has additional interest when we remember that December 14th has been a black day in the annals of our Royal House, marking as it does the anniversary of the death of the Prince Consort and also that of Princess Alice. Henceforth it is permissible to hope that the august lady, in whose joys and sorrows the nation claims a right to share, may find in the felicitous event of December 14th, 1895, a solace for the mournful memories of December 14th, 1861, and December 14th, 1878.

The Queen's diary contains a prophecy that that hope would be generously fulfilled:

This terrible anniversary returned for the thirty-fourth time

[1] All his diary references to the Emperor William are friendly and appreciative right up to the Great War.

[2] Duke of Sutherland's.

[3] Prince Albert, now King George VI.

[4] " S.T."—Sandringham (not Summer) Time. The Prince of Wales was a pioneer in saving daylight for the purposes of sport, and kept all clocks advanced by half an hour. The practice, which had obvious disadvantages, was abolished after the death of King George V.

. . . found telegrams from Georgie and Sir J. Williams, saying that dear May had been safely delivered of a son at three this morning. Georgie's first feeling was regret that this dear child should be born on such a sad day. I have a feeling it may be a blessing for the dear little boy, and may be looked upon as a gift from God!

§ 4

Elderly men to-day may well look back on the last decade of the nineteenth century as children who seek on waking to recapture the details of a delightful, impossible dream. There seems to remain in our lives little to connect the dream with the reality. An unhealthy calm before the tornado it may have been, but there was justification for its easy accept- ance every day by a section of the nation, justification for the *hubris* which present prosperity, settled peace and hopes of still greater advances induced. Above all, the thing which so utterly separates that decade (and the next) from modern life is the sense of permanence and security which still invested it.

The Great Queen had been on the throne longer than the majority of living men could remember. She was an insti- tution. The Monarchy was feminine. England without Victoria was unthinkable. She had, it is true, reigned in troublous times, she had had her years of unpopularity and had lived through crises. But for a long time past her rela- tions with foreign Powers had been friendly and peaceful, so peaceful that for years the country had been able to con- centrate its energies with much bitterness and zest on a domestic controversy—Home Rule. And now even that controversy was in abeyance. Since 1886 a settled Conserva- tive Government, with Liberal-Unionist support, had had charge of affairs. Mr. Gladstone was in the wilderness, and Lord Salisbury, with a brief and abortive interlude of Liberal- ism and Home Rule (1892–95), held the reins into the new century. His was not an unliberal administration. It was, on the contrary, far-sighted and democratic. England was still the richest country in the world; still growing richer. Trade improved again after the recession during the Rosebery interlude, and civic pride demanded and required a great impetus to social reforms. The label would have sounded odd in his ears, but Lord Salisbury's domestic programme was what we should call advanced municipal socialism. Social and cultural amenities sprang up everywhere in the great cities, Local Government emerged on a dignified modern basis, public undertakings and utilities were proudly developed.

It was an age of sharp contrasts, of unrestrained luxury and great privation, of the brilliant and the sordid. Yet for every class in the State there was the compensation of hope and evidence of improvement to come. The workers saw a new light of dawn, the privileged a summer sun still high in the heavens. For the latter, there was some excuse for confidence, ease and even political apathy. There was no apathy about the enjoyment of the good things which life offered. There was excuse for national pride and vainglory in the ever-increasing ease of living, the ever-widening vista of interests which the inventions of science and the initiative of industry afforded. Signs were not wanting that Democracy was knocking at the door, but, inside, the Age of Privilege was enjoying its last high, careless kick. The machine still ran on oiled wheels, the sound of the grinding was low. An income-tax, still adjusted from time to time in pennies, below a shilling, left to the newly rich and the owners of ancient wealth, newly recruited, plenty over for luxurious living and only a scintilla of justification for crying *Ichabod*.

True, the voice of the demagogue was heard in the land, but at the moment such voices and their Jeremiads were rather stimulating than terrifying. The Fabians wrote their books and held their discussions, but the knocking at the door was drowned by the triumphant strains of the dance orchestra. And even for the working classes there was hope of better things and some slight evidence of progress made. The Trade Union Movement had already advanced from an organisation of mute appeal against intolerable conditions of living to a clamant force in politics as well as in social life. The Dockers had recently shown what organisation and determination could win for the workers. And when trade is good, all classes benefit in some degree, and the voice of the agitator loses much of its appeal.

In that age, men asked for no leadership at the head. They were content to follow each his own star. Their houses might be in need of repair, but at least they were built upon the rock. There was permanence, world order and a sense of security. Whatever they might wrest for themselves from the good things which the Age offered, that they would hold. Of the inner circle of the privileged class the Prince of Wales —for lack of more responsible outlets for his ambition and abilities—was the acknowledged head and arbiter. No one in those days looked to the Sovereign and the Royal Family for that spiritual leadership in the pursuit of the more serious aims of life which a "father of his country" can give. Fashionable leadership, perhaps. From Queen Victoria neither form of leadership was asked (nor offered). She was above and outside society. King Edward, when his time came, offered and gave, in the first years of his reign, a leadership of the lesser kind. It was to be King George's achievement once more to revive the great function of spiritual leadership from the Throne.

Of that inner circle led by his father in the 'nineties, the Duke was a part. He was of it but not in it. The stream flowed gaily by. The Duke and Duchess were in a backwater by choice. The best of everything, whatever the age and conditions obtaining, is naturally at the disposal of a Royal Family, is taken as a matter of course, and means no more to them than punctual meals and adequate light and heat mean to ordinary folk of average means with responsible work to do. The good things of life can never achieve happiness, even for those who have not always accepted them as of right. It is a commonplace; yet in that golden age there were scores of men and women who found a life's work in the enjoyment of the new luxuries and the broadening avenues of social interests and distractions. The Duke took without question the age in which he was living and the opportunities which it offered, and, never going with the stream, never losing his head, enjoyed that calm before the storm with all the simplicity and common sense that were in his nature. For months of the year he lived the life of the squire to whom money was no object, and business duties but an interlude of no grievous length.

He and the Duchess were now making many new friends; they constantly visited those country houses which they chose not for their social brilliance, for the wit or sparkle or novelty which their hospitality offered, but for the more solid qualities based on old traditions which appealed to them and which they met there. They took up one by one such of the new inventions as pleased them—the bicycle, bridge, the motor-car, as in turn they arrived. Reading his journals, one cannot help remarking the absence of high lights. He took everything in his stride; he took everything in its turn and as it came, whether it were ceremonial duty or recreation; he took everything for granted. One day he " topped the score " at a record partridge drive. The next he carried out an important ceremonial function. The third day he bathed the baby and read Greville to the Duchess. His lamp burned with a steady flame. He was quietly happy and never excited, uplifted or surprised. He never lost his balance.

§ 5

Throughout the remainder of 1896, throughout 1897 and 1898, his life went on on an ordered plan. In Turf history, 1896 was Persimmon's [1] year. That great horse swept the board with the Derby and the St. Leger and continued his successes at Ascot in 1897. The Royal Family, needless to say, backed him confidently but with moderation. The Duke and Duchess went out to Coburg for a family wedding in April 1896,[2] where they met the Kaiser and Kaiserin, and passed on to Copenhagen, to return home through Paris. The chief event of the end of that season was the marriage of Princess Maud to Prince Charles of Denmark.[3] The next family event of importance was the birth, at York Cottage on the 25th April, 1897, of Princess Mary.

The season of 1897 was made brilliant by the Diamond Jubilee celebrations of the 22nd June. The Duke, with the

[1] Sired in 1893 by St. Simon out of Perdita II, the second of three great horses similarly bred by the Prince.

[2] Marriage of Princess Alexandra (of Saxe-Coburg and Edinburgh) to Ernest, Prince of Hohenlohe Langenburg.

[3] Afterwards King Haakon of Norway.

rest of the Queen's available sons and grandsons, rode in the procession to St. Paul's. " The service on the steps of St. Paul's was magnificent. . . .   The most wonderful crowd I ever saw, perfect order and no accidents, 8 miles of streets we passed through, never heard anything like the cheering. . . ." It is clear that he felt that day a sense of admiration, of awe, of wonder, for that tiny figure, bent with age, the central figure of a glittering throng, whose dynamic will-power had achieved such records.   There followed the Gala Performance at the Opera, ceremonies in London and Windsor, a State Ball and the Naval Review at Portsmouth.

On the 27th October he was at Elveden, shooting with Lord Iveagh, when he recevied a telegram from the Duchess announcing the sudden death of the Duchess of Teck.   It was unexpected, and was a blow to the daughter who loved her dearly.   Mr. Gladstone died on the 19th May, 1898, at the great age of 88.   On the 28th May he was buried in the Abbey. The Prince and the Duke both acted as Pall-bearers.   For the rest, the journal of these years is largely a record of country pursuits and a catalogue of the great variety of plays and operas which the Duke and Duchess attended when in London.

§ 6

For the Duke, at any rate, life was an idyll in the 'nineties. If it were not a biographer's first duty to seek the truth and fearlessly to set it forth, one might leave it there, an idyll unalloyed for the royal couple.   Perhaps, with a little more sympathy from the Prince and Princess and Princess Victoria, it might have been so no less for the Duchess.   She knew and valued and constantly deserved the great gifts that had come to her—the love and trust of an utterly honest, loyal and good man, the founding of a family of healthy and attractive children, the lively interest in preparing them for the destiny that was to be theirs.   Yet in the most ideal marriages, if hearts may become as one, minds never can, and the nature of one individual is never wholly fusible with another's.   The Duchess had married into a family which for years had been self-sufficient, a family which the Princess's genius for affection had turned into something that was certainly a closely guarded clique and was not far short of a mutual-admiration society. It was a family little given to intellectual pursuits, without much in the way of artistic tastes or taste, a family not easily to be converted to any other manner of life than that which they had found all-sufficing in an age wherein privilege vigorously survived.

The Duchess was intellectually on a higher plane; she was already well educated and constantly seeking to increase her store of knowledge in many fields beyond the range of the Princess of Wales and Princess Victoria. She was full of initiative, of intellectual curiosity, of energy, which needed outlets and wider horizons. Their recreations were not hers. Their manner of life could not satisfy her notions of the ideal. And she was living in a small house on an estate which drew its inspiration wholly from the Prince and Princess, whereon every smallest happening or alteration was ordered and taken note of by the Prince. The very arrangement of her rooms, the planting of her small garden, were matters which required reference to Sandringham House, and the smallest innovation would be regarded with distrust. There was so much that she might usefully have done on the estate. Her ideas might have influenced a score of local institutions and increased the well-being of the neighbourhood. But such matters were the prerogative of the Princess, whose charm and kindliness often made up for her lack of system and order.

Sometimes the Duchess's intellectual life may have been starved and her energies atrophied in those early years. For she came of a younger, more liberal generation, with far more serious notions of woman's sphere of usefulness, and very strong ideas of the responsibilities demanded of the first ladies in the realm. For many women, then as now, the daily call to follow the shooters, to watch the killing, however faultless, to take always a cheerful, appreciative part in man-made, man-valued amusements, must have been answered at the sacrifice of many cherished, many constructive and liberal ambitions. It is fair to assume that the self-effacement which conditions at Sandringham in those years demanded of a fine and energetic character must have fallen hardly on her, and fair also to suggest that the Prince and Princess might have done more to encourage her initiative and to fill her days, and with a more understanding sympathy to have alleviated the shyness with which she entered upon her ceremonial duties.

The Duke, no doubt, realised something of the difficulties of living so close to the big house, and did all he could to harmonise the two mighty loyalties of his life: to the wife on the one hand, and to the mother and sister, whom he loved so much, on the other; to the old life of Sandringham, which was perfect in his eyes, because it was a changeless memory of his joyous youth, and to the new life which was opening for him, full of promise of enduring happiness. One notes how in those years the matter of his reading—for he loved reading aloud to the Duchess—gained in solidity and seriousness. He read more history and less fiction, and was at pains to keep abreast of current thought and to list the books which he read. But he was careful to remain in a subordinate position and never to prefer requests or to make demands. At heart he was utterly satisfied with Sandringham ways and Sandringham days, with Sandringham taste and habits, and in a word was not only the most loyal of men, but—leaving politics out of consideration—the most staunch of Conservatives. On the 22nd June, 1898, the Duke took command of the 1st-class cruiser *Crescent*, his last spell of sea service and of eight weeks' duration. He referred in his diary only very briefly and without emotion to his farewell to the Navy.

CHAPTER IV

The Boer War and the Queen's Death. 1899-1901

§ 1

THE year 1899 was a grim one for Britain. Wars of any magnitude involving the country were in the memory only of the elderly, and an unsubstantially based optimism had not conduced to any vigorous efforts of reform at the War Office. All through the Spring and Summer the shadow of coming events in South Africa fell across the sunlit path, disturbing the peace of mind only of those most closely engaged in the guidance of the nation's affairs. The London Season was as brilliant as usual. Flying Fox carried off the Blue Ribbon, Ascot yielded to Goodwood, Goodwood to Cowes, and the Twelfth gave evidence of a bumper grouse year.

But Lord Salisbury was alive to the dangers ahead, and his constant exchanges with the Queen reveal that on her eightieth birthday she was still resolutely shouldering the full burden of her responsibility. It is curious to compare her own diary and that of her grandson, to read her letters and notes and such as survive from the Duke of York's pen. But if in the length and breadth of his diary there is no reference to the shadow ahead, he and the Duchess were perfectly aware of it. To a limited extent, he was now assuming royal responsibilities, sharing or taking over some of the Queen's ceremonial duties. Three or four times that year he attended her at investitures, and notes on each occasion that " Grandmama used my sword for Knighting." In the summer of 1898 the Prince of Wales had been laid up for some time with a fractured knee-cap, and the Duke had been called on occasionally to take his place.

Nevertheless, the ceremonial duties entailed were light enough—for the Prince's public appearances, even so shortly before his reign began, were of the rarest. As was known to his medical advisers, he was in a mood of despondency, which indeed persisted into his accession and may well have aggravated his serious illness before his coronation. In the last three years of the Queen's reign he developed a certain obstinacy that arose from the continued frustration of his hopes of service and from the ambiguity of his position. In her relations with her ministers, in her constitutional functions, the Queen must still, in her eighty-first year, bear the burden alone and jealously guard her prerogatives. And such crumbs of those lesser duties of ceremonial as she was willing to concede, the Prince was no longer anxious to take up. Than the Duke there was no more willing instrument of service. Whatever he was called on to perform, he carried out punctually, cheerfully and dutifully. But very little of any importance came his way, and indeed, during the year the Duchess was more busily engaged than he in labours for various hospitals which she had taken under her wing.

§ 2

On the 9th October the Boer ultimatum could only be interpreted as a declaration of war. The Transvaal and the Orange Free State invaded the British Colonies while the forces of the Empire were still assembling. There was little uneasiness then as to the moral issues of the war in South Africa. The British Government, in the opinion of a large majority of the country and of the Empire, had, latterly at least, shown moderation, and there was almost complete unanimity in Parliament in support of the war. Most people who remember the Boer War have forgotten the appalling swiftness of the march of events which led up to the " black week " of December 1899. During the months of October and November, Sir George White had been hemmed in in Ladysmith, Kekewich in Kimberley, Baden-Powell in Mafeking. Methuen had been thrice checked in Belmont, Euston and Modder River with heavy losses. Early in December came Stormberg, Magersfontein and Colenso. Lord Roberts was called on to save the situation after only two months of that long war.

There were many other political events during this black year to give the Queen and her ministers anxiety, and indeed to cast a shadow over the brilliance of the fashionable world. If in England there was no serious criticism concerning the morality of the war, it was otherwise on the Continent. In Germany, France and Belgium the name of Britain was vilified. The Kaiser had earned a strong and courageous rebuke from his Grandmother for his unrestrained public utterances; Parisians were getting their own back for the trenchant criticisms in the British Press of the scandal of the Dreyfus verdict; while in Brussels the bitterness of Anglophobia drew strength from the memory of British diatribes on Congo maladministration. It became unwise, if not dangerous, for the Royal Family to travel in Europe.

The Duke's diary during the last months of 1899 is a mirror of the times in which he was living and of the manner of thought of his generation rather than evidence of his own opinions. Having very little information on the conduct of State business and no access to ministers, he could do no more than was asked of him. His life went on outwardly as before. His first mention of the war was a note of the departure of one of his brothers-in-law for the Front.

§ 3

Yet in the early part of that year, while the shadow of war was but a cloud like a man's hand in the sky, the Duke had begun to make contacts with some of the leading figures in public life. If his February diary is largely a record of plays and operas seen, if March is a woeful catalogue of blank days on the Dee at Abergeldie, in April 1899 a ceremonial visit which he and the Duchess paid to Ireland gave him opportunities for many talks with Lord Roberts at Viceregal Lodge, and the Curragh. The Duke and Duchess both made a very good impression in Ireland, and were warmly received at Punchestown and Leopardstown and later in Kilkenny. Thence they went over to Wales and visited Carnarvon and Llandudno, where their welcome was not less warm.

In the latter part of November the Kaiser and Kaiserin paid their postponed visit to the Queen. The Duke went to Windsor to help to entertain the visitors, and a day or two later shared with his father and mother the duties of entertaining them at Sandringham. Tact was required all the time, for relations between the Kaiser and his uncle had almost reached breaking-point when the Royal party arrived in England. But the programme was carried through without any unpleasant incident. During the visit the Duke engaged the Kaiser at bowls, and writes appreciatively of his prowess as a shot.[1]

And so in the everlasting round of sporting engagements the black year ended. Reading between the lines of his journal it is not difficult to perceive that, if the country houses were as luxurious, the entertainment provided as rich and varied, the bags of pheasants as heavy as ever, much of the zest had gone out of the business of social pleasure. Somehow the pheasants did not rise as before, and one by one the men of his circle slipped silently away to another and grimmer sport. For many reasons, it was a sorry year for the Duke and for the Prince, and the Duke's *envoi* was written from his heart: " I trust the New Year will be a happier one for us all than the end of this one has been, and that this horrid war in S. Africa may soon be brought to a successful conclusion. Good-bye 1899."

§ 4

He had a greater share of responsibility in 1900, and his journal, reflecting the welcome change,[2] contains constant references to the war. When " the first good news for a long time " came in a telegram of the 16th February reporting the relief of Kimberley by General French, the country had come to realise that it was no picnic in which the flower of its army was engaged. Prince and Duke were both kept busy on duties arising out of the war, in the inspection of hospitals and hospital ships filled with returned casualties, in presiding at meetings of the War Fund, and in many other schemes. There were drafts to speed, troops to review and heroes to invest with decorations.

[1] " William shot remarkably well at Wolferton Wood, considering he has only one arm."
[2] But the year began sadly enough for the Duchess and for him. On the 21st January the Duke of Teck died very suddenly.

The Great Queen's reign was drawing to its close. There were now signs, clearly to be seen by those nearest her, that her physical powers were fast waning, and some part of her burden fell at last on shoulders better fitted to bear it. In the Duke's diary the game-cards give place to weightier documents. In quick succession he was to gum in copies of Roberts's telegrams announcing Cronje's surrender at Paardeberg on the 27th February, the anniversary of Majuba, and Buller's relief of Ladysmith on the 1st March. On the 8th the Queen came up to Buckingham Palace from Windsor, when London, realising no doubt that the chance might never come again, put into its welcome of her a warmth which expressed its unbounded admiration. On the following day the Duke stood in the crowd to watch her drive through London in a hurricane of cheers.

Good news continued to come in. On the 13th another telegram was gummed into the diary—the announcement of the capture of Bloemfontein. The nation was in more cheerful mood now, and the Royal Family was very popular throughout England. March ended with two particularly happy events. On the 30th the Prince's Ambush II won the Grand National at Aintree, and early next morning, the Duke's third son, Prince Henry, was born at the Cottage.

A series of telegrams document the next few days in the Duke's diary. Lord Roberts telegraphed from Bloemfontein, accepting the honour of standing godfather to the new Prince, and there were a number of messages from Belgium of a less auspicious kind. The Prince and Princess, on their way to Denmark, were fired at by a youth, a mere child, named Sipido, as they sat in their carriage at the Gare du Nord in Brussels. They were unhurt, and the Prince behaved very coolly. He wired brief details to the Duke from Louvain before the extent of the danger they had escaped was fully known. The next day the Princess telegraphed: " Thank God for His mercy, who saved us both. The ball was found in the carriage to-day, having passed between our two heads. I felt it wizzing across my eyes."

Early in May the Duke travelled to Berlin to attend the celebrations attending the eighteenth birthday of the Kaiser's eldest son, who took the oath of allegiance as Crown Prince after a religious ceremony. " A charming boy, goodlooking and much taller than William " is the Duke's favourable comment. There was a gala performance at the Opera, some inspections of regiments, and a grievous round of ceremonial calls to be carried out before he returned to London to resume his committees.

He was in London on Mafeking night, the 18th May, and was held up by the enormous crowds of revellers and flag-wavers as he tried to get from York House to the Marl-borough Club. He was with the Prince a few days later when the City gave them a tremendous reception, and the Prince's star shone brighter still on that famous 30th May, when he led in Diamond Jubilee after his victory at Epsom through a crowd mad with enthusiasm. The Prince had made Turf history by winning the National and the Derby in one year.[1]

The Duke had travelled up to Balmoral for the Queen's birthday, and climbed Craig Gowan to light the bonfire in celebration of the occupation of Pretoria. On 31st May Johannesburg was occupied. The Duke attended the Ascot meeting—the first " motor " Ascot—staying near the course with the Duke of Cambridge. There was a great heat-wave that Summer, and he was here, there and everywhere on official duties; in York, in London, where he met the Khedive on his arrival at Charing Cross; now receiving wounded heroes, Captain Lambton,[2] Captain Towse, V.C., an old friend of Malta days, and many others. There were investitures and constant committees and a ceremonial visit to Wolver-hampton. The Duke began at this time to see a good deal of Sir Arthur Bigge, one of the Queen's Secretaries, who was to play an important part in preparing him for kingship.

At the end of July came the news of the assassination of the King of Italy near Milan, and on the next day (30th) of the death of the Duke of Saxe-Coburg and Edinburgh. The Prince went to Germany for his brother's funeral and the

---

[1] Diamond Jubilee's time for the Derby was 2 minutes 42 seconds—exactly the same as Persimmon's time and a record for the course.
[2] Afterwards Admiral Sir Hedworth Meux.

Duke went with him. They were at Osborne for the Regatta, and then went to Balmoral for a long holiday, which both had earned.

§ 5

The last complete year of the Queen's life was one of considerable movement and activity, considering her age and the state of her health. All the winter she had remained at Windsor, indefatigable in war duties. No doubt the greatest achievement of the year was her visit to Ireland in April. It was her own decision to substitute a visit to Dublin for her customary holiday in the South of France, which the then state of Europe precluded. It was her first visit to Ireland for forty years, and the fourth of her reign. She spent three weeks at Viceregal Lodge, keeping many public engagements and entertaining the leaders of Irish Society, and everywhere she received a great welcome. It was a tribute to her courage from a warm-hearted people. She came to them crippled by rheumatism and almost blind.

On her return to Windsor she kept several engagements connected with the war, and entertained the King of Sweden and Norway.[1] She held her last Drawing-room at Buckingham Palace on the 11th May, and in person stood sponsor at the christening of Prince Henry. She was at Balmoral as usual during a part of May and June, and on her return entertained the Khedive both in London and at Windsor.

Throughout the year her chief anxiety was for the conduct and progress of the war and for the welfare of her soldiers, but many personal sorrows crowded in upon her. The murder of King Humbert and her second son's death, following upon it, were shocks which affected her deeply. Not long afterwards she learned of the serious illness of her eldest child, the Empress Frederick,[2] and of the death in South Africa of her grandson, Prince Christian Victor of Schleswig-Holstein. At the end of August she gave her assent to the proposal that the Duke and Duchess of York should visit Australia the following year to open on her behalf the new Federal Parliament.

[1] These Crowns were at that time still united.
[2] She died in August 1901.

Her last visit to Balmoral in October was among the saddest of her life, and all the usual seasonal festivities were abandoned by her wish. While she was there a General Election took place, which confirmed Lord Salisbury's Government for a further period. On the 6th November she took leave of the place which she had planned, created and for half a century loved beyond all her houses, and returned to Windsor to comfort her bereaved daughter, Princess Christian. The thirty-ninth anniversary of the Prince Consort's death was celebrated at Frogmore as usual, and on the 18th December she made her last journey—to Osborne. It was obvious to those nearest her that now the sands were fast running out.

The Duke and Duchess of York were back at the Cottage on the 5th October, and the customary shooting parties were entertained at Sandringham up to Christmas.

On the 16th January, 1901, the Duke and Duchess went up to London to carry out a short programme of duties. The next evening the Prince and Duke attended a dinner given to Lord Roberts, who had now returned from South Africa, by the United Services Club. There were 300 people present, and the Duke sat next to the guest of honour.

When we got to the Club [he records], Papa told me that darling Grandmama had had a slight stroke this morning. He got a cypher telegram tonight from Aunt Helena saying her condition was precarious but no immediate danger. It makes us all very anxious, told May when I came to bed.

For a day or two the doctors kept their worst fears to themselves. The Prince did not at once leave London, and the Duke travelled up to Sandringham on the 18th to see his mother, and on the next day, a Saturday, he began to shoot at Grimston Carr. But soon after luncheon the news came that the Queen was worse and that the Prince had left for Osborne. The Duke instantly went back to London, and the Prince returned there from Osborne. On the night of the 20th the news was very grave, and next morning the Prince, with the Kaiser, the Duke and Duchess of Connaught and the Duke, left London and crossed in the *Alberta* to Osborne. For another day the Royal Family did not abandon hope. The

Queen rallied once or twice, and one by one available members of her family gathered at Osborne.

On the 22nd January:

at 2.30 [the Duke wrote], we were all again sent for and remained with darling Grandmama almost the whole time until 6.30, when our beloved Queen and Grandmama, one of the greatest women that ever lived, passed peacefully away, surrounded by her sorrowing children and grandchildren. She was conscious up to 5 o'clock and called each of us by name and we took leave of her and kissed her hand, it was terribly distressing. Thank God darling May arrived in time at 5.30 to see her. I shall never forget that scene in her room with all of us sobbing and heartbroken round her bed. We all went to her room at 10 and there she lay covered with flowers, looking so beautiful and peaceful; the Bishop of Winchester read some prayers and we knelt all round the bed.

§ 6

The significance of the reign and death of Queen Victoria is not a subject that lends itself to treatment in a few words, even felicitous words. The reigns of sovereigns are convenient as subdivisions or chapters in history; but a reign is not usually coterminous with an " epoch " in any sense that will bear close examination. Exceptionally the reign of Victoria *was* so, and its significance was as clear to Creevey when he was writing his last comments on his world at her accession in 1837 as it was clear at her death in January 1901 to every thinking person in England. Nothing could ever be the same again. It almost seemed as if that strong, slender thread alone had of late held the sword of Damocles that hung over England, Europe and Civilisation. There had never before been a sovereign like Queen Victoria in our history as a democracy, and there would never again be another. Little by little she had built up for herself a position undreamed of as a constitutional possibility in 1837, unthinkable in and after 1901. She was unique, a legend. She was a benevolent autocrat whose power was usually shrewdly directed. She was a great statesman of the old Conservative type, and she knew her country and countrymen better than did the wisest of her ministers. As the years passed, the store of her experience on constitutional questions bulked ever larger and lent increasing weight to the authority of her views. Heaven had given into her charge—as she confidently believed—the guidance of Britain; for sixty years she had spent herself in the trust, and at the end she *was* Britain.

These things are a commonplace. It is more relevant here to consider her in her relations with her own family. She had in her many qualities which make for happy family life. She was by nature genial, sympathetic, high-spirited and perpetually interested in the welfare of her immediate family and of her widespread kin. But her private life in her opinion was consecrated to the service of her mighty office. As she was above and outside Society, so was she above and outside family life in any ordinary sense. Her children were but lesser stars circling round the sun. Their orbits were controlled and defined by it. Their lives, their aspirations, were sacrified to the great trust which reposed in her. The awe she inspired in her ministers was as nothing to the awe she inspired in her children, the sacrifices entailed on her family outweighed the sacrifices of those who served her as ministers or secretaries. Sons, daughters and sons-in-law, grandchildren and remoter relations, gave up their lives and inclinations—and could not choose but do so—to make for her sovereignty the background she deemed fitting. For all concerned that background was lacking in colour and variety. Her children went in awe of her, but they never ceased to love her, never ceased to admire her with a veneration which was almost a religion. Her example or her will shaped their lives for better or worse.

The Duke of York was aware of her greatness. She had in the last few years recognised his merits. She saw in him an instrument finely tempered for the mighty task to which he would one day succeed. The last volumes of her journal are full of tributes to the Duke and Duchess and to the great qualities which she clearly saw in them. If the flower of our modern ideal of constitutional monarchy bears the name of George V, the seed was sown by his grandmother. It is fitting here to see the end of her life and reign only through the eyes of her grandson and ultimate successor, who had never been wanting in sympathy and true affection for her, and in veneration for her high qualities; above all, for that sense of duty which, if it made for tyranny and egotism, yet transcended all petty and personal selfishness, and which he, beyond all her descendants, most clearly appreciated and admired, being best qualified by nature to do so. Indeed, they had understood each other very well.

CHAPTER V

The New Reign—Sir Arthur Bigge—" Ophir " Tour. 1901

§ 1

THE Duke had been too ill to take his fit place at his brother's funeral in 1892. Now Fate struck him down again and prevented him from attending the funeral of the great Queen. He was feeling far from well when, with his father and uncle, he travelled to London on the 23rd January to attend the Privy Council Meeting in the Banqueting Hall at St. James's Palace, summoned to approve the Royal Proclamation and to take the Oath of Allegiance.

Papa [he wrote] made a beautiful speech in which he said he wished to be called Edward VII. We then took the oath of allegiance, I kissing his hand first, and then the oath as a Privy Councillor. Saw Holzmann [1] about the Duchy of Cornwall. I have now succeeded papa as the Duke of Cornwall.

An hour or two later he took the oath in the House of Lords with his uncle, the Duke of Connaught. Next day, after the Proclamation, he left with the King and other Royalties for Osborne again.

At 4, we all received the Holy Communion in darling Grandmama's room with Her lying in our midst.

That night he fell seriously ill. His complaint was diagnosed as German measles, a severe attack, caught probably from Prince Edward, who had developed it soon after Christmas.

---

[1] Maurice Holzmann, a German by birth, had been private secretary to Queen Alexandra. He nursed the Duchy revenues with shrewdness and devotion, but lacked that personal touch with the tenants which the Duke and Duchess soon began to insist on.

He remained at Osborne in his bedroom until the 10th February, by which time the last ceremonies were completed. He expressed in his diary his grief that of all available members of the family only he and the Duchess were absent, and his satisfaction that his eldest son should represent him.

While he was still weak in the first stage of convalescence, much necessary work had to be done. His personal Staff fell to be reorganised. Sir Arthur Bigge was appointed his private secretary, and in the new arrangement no place remained for Sir F. de Winton, who had long served him. He disliked changes, and the necessity which required him to part with a faithful servant fell hardly on him. The *Ophir* was even now being prepared for the Australian visit, her great hull dazzlingly white in the dingy surroundings of Tilbury. The Duke had daily conversations with the chiefs of his Staff and with Commodore Winsloe, who was to command the big liner, now temporarily converted into one of H.M.'s ships commissioned like any ship of war. Before the Queen's death, the lists of his personal Staff for the tour and of the ship's officers had been completed to the Duke's satisfaction.

From the first formation of a personal Household down to the last day of his life and reign, he was invariably loved by those who served him. Those men, who saw him most often, stood nearest him and lived with him on terms of intimacy and informality, were the best judges of his character. Their testimony is consistent and unanimous. In his relations with them, his simple kindliness, his intense loyalty, his straightness, honesty and devotion to duty, his great qualities as a friend and good companion, stood out across the years like rocks in a changing sea. Nothing mean could ever live in his presence. They could see his faults. He was even then sometimes explosive, sometimes indiscreet in his utterances (a habit which in part grew out of the complete faith which he reposed in the discretion of *all* his servants of every rank; and which increased indeed with the years); he was neither highly educated nor much inclined to go below the surface in political, constitutional, economic, or intellectual questions. But his common sense was sound, he was balanced, level-headed and fundamentally disciplined, and his practical kindliness and loyalty never varied by a hair's-breadth. To one and all he was a master in a million, a man whom they were proud to serve, a man to whose interests they devoted their lives without question.

§ 2

It is fitting at this point to refer in some detail to the career and qualities of the Duke's new secretary, who was to exercise a powerful influence over his life, his character and his reign. That influence has been widely acknowledged, by none more generously and constantly than by the master he served for thirty years.

One of the twelve children of the Rev. J. Bigge, Vicar of Stamfordham in Northumberland, Arthur Bigge was born in 1849 on the anniversary of Waterloo, and was named after the Iron Duke. He was educated at Rossall, having determined to be a soldier. He worked immensely hard during his school holidays at various crammers, and eventually passed through the Academy into the Royal Artillery. His life as a subaltern in the Gunners was very pleasant. His was a happy nature. He was not particularly quick or brilliant. Rather, he was sound and painstaking; simplicity and honesty, good sense, loyalty and keenness were all his life the chief features of his character, and they made for him powerful and lasting friendships.

A friendship between him and the Prince Imperial led indirectly to his presentation to Queen Victoria. He had known the Prince as a fellow student and subaltern for many years before they saw service in the Zulu War of 1879, but he was not present—as it is often said he was—when the Prince met his death. At that time Arthur Bigge was down with enteric. When, in 1880, the Empress decided to visit the spot where the Prince died, Bigge, as a personal friend of her son, was chosen to go out in her party. Later in the year the Empress stayed at Abergeldie, where Bigge visited her, and it was then that he was presented to Queen Victoria, who instantly took to him, for she was a shrewd judge of character, and soon afterwards invited him to enter her Household. He had no thought to decline the invitation, but he regretted the severance from the royal regiment, in whose welfare he continued to take a deep interest all his life.

From that year, 1880, onwards, for fifty-one years his life was solely and almost continuously devoted to Queen Victoria and her grandson. It was indeed rather a dedication of his life than a contract of service, and he entered upon it with his whole heart and soul. He allowed himself no serious interests outside the secretariat, his annual holiday was a matter not of weeks but of days, and his Sundays were usually the busiest times of the working week. The Queen's death came to him —to a greater degree no doubt than to most—as the end of his world. He was then fifty-two years old and admirably fitted for the duties of private secretary to the Sovereign, a post which he had filled for the Queen since Sir Henry Ponsonby's retirement in 1895. It was not without heartsearchings that he accepted the offer from the King that he should transfer his services to the Duke. There was urgent and important work waiting for him, for the *Ophir* tour was to start within eight weeks of his appointment, and although he was already familiar with the broad outline of the cruise which long since had been planned in the Queen's Secretariat, there was a mass of business to be done at short notice.

From the first the Duke and Sir Arthur were in the position of pupil and teacher. The Duke was in 1901 thirty-six years of age, but, as has been said, had had the minimum of experience of ceremonial functions, and was far from conversant with the technique which they call for; he had interested himself hardly at all in matters of State, or in political and constitutional questions. His education had been constantly handicapped by his naval service and little effort had been since made to repair the gaps. Bigge found him a willing pupil. He had, of course, known the Duke for over twenty years, but his first close intercourse with him brought surprises and encouragement. He found a readiness to learn and a rare humility of heart, which are half the battle with a keen and conscientious instructor. These qualities in the Duke, combined with an unquestioning belief in his grandmother's greatness, enhanced the influence which Sir Arthur could bring to bear. The pupil from the first accepted his secretary's prestige, relied on his advice and listened with attention to his criticisms. Accordingly, it usually fell to the secretary to convey to the Duke criticism from any quarter. Bigge came to be accepted as one of the first of his age in the composition of speeches and memoranda. He was already a master in the right choice of words,[1] and throughout the *Ophir* tour the two, working long hours together, achieved rapid and valuable progress in their different functions to a single end.

At the time of Sir Arthur's appointment as secretary the Duke's character was still in a transitional stage. Some of the faults of youth remained, some, naturally, were never wholly eradicated. In boyhood he had been hot-tempered and impatient, and now, when the first serious call was made on all the patience and discipline in his nature, he sometimes gave Sir Arthur cause for criticism. Bigge made it his business to hear what the outside world was saying, and once or twice in the first months of his service it came to his ears that the Prince was criticised for looking cross or bored. He appealed to him, urged the supreme importance of a smiling face, and once at least was met with the reply: " We sailors never smile on duty."

About Bigge there was nothing shadowy, nothing of the " courtier " (in the lowest sense of that much-abused term); he was a man of decided and clear-cut views and would fight strenuously for any policy in which he believed. He strongly dissented at the very start from King Edward's decision to defer creating the Duke Prince of Wales until after the *Ophir* tour was made. He felt that greater honour would have been done to the Dominions by the earlier conferment of what was the fit title for the King's only son.[2] He possessed, in a word, the character of the ideal secretary. Wise, strong, careful, discreet, utterly selfless, loyal to the core, immensely

[1] The Duke was early aware of Sir Arthur's mastery of phrase, and sometimes objected to passages in drafts on the ground that " Everybody will know that that is not the sort of thing I should say."

[2] As another instance of his moral courage, he constantly voiced his dissatisfaction with York Cottage as a suitable country house for the heir to the Throne, in the face of his master's devotion to it. In Sir Arthur's view its limitations encouraged the Duke's dislike of entertaining on a scale which his position demanded.

experienced, constantly informed, a masterly draftsman, a good comrade, a great gentleman, he soon won and retained the Duke's trust and friendship, and as soon found himself transferring to her grandson all that devotion and admiration which he had felt for the Queen.

§ 3

The beginning of the new reign and era found the chief figures in no mood of optimism. The King had been depressed for some time. The events of the last two years of the Queen's reign had brought to a head the cruel anomaly of his position, and at this time he may well have felt that his hour had struck at last too late. It may be that the customary and universal outburst of encomium which usually follows the death of a Sovereign, while it is a tribute to the dead and a source of pride to the family, is no encouragement to a successor called to a post of tremendous responsibility and too long denied experience of its functions. Certain, at least, it is (for the evidence of those best qualified to judge of the state of his mind is decisive on the point) that King Edward entered upon his reign in the lowest spirits, in a condition of mind which affected his bodily health.

And his son was, for the moment, in little better case. He had been often unwell in the past two years, one illness having aggravated another. Now a serious attack of measles had brought a return of minor ills from which he had recently suffered, and his restoration to normal health was slow at a time of unusual worry. He was very much a family man, was devoted to his small children and found in his quiet home life at Sandringham all that he could ask of Fate. The coming separation weighed heavily on his heart.

On the 21st February he and the Duchess went down to Tilbury to inspect their quarters in the *Ophir*, and found them very satisfactory. Two days later King Edward paid a brief visit to Berlin to see his sister, who was dying, and the Duke and Duchess of Cornwall [1] and York went to Sandringham for

[1] On his father's accession he became Duke of Cornwall in the peerage of England, in accordance with a charter of the year 1337. His new title took precedence of the old.

a last few days of peace and quiet, to take leave and to plan one more enlargement of the Cottage to meet the needs of a growing family and new circumstances. They were back in London on the 15th March for a round of farewell visits and last purchases. "It is horrible," he wrote, "saying good-bye to the sweet children."

The royal yacht now lay beside the *Ophir* in Portsmouth Harbour and the King and Queen travelled down with them and went on board the yacht while the Duke and Duchess were received in the *Ophir*. There was a big luncheon-party in the *Ophir*, at which Mr. Joseph Chamberlain (then Colonial Secretary) and other Ministers were present, when the King proposed the healths of the Duke and Duchess, and the Duke replied. "Very much affected and could hardly speak. The leave taking was terrible. I went back with them to the Yacht when I said Good-bye and broke down quite." Soon after, led by the *Alberta*, with attendant cruisers and torpedo-boats, the *Ophir* steamed out of Portsmouth and proceeded on her voyage to Gibraltar, the shore lined with enthusiastic crowds. "About 5 we passed the *Alberta* quite close and cheered, a terrible moment, we felt terribly sad leaving all our darlings, and the *Alberta* returned to Portsmouth and we went on with the two cruisers." The Duke's narrative may not be literature, but it contains the first essentials of literature.

There was much to inspire interest and to lend enchantment to the long cruise. The project was a great one and had been many years in reaching fulfilment. The idea had been first broached in 1893 by the Australian Colonies; it was revived by New Zealand after the Diamond Jubilee Celebrations. The Duke had always favoured it and regretted the circumstances which had hitherto precluded acceptance. His marriage, the Queen's health, the Boer War, all these circumstances at various times postponed the visit he was now to make. The inconveniences of so long an absence from England were not less real in the Spring of 1901. The new King had indeed no one to rely on to share the burden of ceremonial save his son and his brother, the Duke of Connaught. But recent events had increased the urgency of the

Empire Tour. The Proclamation of September 1900, which announced the formation of a Federal Commonwealth in Australia, and the splendid response of the Dominions to Britain's war efforts in South Africa, both seemed to require that the visit should not be further postponed. The supreme importance of the Empire was just beginning to be appreciated in the Mother Country. It was fitting that the heir to the Throne should open the new Federal Parliament and deliver in person the King's thanks to the Dominions and Colonies for their generous support. Moreover, the completion of the great Jubilee bridge at Montreal was a significant achievement which called for recognition.

For the Duke, the tour was a turning-point in his career and a test of character, as indeed for the Duchess also. It was his first important and " independent command," constitutionally. Hitherto he and the Duchess had been overshadowed by his parents, as had been the Prince and Princess, in matters of State, by the Queen. Neither the Duke nor the Duchess had yet had any real opportunity to test themselves or to gain confidence, and though King Edward had long realised the evils of discouragement and frustration induced by the Queen's policy towards himself, he had not, since the Duke's marriage, succeeded in giving his son and daughter-in-law adequate opportunities to gain experience. Now at last they were to stand on their own feet, to make a success by the exercise of their qualities of a project of accepted importance; and as the first stages in the long programme were reached and triumphantly passed, their spirits rose and confidence increased.

For the Duke every port visited, every coastline sighted, brought new interest and revived old memories. Whenever he fell in with the ships of the Fleets, the Channel Fleet at Gibraltar, the Mediterranean Fleet at Malta, he met old shipmates who had served with him on Atlantic and Mediterranean stations. On board the *Ophir* he was among old and tried friends. She was already a happy ship. He himself had helped to choose her officers. His Staff was composed of men he had supreme faith in and of personal friends, many of whom had known him from boyhood.

44

§ 4

The chief item in the immense programme of duties throughout the Empire was no doubt the opening of the first Session of the new Commonwealth Parliament, and that item fell early in the tour and was admirably carried out. But the Duke and Duchess had got through a great deal of work before Australia was reached. At each Colony visited the programme was broadly the same, but varied according to local conditions. Always there were official receptions on landing, addresses received and replied to, deputations met, Durbars and meetings with native rulers and chiefs, receptions of local officials and their wives, visits to new works and famous buildings and beauty-spots, the laying of foundation-stones, inspections of hospitals, reviews of troops, investitures, presentations of colours and medals, openings of trade and other exhibitions, banquets.

In a memoir of this scope it is impracticable to follow in detail the eight-months' programme. Statistically set forth, the figures and fixtures are imposing enough. The tour extended to the five continents, and by sea and land covered a distance of nearly twice the circumference of the earth. Of the 45,000 miles travelled, 33,000 were by sea and 12,000 by land. Ceremonial visits of longer or shorter duration were made to Gibraltar, Malta, Port Said (the only land over which the British Flag did not fly),[1] Aden, Ceylon, Singapore, Melbourne, Sydney, Brisbane, Auckland, Wellington, Christchurch, Dunedin, Hobart, Adelaide, Albany, Perth, Mauritius, Durban, Cape Town, Quebec. Thence the party travelled by rail across Canada, with calls at all the principal cities to Victoria, returning home via Halifax and St. John's.

But the chief fruits of the tour were probably not all anticipated. England in the 'nineties was no doubt beginning to grow Empire-minded. The poetic ideas of dominion over palm and pine, of an Empire on which the sun never set, were pleasing to a nation not lacking in national vanity. The

[1] Their Royal Highnesses did not land at St. Vincent, Cape Verde Islands, at which the *Ophir* touched on the 3rd September.

45

England of the new century was no doubt very rich, very powerful, very secure, very sure of itself, but its national life was not everywhere accepted as wholly edifying. Among a majority of the educated classes and in Society, England was regarded as the chief sun of the universe and London the hub of the great wheel. It was natural for such a sun to attract satellites and gratifying to observe them conforming to the magnetism of their directing force. But the conception of Empire, as it exists to-day, was very far from the minds of even thoughtful English people in 1900; their notions of life in the Dominions were vague, and it cannot be denied that a certain patronage was present in their voices and manner when they spoke of the Empire. The Duke and those who in various capacities accompanied him were to bring home with them a good many interesting discoveries, which would revise many out-of-date ideas held in England about the Empire, and would possibly correct some of the false pride of the Mother Country.

Among the impressions of lasting importance made on the Duke were, first and foremost, the loyalty to the Crown shown by all classes and creeds and races in every Colony visited. It surprised him to hear from the lips of those who had never seen England even in childhood constant and loving references to Home, references natural enough from settlers born in the Old Country. It was forced in upon him that nothing had contributed so much to produce those unmistakable manifestations of loyalty and of love of England as the life and example of Queen Victoria. Everywhere she was a legend; among the more primitive races she had become invested with almost divine qualities. She had been on the Throne when the oldest among them were still infants, she had reigned throughout the most important decades in the development of many of their countries from settlements to modern nations, and she was the first British Monarch whose character and personal influence had suggested the idea of the Throne as a symbol of Imperial unity. Her grandson now formed from what he heard and saw a lasting impression of the importance which must henceforth attach to the private lives and examples of those called on to fill her place and

46

assume the power and symbolism of her great office. Possibly the discovery surprised him less than some of those round him.

He was, too, deeply impressed by the efficiency of the troops he reviewed in the countries visited. That the material would be of a high physical excellence was to be expected. It was a surprise to many soldiers, British and foreign alike, to observe the admirable discipline of the parades and to study the methods of training in the Dominions. If such methods differed in detail from those still in practice in England, it did not appear that they produced inferior results. On the contrary, experience of military training in Australia, New Zealand and Canada brought home to all capable of judging how urgent still was the need for Army reform on modern lines in the Old Country. And as with the fighting, so with the Civil Services and with Industry. The educational system of Australia produced results which England might envy and would do well to imitate. In brief, in every sphere of political, industrial and social life, there was evidence of an efficiency, a far-sightedness, a dignity, a sure foundation, which somehow surpassed the expectations of the majority of the visitors. A letter written by Bigge to his family describes the salient features of the chief function of the *Ophir* tour:

GOVERNMENT HOUSE, MELBOURNE, 11*th May* 1901.—. . . The next day was the opening of Parliament, in fact the whole object of our coming here. You will probably read and hear much about it. From here to the Exhibition Building where the function took place, about two miles, the streets were pretty well crammed and lined with soldiers; there was a cold and strong wind blowing; but otherwise it was fine. The building held, they say, 15,000 people!

Directly we got on to the dais the Old Hundredth was sung, but in that enormous building no sound seemed adequate. Then Black Rod was told to bring the members of the House of Representatives. Hopetoun [1] read Prayers. I handed to H.R.H. his speech, which he read remarkably well: the M.P.s standing just in front, below and facing the dais. At the end of speech I handed him a pink telegram paper which was from the King, which he also read and everyone

[1] 1st Marquess of Linlithgow, first Governor-General of the Australian Commonwealth, 1900–1902.

cheered. The Orchestra played the Hallelujah Chorus, which we all wished had been sung. Rule Britannia sung and all was over. I forgot to say that when H. declared the Parliament Open there was a blast of Trumpeters! which I ventured to suggest! The whole function was beautifully done, and with dignity, and was in all ways worthy of the occasion. Before leaving, the Duke and Duchess bowed and curtsied several times. We had a telegram all ready written to the King, which was flashed off directly the ceremony was over and which of course got to London before he was up! . . .

In the evening held our Privy Council, at which I acted as Clerk and swore in the " jimplies " [1] on their knees; then an Investiture, and I say seriously I never in England saw a better done function—made successful by the other chaps, especially Crichton, who walked before each fellow carrying the Insignia on a Cushion. He is a splendid-looking chap, and his walk and bows were admirable: the Colonists were inspired, and took their cue from him—the result was dignity and order: all the Ministers and wives and wives of recipients were present: the Duchess and our ladies. . . .

In New Zealand, among impressions which went deepest, were the informal visit paid to Rotorua, and the Maori welcome. In Canada the journey across the Rocky Mountains and the charms of Vancouver Island were new in the experience of the Duke as well as of the Duchess. The welcome of Toronto and the big review there also stood out in memory, as last, but not least, did the great reception prepared by the Newfoundlanders. In a letter to Queen Alexandra from Sydney, dated the 2nd June, the Duke pays a tribute to the help given him by the Duchess:

You will have read the accounts in the papers of our doings here and at Brisbane, we have certainly had a very busy time, we have tried our best to be civil to and please everyone. Darling May is of the greatest possible help to me and works very hard, I don't think I could have done all this without her. Everybody admires her very much, which is very pleasing to me. I hope you are as proud of your daughter-in-law as I am of my wife.

[1] " Jimply " was a nursery term in the Bigge family signifying " Gentleman."

So glad to hear that the sweet children are well and flourishing and that you have had them with you at Sandringham; but I think it was a pity that Bricka [1] did not go too as David really ought to do a few lessons each day; he is 7 years old already.

Tomorrow I am going up country . . . I shall indeed be glad to have a change after all these functions and receptions. . . .

Some idea of the strain imposed on the Duke and Duchess is conveyed in a letter he wrote to his mother on the 8th July, after the New Zealand visit:

I have sent Papa a short diary of our doings there written by Sir Donald Wallace. . . . I certainly never had such hard work for 17 consecutive days before but, strange to say, neither May nor I were any the worse. We were occasionally a bit tired. We do rest whenever we can. It is all very well for you and Papa to say we mustn't do too much but it is impossible to help it. Our stay at each place is so short that everything has to be crammed into it, otherwise the people would be offended and our great object is to please as many people as possible. . . .

The Duke's character, of course, made a strong appeal to the men of the Empire. Those (in Australia) who remembered him as a boy found him little changed in essentials. Whenever opportunity came to him, he delighted to put aside the formality which ceremonial imposed and to talk with the people he met as man to man. They appreciated his simplicity and directness of approach and understood his frank and breezy manner. They liked his loud laugh and occasionally explosive comments. There was none of the " Oxford manner " about the Duke. They knew him for a sportsman. They saw his graceful seat on a horse,[2] and his reputation as a

---

[1] Mdlle Bricka—an Alsatian lady—had been companion to the Duchess in her girlhood at White Lodge. She was highly educated and politically liberal and was remarkable for her strength of character and devotion to her pupil. She had come to Princess May to assist in her self-imposed finishing education and at this time she was superintending Prince Edward's first lessons.

[2] The Duke was never a fine horseman, though he was fond of hunting and had played polo in his younger days. He sat his horse well and managed it adequately on ceremonial occasions, but horsemanship was not in him.

crack shot had, of course, gone out before him. To farmers he could speak as a farmer himself " in a small way," and they were won over by his keen anxiety to learn from their methods. He was often tired, but throughout the tour few ever saw him bored or giving divided attention to what he was engaged in. It was not otherwise with the Duchess. Her energy and interest in all she saw left no room for doubt that she was a genuine searcher after knowledge, which she would add to a store of experience already remarkable. She had theories soundly based, and sometimes in advance of the age, in many branches of social welfare, not to say in matters of art and taste, and those who received her were quick to realise that her interest and knowledge went below the surface.

They were, no doubt, sometimes strained to the limit of endurance by an overloaded programme, and by their determination to give satisfaction and pleasure to as many as possible. In those days, of course, before wireless was invented or even typewriters were in general use, the difficulties of preparing speeches were even greater than now. To-day, a ship with a mission such as the *Ophir's* would be in constant touch by wireless with the next port of call, and any change in the programme or circumstances could be instantly given effect to in the speeches preparing aboard. But in 1901, as in later years King George would ruefully recall, he and Sir Arthur often spent anxious hours at very short notice revising speeches and writing them out again in long-hand. By the end of the Canadian programme, the Duke was very near the end of his powers of endurance, and once at least, at Quebec, the Duchess stepped into the breach at the last moment.

§ 5

When at last at the end of October the *Ophir* felt her way home through the fogs off the Newfoundland Bank and took the green rollers of the Atlantic over her decks, the Duke's mind was as heavily stored with new impressions and experiences as was the *Ophir* with presents and mementoes of his visits to many lands.[1] But of all these confused memories those

[1] He had added greatly to his collection of British Empire stamps, with the ready help of the Postmasters-General in every territory visited.

graven deepest perhaps on the Duke's orderly, statistical mind were the tell-tale figures of " business done "—45,000 miles of sea steamed, 12,000 miles by rail, 24,855 hands shaken at public receptions alone, 62,000 troops reviewed, 231 days of absence from England, 125 of them spent at sea, and—not least convincing of hard work—14,500 tons of coal burned from the *Ophir's* bunkers. . . .

The *Ophir* had been their home for eight long months, the only home they had known, which they had left with anxiety for a hundred important ceremonies, and to which they had returned as often with the satisfaction that comes from duty done. Those on board her had become a happy circle of intimate friends; old ties had been strengthened and new and enduring links of friendship forged by great experiences shared and common difficulties overcome. When at last the familiar coastline of England was sighted across an angry sea, the Duke and Duchess were justified in feeling that they had done their part in making a success of a great undertaking and that they returned home bringing their sheaves with them.

They had a wonderful reception. The reunion with their family held in it all the joy to which they had so long looked forward. Throughout the long tour the Press of the country had been fed with first-hand information of the progress of events in every territory visited, and the leader-writers of the chief newspapers on the day of the Duke's return summarised the achievements of a programme grandly conceived and admirably carried out, and announced a fact which the public had already learned for themselves, that the Duke and Duchess of Cornwall and York had proved themselves in a test of a magnitude which left no doubt of their qualities. Certainly the heir to the Throne returned home with a knowledge and an experience of Empire which none of his father's ministers could equal and with ideas concerning it which might surprise many and benefit all of them.

Upon the 9th of November the King created him Prince of Wales. Three weeks later he went in State to the Guildhall to deliver a public summary of the impressions of his tour. That speech, delivered on the 5th December, 1901, has gone down to history with a label attached to it. Like most labels, it does not very exactly describe the contents. It is called the " Wake-up, England " speech. The label is rather a documentation of the manner of thought in England at the close of last century. It was news to many in the Old Country that England needed to wake up, news that she would do well to learn valuable lessons at the feet of her young daughters, news that the strengthening of Empire ties was henceforth to be a chief item in the policy of British Governments, and news that that great ideal had already blossomed long since in the outposts of Empire. In truth the label was derived from no clarion call in the speech; other points made by the Prince had no less prominence in his mind and in his address. The only reference to " waking up " was made discreetly enough in the final paragraph of a short but admirably balanced survey:

To the distinguished representatives of the commercial interests of the Empire whom I have the pleasure of meeting here to-day, I venture to allude to the impression which seemed generally to prevail among their brethren across the seas, that the Old Country must wake up if she intends to maintain her old position of pre-eminence in her Colonial trade against foreign competitors.

That, and no more. But the words stuck, and were taken up as the keynote of the speech and shaped the wording of the label. The children had given advice to the parent who had so long believed in her directing force and in her mission as exemplar and adviser-in-chief. The younger generation was knocking on the door.

The speech was as well received as it was admirably delivered. No doubt Sir Arthur Bigge heard it with more satisfaction than surprise. He and those who had observed the Duke during the tour had formed a high opinion of his qualities as a speaker. From the day of the great test at Melbourne he had consistently abated any anxiety they may have felt, and his delivery had constantly improved. He spoke without hesitation, in a clear, ringing voice, with a great deal of understanding of the value of words and sentences and with effective changes of tone. Sir Arthur had good reason to be pleased with the results of eight months of careful coaching in matters of State and kingship.

A day or two later the Prince of Wales was released and began to shoot again. There is a letter of his to his father, written from Elveden on the 10th December, which is revealing of his character. Soon after the Guildhall speech, the King wrote to him to congratulate him on it and to thank him for the excellent way in which he had carried out the vast programme of the *Ophir* tour. To this the Prince replied:

MY DEAREST PAPA,—I hasten to thank you from the bottom of my heart for the more than kind letter which you gave me yesterday. It has touched me more than I can say. And it makes me very happy to know that you are pleased with the way that May and I carried out the very important mission which you entrusted to us and that you approved of my speech at the Guildhall. If I have gained your approval, I am quite satisfied.

That letter could have come only from a humble heart. It may be taken as evidence that the Prince was not of a character ever likely to be changed by success, as evidence indeed that he was unspoilable and that his natural simplicity would last his life, however distinguished it might be.

CHAPTER VI

Politics and Social Life—King Edward's Illness and Coronation. 1901‑3

§ 1

THE new reign was (in the easy phrase which may with more or less truth be applied to every decade in human history) a period of transition. England at the close of the Victorian era was a nation in " splendid isolation." About the isolation there was no sort of doubt. The country had entered into no major commitments in Europe and still stood aloof from the policy of defensive alliances with European or Eastern States. The balance of power had been adequately maintained without her weight in the scales. There were elements of splendour about her position. She was immensely rich and she had long enjoyed an unchallenged sea-power. On the other hand, the South African War dragged on and had done much to tarnish her reputation in Europe and to stimulate the jealousies and aspirations of nations less favoured and privileged. When Lord Roberts returned in triumph from the seat of war to receive with almost her last breath the thanks of his Queen, he himself shared the common belief that the war was practically over. But only a few days afterwards that easy belief was blown away. The war dragged wearily on well into the new reign and was to cost the Empire 20,000 lives and 200 millions of money. The reign began in a spirit of disillusion and war-weariness which weighed on the nation from the King downwards.

The war had had its effect on trade. A marked recession had been in evidence for six months, the heavy industries were acutely depressed and a War Budget of more than usual severity would necessitate higher taxation. In the first Budget of the reign the income-tax was raised to 1s. 2d., with increased taxes on the people's breakfast-table. Naturally, the criticism of Britain and her Government was not confined to foreigners. The cry of inefficiency was heard in the land.

The Government inherited by King Edward was still led by Lord Salisbury, whose approaching retirement was already anticipated. The chief strength of the Ministry lay in Mr. Chamberlain, the Colonial Secretary, whose energy and vision in matters reaching far beyond his department seemed to mark him out for still higher preferment, and assured him, once the issues of the war were clear beyond all doubt, a popularity reserved for the heroic figures in our history. To that position he had not won without years of hard work and disappointments. Lord Lansdowne was at the Foreign Office, Sir Michael Hicks Beach was Chancellor, Lord Selborne was at the Admiralty. On Mr. Brodrick (Earl of Midleton) at the War Office and Mr. Gerald Balfour (2nd Earl of Balfour) at the Board of Trade the brunt of the attack fell, and there were many gaping joints through which it could be pressed home.

In indifferent health and low spirits, King Edward was beset by worries from the day of his accession. He was deeply wounded by the doubts expressed in some quarters—both expected and unexpected—as to his own fitness for the great office to which he had at last been called, and he could not but realise that he had had hitherto the minimum of training in the conduct of State business. Matters of ceremonial and of lesser moment, on which he was an acknowledged authority, perhaps received an undue share of his attention. He showed from the first days of his reign a determination to revive the ceremonial circumstance of the Monarchy, and to give back to it the splendours and parade which had declined with every decade since the death of his father. No details of the Coronation ritual were too unimportant to claim his attention.

He was deeply concerned, too, with the condition of the royal residences. Buckingham Palace had degenerated into an antiquated museum, quite unfit for occupation by modern standards of comfort and hygiene. Windsor was in little better case and demanded any amount of attention, and there was, besides, the embarrassing question of Osborne, which the Queen had left to him as a family residence in perpetuity and *in piam memoriam*. He could not satisfactorily solve the problem it created—since he was determined not to live in it—without wounding the feelings of some of his sisters.

He entered upon all these matters with great energy and promptness, which left him all too little time to spare to affairs of State. In his contacts with his ministers in those early days he made one or two false starts. They were due to inexperience, as he generously acknowledged, and he very soon put those relations on a firm basis. His methods were very different from his mother's. Throughout his reign he relied very much more on expert judgment and largely reduced the bulk of exchanges of views between King and ministers. In certain fields of first-rate and of secondary importance in which he was, or soon became, an acknowledged master, he was sometimes more autocratic than Queen Victoria. He became a model of punctuality in the business of State, if his interest in its various aspects was not uniformly sustained; and his conception of the functions of his office well suited the times and conditions in which he reigned. Meanwhile he was worried and overworked, and often wounded or irritated by the pinpricks of radical critics whose heads are invariably raised during debates on the financial provisions necessitated by a demise of the Crown; and his health steadily declined.

The dawn of the new century was obscured by fog, but there were many indications that, exceptionally, the late reign was coterminous with an era, and that with the new reign and century a new age had come in. The motor-car had made no startlingly rapid strides during the last few years, but by 1901 public dislike or ridicule of the new transport was beginning to be tempered with respect for its possibilities and even for its performance; and already the uses of the internal-combustion engine for a submarine arm of the Navy had been accepted. Marconi's wireless system, too, was now being operated between Newfoundland and a station at Poldhu in Cornwall; and one or two pioneers were experimenting with dirigible balloons. In London a brand-new electrically driven underground railway system was running, revolutionising the slow and dingy methods which Londoners had too long endured. The telephone system was being largely extended in private service, and businesses were everywhere being modernised by telephones, typewriters and up-to-date index and filing systems. Some of these things were still but toys for the wealthy and privileged. But to the nation at large they afforded grounds for an unhealthy pride and self-satisfaction in the progress and wisdom of civilised men. No one had yet realised the danger to the nation's health from so much rich, new fare so greedily gobbled, nor imagined the devastation which would come in the train of these triumphs and would soon outweigh the benefits they might confer on the human race. The heart of the nation was a battleground in which pride fought with doubt, vainglory with distrust, security with anxiety, disillusion with a new hope of wider horizons political and cultural.

In social life the barriers between class and class seemed to stand as high and impregnable as at any time in the last hundred years, even if, under the leadership of the new King, the circle of Privilege had been liberally recruited for some years from a new aristocracy of wealth and initiative which was busily engaged in consolidating its position behind the barriers. In politics the Opposition was making its voice heard with more confidence, and in industry the voice of Trade Union leaders continually challenged the policy of masters.

In social evolution the new Prince of Wales accepted what came without question and enjoyed what was new where it marched with his inclinations, turning his back on such innovations as did not suit his conservatism. This indeed applied to persons and to things alike. He took up golf and bicycling, bridge and motoring, being an early pioneer in electric and petrol-driven cars; he raced, played and betted in moderation, and was a staunch patron of the stage and the opera. His loyalty to his father was absolute, his admiration for him intense. But he did not slavishly follow his father in the gamut of new fashions or unquestioningly adopt his father's circle of friends as his own. He was by nature far more conservative than the King, and his conservatism now

57

embraced a dislike of foreign travel, of foreign ways, of cosmopolitan society, of the breaking down of social conventions. In his attitude to Society he was a Victorian in an Edwardian setting, and he still chose his own intimates chiefly from the ranks of the Old Guard. The world of men and women were all the books which the King used or needed. He read little and thought and learned a good deal. The Prince, on the other hand, under the influence of the Princess and of Sir Arthur Bigge, began now to read a good deal and to study the problems of the day by that means, not indeed deeply, but in a sincere and humble search after knowledge. King Edward's circle of intimates, accordingly, was inclined already to whisper that the Prince and Princess lived rather dull and colourless lives.

While his grandmother reigned he had probably concerned himself as little as any of his age and abilities and opportunities with the political questions and events of the day and had indeed rather less than more occasion and inclination to do so. That was now changed and the story of his private life will be made clearer by a very brief summary of the political events of the early part of his father's reign both abroad and at home.

§ 2

The latter half of King Edward's reign was passed under Liberal Governments. During the earlier part Mr. Balfour's administration was responsible for a radical change in our foreign policy. The King was in full agreement with his Foreign Minister, Lord Lansdowne, that with the new century the era of Splendid Isolation was at an end. Unchallenged sea-power could no longer be a decisive factor in Britain's foreign policy. That power was threatened by the growing navies of other nations which, in combination, might seriously menace the integrity of our Empire. It behoved us therefore to seek alliances and, if need be, to throw our weight into the balance of power in Europe. From this new policy came first in 1902 the Japanese Alliance which was to serve us so well in the First Great War and which at the time saved us from a heavy expenditure on defence in the Pacific.

More dear to the King's heart was the understanding with France which came to be so closely linked with his name. Germany had for some years been throwing a menacing shadow over Europe. A vigorous, disciplined, strongly led nation, her population and wealth and ambition were all growing fast. Her Army was already feared in Europe, and now she was seeking to rival the naval power of Britain. German ambition threw us into the arms of France and brought us back into the balance of power in Europe. It is beyond the scope of a summary to consider the extent to which the personal relations of individuals may affect in modern times the destinies of the nations which they lead. No doubt Lord Lansdowne had hereditary affinities with France, no doubt King Edward's justifiable antipathy to his nephew added zest to his own efforts to bring about the Entente. All his charm was required, for the arms of the Republic were by no means opened to receive us. Englishmen were still received coldly in Paris if no longer hooted in the streets, and the memory of the Boer War and the " Affaire Dreyfus " were not the only causes of friction. There were clashes of interest between the two countries in Egypt and in Morocco, and the way to smoother words and closer understanding was not opened until Lord Lansdowne had succeeded in composing those differences. The King, it is true, won back his own popularity in France in a personal triumph before the defensive Entente—which was a broad ideal rather than an exactly defined alliance—was brought about. Its achievement was the signal for a ten years' race in armaments to begin in Europe, and war became a practical certainty within a very few years.

In the chequered history of the relations of European States it is difficult to find anything new. Situations are quickly repeated and the slogans of to-day are but the half-forgotten heart-cries of yesterday. The situation in Europe between 1904 and 1914 was often an ominous and faithful parallel with that of 1939. The decade which preceded the First Great War heard from Germany the loud and constant cry of encirclement. Britain, France and Russia were attempting to encircle Germany and to strangle her legitimate and essential expansion. By every means then available the leaders of Germany sought, while they piled up armaments, to persuade the world and their people of the reality of this nefarious purpose. And then, as now, a majority of the German people believed it.

At home, as has been said, the King inherited a Conservative Government kept in power by Liberal-Unionist support. It still possessed a substantial majority in 1901, and when the South African War had been at last brought to an end, it could look back, not without satisfaction, to the record of legislation it had sponsored and carried through Parliament. It had passed into law a number of important measures greatly improving conditions of life for people in every class. It was Mr. Balfour's Education Bill of 1902 which was to do much to bring the reign of Conservatism to an end. For the bitterness evoked among the Nonconformists by the Government's half-measures with the Church voluntary schools in the transfer of primary and secondary schools to the County Councils did more than anything else to revive Liberalism and establish the sporadic Labour movements on a firm and united basis. Unionist Conservatism was no doubt due for a period of eclipse, having served its turn. The Education Bill jolted it. Tariff Reform gave it its knock-out, as in 1886 Home Rule had shattered the Liberal Party.

Mr. Chamberlain, still the Government's key-man, had nursed his theories for a considerable time. The Prince's " Wake-up, England " speech had with reasonable exactness anticipated the chief arguments in Mr. Chamberlain's Protection proposals which were the fruits of the Colonial Conference held in London during the Summer of the Coronation. The Empire was to be united and cemented by Imperial Preference, Britain to be protected against ever more stringent foreign competition by means of tariffs on foreign imports. Tariff Reform, as propounded by Mr. Chamberlain, implied some taxation of food. While imports from the Colonies would be free, foreign foodstuffs would be subject to tariffs. The " people's breakfast-table," already taxed by a War Budget duty on imported corn, was menaced again. Mr. Ritchie, the new Chancellor, led the Free Trade Opposition with a relentless determination which Mr. Chamberlain's persuasive oratory could not shake. Mr. Balfour's desperate expedient of purging his Cabinet of the extremists on both sides in the issue was unavailing. His Government resigned, and in the General Election of 1906 his party was routed.

A Liberal Government, under Sir H. Campbell-Bannerman, united against Tariff Reform with the Irish Nationalists and the Socialist group which had obtained fifty seats in the new House, came into office and Liberalism remained in power throughout King Edward's reign and well into the Great War.[1] Many rising politicians came into prominence during the bitter phase of the Protection issue. Lord Hugh Cecil and Mr. Winston Churchill were protagonists in the Free Food League, Mr. Amery sponsored the Tariff Reform League, while Mr. Austen Chamberlain filled an uneasy gap in Mr. Balfour's purged Cabinet, becoming Chancellor of the Exchequer at the early age of forty. The name of Mr. Lloyd George was already familiar to the man in the street as a shrewd debater and orator on the Liberal side since the Education controversies, and in Sir Henry Campbell-Bannerman's Ministry his services were rewarded with office.

The formation of that Ministry presented no great difficulty and few major surprises. Mr. Asquith was Chancellor of the Exchequer, Sir Edward Grey went to the Foreign Office, Mr. Haldane to the War Office, Mr. Morley to the India Office, Mr. Herbert Gladstone to the Home Office. Sir Robert Reid became Lord Chancellor as Lord Loreburn. A place was found for one Socialist in the Cabinet—Mr. John Burns at the Local Government Board. Mr. Winston Churchill, as Under-Secretary for the Colonies, was given a chance to try his wings, and among other rising juniors who secured minor offices were Mr. McKenna, Mr. Runciman and Mr. Herbert Samuel.

[1] Mr. Balfour had never attempted to make himself intelligible to King Edward, whose relations with his next Prime Minister, Sir Henry Campbell-Bannerman—the first to be constitutionally confirmed as such—were very much easier. It is interesting to note that Mr. Balfour was always at ease with the Prince of Wales. According to Lord Esher, he said to him in 1909: " Except the German Emperor, the Prince of Wales is the only prince to whom I find I can talk as man to man. He is really clever."

Such, very briefly and simply set forth, were the political situation and social conditions during the earlier part of the new reign. And so no doubt, broadly and superficially, the Prince saw and appreciated them. At a later stage the actions of the House of Lords, and the political events which shaped those actions, will come to be considered.

§ 3

To return to 1901. The Duke had been created Prince of Wales on the 9th November. The composition of his new Household was soon afterwards announced. Lords Wenlock and Chesham became Lords of the Bedchamber, Sir William Carington Comptroller, Sir Arthur Bigge was confirmed as Private Secretary, Captain Wentworth-Fitzwilliam [1] was Master of the Stables, Sir Charles Cust and Mr. Derek Keppel remained Equerries, with Lord Crichton and Commander Bryan Godfrey-Faussett. Canon Dalton became Domestic Chaplain. He was in the sixties now, and a mine of knowledge about all that concerned the history of Windsor; the happy relations between tutor and pupil were as enduring as ever.

The Court remained in London that Christmas. The Queen was suffering from an attack of chicken-pox, and she and the King stayed on at the Palace. The Prince and Princess settled into the Cottage, which, now enlarged for the last time, presented a wonderful amalgamation of styles. But it was in a better condition to cope with the increasing demands to be made on it. Mr. Hansell [2] had been appointed tutor to the elder princes. Nursery and schoolroom needs took up a good deal of the available space, but there was accommodation for a few guests and for an enlarged Household, as well as for a majority of the servants. There were occasions when as many as fifty people were put up in the Cottage. The necessary alterations to Marlborough House,

[1] Captain the Honourable (afterwards Sir) Charles Wentworth-Fitzwilliam, son of 6th Earl Fitzwilliam.

[2] Mr. Henry P. Hansell was tutor to all the sons of King George V and later to Prince Nicolas of Roumania. He was immensely liked by all his pupils without exception. A Norfolk man, educated at Magdalen College, Oxford, he had spent several years as a public-school and private-school master.

which the Prince and Princess were to take over, were also in hand at this time.

And so 1901 ended and the Prince gave it the customary envoi in his journal: " So endeth 1901. A very eventful year to us."

§ 4

The first year of the new century had certainly been a very important one in the lives of the Prince and Princess. When it began they were, considering the positions they occupied, peculiarly inexperienced and unproved in matters of State and in responsibility. Before the year ended he had become the immediate heir to the Throne and both had proved their merits and ability in a testing programme of great magnitude and real importance to the Empire, the results of which had exceeded expectations. He was a changed man. A new authority was already observable in his writings and utterances. He had begun to assume his appropriate responsibilities. From the first days of the formation of his new Household relations between it and the King's were harmonious. It was the King's policy to trust his heir without reserve, and he soon gave orders that, as far as might be, no confidential matters should be withheld from the Prince. Certainly Sir Francis Knollys and Sir Arthur Bigge worked together throughout the reign in the same harmony and trust which distinguished the relations of their royal masters.

Certain letters which the Prince addressed to Sir Arthur Bigge in January 1902 throw a light on several matters of importance in such a memoir as this. They indicate the great trust which the Prince reposed in his secretary from the beginning; they show the continued development of the Prince's character and the progress to the attainment of that mutual confidence between the Sovereign and his heir which the King had never enjoyed as Prince, which he intended that his son should enjoy, but which he could not instantly concede.

Prince of Wales to Sir Arthur Bigge

YORK COTTAGE, *1st January* 1902.

My DEAR BIGGE,—First let me thank you for your most kind letter receivd. this morning & for all yr good wishes to

63

us for the New Year. The one that is now over has indeed been an eventful one for me & mine; it has been a sad one and a happy one & there is much to be thankful for, as you say. I must again repeat how grateful I am to you for all you have done for me during this past year. I thank you for yr kind help & advice & for yr great loyalty. I feel that I can always rely on you to tell me the truth however disagreeable & that you are entirely in my confidence. To a person in my position it is of enormous help to me. I thank you again for it from the bottom of my heart. . . .

YORK COTTAGE, *4th Jan.*—. . . A Colonial Office Box has just arrived but I had no key to open it with, I sent it up to Sidney Greville to unlock it; it only contained a telegram from Hely-Hutchinson expressing thanks from officers & men of Cape Peninsula Regiment to me for becoming their Col. in Chief. You had better get a key for me if they are going to send me boxes, otherwise I can't open them. I am returning you all the letters and papers you sent me & have written on them all. I am sending this pouche by the messenger. Believe me, Your sincere friend, GEORGE.

9th Jan.—. . . I don't think Bulow's speech will in any way tend to improve the relations of the two countries, he missed his opportunity of repudiating these foul lies about our Army made in Germany. *The Times* gives it him hot & says that his speech will only make matters worse. It makes it all the more pleasant for my journey to Berlin.[1] I hate the very idea of going. . . .

WINDSOR CASTLE, *22nd Jan.*—. . . I thought the little service [2] was charming, the singing beautiful and the Bishop's words simple & dignified. I am afraid it was a very sad day for you & brought back all the sad trying days which happened a year ago. I don't know yet if I am going to Berlin. But Lascelles has just telegraphed that he saw the Emperor today who informed him that he had not receiv'd my father's letter, I can hardly believe that possible, Lascelles sent it himself to the Palace last Thursday & got a receipt for it. Lord Salisbury strongly urges that I should not go unless the King receives a satisfactory answer to his letter from the Emperor. This is most disagreeable for me & especially if I have to go in the end. . . .

[1] For the Kaiser's birthday celebrations.
[2] Anniversary of Queen Victoria's death.

The Prince seldom wrote to Sir Arthur, for the good reason that his secretary was so rarely absent from his post. The King was, on the other hand, often away from England, and long and frequent letters were exchanged between father and son during the reign. Yet the confidence and freedom of expression observable in the Prince's letters to Sir Arthur were lacking still in those addressed to his father. The point is worth re-stating. In writing to Queen Alexandra, the Prince was always free and forceful enough in expressing (not without humour) his views, to Sir Arthur he wrote with increasing good sense, but to the King it was not so. Always there is something of the copybook in the matter and the manner of his letters which the obvious care taken in their preparation renders somewhat stilted and colourless, so that it is hard to select passages from them for quotation. It is an artificiality foreign to the Prince's frank and straightforward nature and it is on one side only in the correspondence. The King wrote to his son in his characteristic way naturally enough. But somehow the Prince could not respond in like manner.

But the fruits of the first year of Sir Arthur's intensive training were already visible in the Prince's diary. He is much more concerned to record matters of duty, and sport hereafter takes second place. There is also a very noticeable improvement in his style of writing and in his spelling. Indeed, henceforth errors in spelling become rarities.[1]

He began to be assiduous in his attendance at important debates in the Lords, usually in February and March, for during the Season he was generally too busy, and his diary also contains frequent notes of conversations with ministers and leaders in the Services, the Church, Politics and Industry. He spent a good deal of time most days over official business with Sir Arthur and already showed signs of a determination to judge for himself by reading despatches and documents at length, and not to accept précis and marked passages as a short-cut to knowledge. In this respect he differed from his father.

---

[1] But " Mausoleum " and " Academy " defeated him all his life.

§ 5

Towards the end of January he went to Berlin to be present at the Kaiser's birthday celebrations and passed there two strenuous days devoted to huge official dinners (which he detested), and to military ceremonies with his Imperial host. Anti-British feeling in Germany was still strong, and the King had indeed tried to postpone the visit. But the Prince made a success of it, and no mention occurs in his diary of difficulties anticipated or realised. He returned home by way of Strelitz for a busy season of official ceremonies and inspections in London and the provinces.

Arrangements for the coming Coronation had now begun to mortgage the time of ministers and functionaries of the Court. All through the Spring the Prince was kept busy, and in April he and the Princess followed the Queen to Copenhagen for the King of Denmark's eighty-fourth birthday celebrations.[1] He came back with a cold, the third severe one he had caught since his return from Canada.

In May he and the Princess paid official visits to Carnarvon and Rhyl, staying at Vaynol,[2] and afterwards went down for a few days to Frogmore House in Windsor Home Park, which the King had put at their disposal. They were delighted with it, and found it very comfortable, but later on the Prince complained of its dampness. Indeed, he used to say that the climate of Windsor never agreed with him. On the 1st June he learned that the war was over. He records in his diary on that day that the King sent for him to the Palace and told him that peace had been signed in Pretoria on 30th May. The Prince copied into his diary Lord Kitchener's secret telegram announcing the event. He added: " War was practically declared by the Boers on Oct. 11. 1899, so that a State of War has existed between us and the South African Republics for 968 days. Thank God, it is over at last." On the 8th June the Royal Family attended a Peace Service in St. Paul's.

[1] The wonderful old man still rode winter and summer for an hour every day and still maintained a Court routine, gruelling to visitors, which entailed dinner at half-past six and much extra eating and standing about onwards until nearly midnight.   [2] Mr. Assheton-Smith's.

§ 6

The great day, the 26th June, was now drawing near, and preparations were well advanced to finality. The streets were already transformed with wooden stands and gay with bunting, and the Parks were a camp for soldiers of the Empire and a magnet for the huge crowds of sightseers who thronged London.

The King's illness and the postponed Coronation are matters of history and medical history, which have been exhaustively described and recorded. The Prince's diary notes relating to his father's illness are short and precise. On the 14th June the King first complained of severe pain. He was better on the 15th, but was unable to go to Ascot although he stayed in the Castle that week. The Prince and Princess went down to Frogmore, and were with the Queen when she drove in State along the Racecourse. On Prince Edward's birthday, the 23rd June, they joined the King and Queen at the Palace to help in the reception of foreign Royalties who were to attend the Coronation.

But the King was in considerable pain again. " I don't think him at all well today," wrote the Prince, " and he suffers more pain. We are getting in despair. Laking is always with him." That night it was decided that an operation for perityphlitis must be performed the next day. Shortly before it was carried out by Sir Frederick Treves the Prince saw his father and had a talk with him. He was struck by his bravery and calmness. He faced all eventualities and was prepared for them. The operation was successful in removing a dangerous abscess. It is significant evidence of the King's vitality that on the very next day the Prince saw his father sitting up and smoking a cigar.

They were busy and anxious days for the Prince. He was constantly engaged in answering telegrams and enquiries and in discussions of moment with ministers and officials. The King's condition remained a matter of great anxiety for some days. The foreign visitors had already begun to disperse on the 25th and the Prince was worked to death.

By the 1st July the worst was over. The King was definitely

better and sleeping satisfactorily. On that day the Prince reviewed the assembled Colonial troops on the Horse Guards parade-ground. " I wore General's uniform for the first time," he noted, " and rode dear old Princess, who still looks beautiful. She is 22." For the next fortnight one duty succeeded another, and many immediate problems claimed his attention, besides the arrangements which were being planned for moving the King when he was pronounced fit for it. When, with the consent of his doctors, it was decided that he should go on board the royal yacht, the King was almost morbidly anxious that the journey to Portsmouth should be made with the utmost secrecy and privacy. The journey was swiftly and smoothly accomplished, and the King was on board the royal yacht in the Solent before the general public was aware that the move was contemplated. On the 16th July the Prince joined the party in the *Victoria and Albert* off Cowes. On the eve of the King's departure Lord Salisbury, who had decided not to delay his retirement any longer, had come to the Palace and placed his resignation in the King's hands, and the latter had sent for Mr. Balfour.

The Prince's relief and thankfulness at his father's safety are reflected in his diary, and confirmed in a vivid and unpublished memoir written down by one of the King's doctors. The Prince wrote: " Found dear Papa lying on deck and looking so well and delighted with the change. He is able to see everything that goes on with glasses." The memoir referred to, which treats at length of the illness and of the arrangements so elaborately made for privacy on the journey to Portsmouth, gives a vivid picture of the Prince's reaction from anxiety and depression. His loud laughter echoed over the yacht. He was heard amid shouts of merriment to read and re-read to the company a " personal character study " of himself by a doubtfully inspired gossip-writer in a weekly journal. His gaiety was infectious. While he remained in the yacht he was the life and soul of the party, and the writer of the memoir decided that he had never seen the Prince in such tearing spirits. The King was resolved that when Sir Frederick Treves left the yacht, he must be accorded a very special, royal send-off, and the Prince was employed to make the arrangements. He did it with a will.

His own gratitude to Sir Frederick and the King's doctors and nurses for their skill and care in his father's illness was immeasurable. He loved his father dearly, admired him intensely. Even then the times seemed to him dark and dangerous and the difficulties of kingship many and great. He was not blind, if deaf, to his father's faults; but he had faith in his father's genius and as yet little or none in his own abilities. In a word, he gave to King Edward that unquestioning hero-worship which is offered to an acknowledged leader in fullest measure by men of humble and loyal heart and of disciplined mind. He felt that his father's life was at that juncture of the utmost value to the country and to himself.

§ 7

More than once in his life King Edward's misfortunes turned unexpectedly to his advantage. Now, not for the first time, he regained his strength in the sunshine of popular esteem. There was no more talk of unfitness; the country was generous in the expression of its relief. In that warm atmosphere the King's health and spirits rapidly improved. The postponed Coronation was fixed for the 9th August, and he was soon as busy as ever with matters of detail. It was not practicable to reassemble all the foreign Royalties. The King designed that the solemn ritual should now be gorgeously and elaborately carried out as the symbol and the centre-piece in a manifestation of the greatness and solidarity of the British Empire, and the idea caught the fancy of a nation newly become Empire-minded. No splendid detail from the pageantry of past Coronations was neglected and when London saw its King and Queen, wearing their crowns, passing back from the Abbey, its enthusiasm knew no bounds, and from that day to this the popularity of the Monarchy has continued to increase and public interest in the doings of the Royal Family to grow. " A never to be forgotten day," the Prince summed it up in his diary, after giving brief details of his own part in the ceremony which his two elder sons watched from the Princess's box.

A Naval Review is always one of the features of a Coronation programme. It chanced that, as the might of Britain's sea-power was taking station off Spithead, the ship that carried to England the three Boer generals who had come to plead for leniency for their defeated countrymen passed down the line. It was an unfortunate coincidence and the Boers refused a well-meant invitation to watch the Review. They went on to London, where the friendly and even boisterous welcome of the crowds did little to soften the bitterness of their spirit or to give them a better understanding of the English character. The King determined to receive them privately, and the meeting took place on board the royal yacht with happy results. It was a very successful stroke in his general policy of appeasement and a good instance of his tact. The Prince was present during the interview, as were Lords Roberts and Kitchener.

§ 8

After the Review the Princess and the Royal children left for Abergeldie, whither the Prince followed them after presiding at a State Banquet in honour of the Shah at Buckingham Palace. He broke his journey to Abergeldie at Studley. It was a good grouse year, and five guns averaged 450 brace a day. On the 23rd August, the bag was 502 brace. " de Grey [his host] shot beautifully as usual and got over 370 birds. I shot badly and only got 245."[1] The Prince remained in Scotland until October, and was able to see a good deal of the King, who took part in deer drives and even went out stalking. In October, after a visit to Netherby[2] where the duck-shooting delighted and tested him, he settled down with his family at the Cottage.

On the 8th November the Kaiser arrived at Sandringham for a visit timed to cover the King's sixty-first birthday. It was naturally an awkward visit from which the Royal Family anticipated more discomfort than pleasure, and the presence of Mr. Chamberlain among the guests seemed likely to in-

[1] The Prince was now approaching his apex as a game shot. His ranking among the cracks of his day will be considered at a later stage.
[2] Sir Richard Graham's.

crease the chances of friction. The Prince bore a big share of the duties which the visit entailed, and clearly appreciated its significance. He went with his father to Wolferton to meet the Kaiser, who brought in his Suite Counts Metternich and Eulenberg and General von Plessen. Sunday was the King's birthday, and there was the ceremony of present-giving on a grand scale, a service and sermon by the Bishop of Ripon and the usual round of the gardens and stables in the afternoon. In the evening there was a big dinner, " after which [the Prince commented] Kubelik played the violin. He is quite wonderful, but I wish didn't have long hair." On the Monday the Prince took the Emperor to shoot in the Marshes and they got 50 duck between them. The next four days were devoted to serious shooting, and the Prince remarked on the Emperor's prowess. Big bags of pheasants and partridges were shot, the guns being the Emperor and his Suite, the King and Prince, Lords Londonderry, Ormonde, Clarendon and Farquhar. There were plays or music performed each night after dinner. On Saturday, the 15th, the visit, which went without a hitch, ended with a State Drive to Wolferton whence the Emperor travelled to Lowther to visit Lord Lonsdale.

The year 1902 ended as usual at Sandringham. Five days before Christmas the Prince's fourth son, Prince George, was born at the Cottage. The Prince saw a good deal of his children in the days that followed. He like to take them out walking with him, and would show them the horses and dogs and the farm animals. The remark attributed to him, " I shall soon have a regiment, not a family," may belong to this period; indeed, there was something of regimental discipline in the elder Princes' walks abroad at Sandringham with their father, for he was very insistent alike on " march discipline " and on the correct payment of courtesies to people on the estate. He was devoted to his children and proud of their childish progress and obviously liked to have them praised with sincerity. Yet already his methods were somewhat disconcerting to them. His banter embarrassed and silenced them, and he had a way of asking what they had been doing and then supplying chaffing answers before the little boys

could find their own words. Such methods, most affection-
ately intended (for his nature was kindly and he was by his
Staff already beloved above all virtues for this thoughtfulness
for others), had an unfortunate effect on his intercourse with
his children, the very reverse of that which he intended.
Early in the new year, towards the end of January, the new
Prince was christened at Windsor, the King and Queen
standing sponsors.

CHAPTER VII

Duties at Home and Abroad—Preparations for India —Sir Walter Lawrence. 1903-5

§ 1

THE year 1903 was to be a busy and important one in the sphere of European politics. Several Sovereigns and heads of States paid official visits to England in the course of it. At the end of March King Edward left England for his first holiday on the Continent since his accession. He saw no reason to alter the habits or to curtail the chief pleasures of his life (among which visits to the Continent ranked high) and, as the reign proceeded, he continued to spend about a quarter of every year abroad, leaving to his Heir the more protracted journeys in the Empire and through him keeping in touch with Imperial problems.

This holiday had important, if oblique, results. It was a tour undertaken entirely on the King's initiative. He travelled in the royal yacht and had on board a party of his own men friends. But, in the inclusion in the party of Mr. Charles Hardinge of the Foreign Office,[1] gossip and the Press found colour for the theory that the cruise would combine business with pleasure. In the course of the tour the King visited Lisbon, Rome and Paris, and had conversations with King Carlos, King Victor Emmanuel, Pope Leo XIII and M. Loubet. Everywhere he was warmly received and found time at each capital to write letters of great length to the Prince detailing his doings. There was some doubt at first about the reception which Paris would accord him. Indeed it was touch-and-go, but the King's courage and *bonhomie* won the day and the hearts of the Parisians, to he satisfaction

---

[1] Afterwards Lord Hardinge of Penshurst. Mr. Hardinge was to make several such holiday visits with the King. " I am so glad," the Prince wrote to the King at this time, " that you find C. Hardinge so useful. He is certainly a charming fellow and I believe a clever one too."

of the President and M. Delcassé and, at home, of Lord Lansdowne. It was a fine diplomatic stroke which almost immediately prepared the way for appeasement between the two nations, and it was made on a purely social occasion. The King returned to England in high spirits.

Meanwhile, throughout April the Prince was busy in London. He and the Princess went into residence at Marlborough House on the 4th, almost exactly forty years since his father and mother had begun to live there. He spent some of his spare time arranging his pictures and furniture with Mr. Guy Laking.

He was now president or member of many important committees and commissions, permanent and temporary. It was a cold and cheerless Spring and the first warm spell was not until the end of June. The Prince and Princess divided their time between Marlborough House and Frogmore, and they were at the latter place when the Khedive was spending a part of his official visit at Windsor. There is a note in the Prince's diary on the 1st June of the fire at Kindersley's House at Eton. He referred to the narrow escape of Canon Dalton's son.[1]

M. Loubet and M. Delcassé were expected at the beginning of July and York House was being redecorated to receive them. The visit of a French President to an English Sovereign broke new ground in diplomatic history. Further exchanges of views between the two nations in the new spirit created by the King's Paris visit were obviously desirable, and a date had been fixed for the visit to London without difficulties on either side. It was on the anniversary of his wedding-day that the Prince drove in State to Victoria to receive the visitors.

The visit, reviewed to-day, bears a curious resemblance to that of M. Lebrun to King George VI in 1939. President and Foreign Minister received a very warm welcome, from none more cordial than from the King who employed all his genius to make the occasion a success. Nor did the good results expected to come of it fall short of anticipation. In the Autumn the two Governments signed an Arbitration

[1] Mr. Hugh Dalton, M.P.

Treaty and before the next Summer (in April 1904) the Anglo-French Agreement was concluded by Lord Lansdowne and M. Delcassé, the main differences in North Africa having by that time been composed and the way smoothed to an understanding between England and France which was to bear strains heavier than any statesman dreamed of, and was to outlive scores of treaties far more exactly defined and with far more contemporary importance attached to them. The Entente has been coupled with the name of King Edward. His title of " the Peacemaker " largely rests on his share in its achievement. That share may have been important, but it was not achieved by intervention in the field of diplomacy. He carried out in his inimitable way his function of Constitutional Sovereign. It was not his practice or his inclination to interfere beyond his brief in matters of State.

In the middle of July, the Princess gave a ball at Marlborough House, which the King and Queen attended. A temporary ballroom was built out in the garden and the occasion was a brilliant one. The Prince records that he " danced almost every dance." The day following he was " the victim," to use his own words, of a record run to Plymouth by the Great Western Express,[1] which carried them to the Duchy for an interesting tour which included a visit to the prison at Dartmoor. Soon afterwards the Princess went for a holiday to Switzerland and the Prince attended a particularly damp Goodwood from West Dean. Thence in the customary rotation he went to Cowes, visiting Whale Island *en route*, where he took the opportunity to examine one of the new submarines. He had a number of " charming sails in dear old *Britannia*," and was at Cowes on the twenty-fourth anniversary of " Eddy and I joining the *Bacchante*."

§ 2

During the year 1904 the Prince's routine and duties followed very much on the lines of the previous year and require no very detailed notice. He continued to be kept busy with his committees, sitting sometimes for four or five

---

[1] Average speed in non-stop run 63·14 m.p.h.

hours at the Foreign Office on the Food-in-War-time Commission. He always gave special attention to Naval matters, and this year he saw a good deal of Sir John Fisher and, while at Portsmouth, made a short submerged cruise in one of the new submarines.

His chief function that Spring was the State visit, which he made with the Princess, to the Emperor of Austria in April. They were met at the station in Vienna by the Emperor and Archdukes and for several days their time was fully occupied with ceremonial calls and sightseeing. The Prince had some opportunities for sport, and both watched and shot capercailzie. He summed up the visit in a diary comment: " Everybody most kind and nice but my goodness this Court is stiff and they are frightened of the Emperor." They returned by way of Stuttgart, where they spent a few days at the Court, and the Prince invested the King of Württemberg with the Garter. There was a ceremonial visit to Bradford in May from Harewood House, after which he stayed with Sir John French at Aldershot, and saw the work of some of the troops in the Command. In November he met the King and Queen of Portugal at Portsmouth and took them to Windsor for a State visit to King Edward.

In the social field, the Prince and Princess were increasingly active. They gave a number of large dinner parties at Marlborough House composed of representative people. For the rest, his diary has many references to hours spent in his office with Sir Arthur Bigge, but it contains no mention of the Russo-Japanese War, of the disasters to the Russian Fleet or of the Dogger Bank incident. But the Prince's letters are always a better guide to his mind and character than is his diary. There is one to Sir Arthur from Abergeldie, written on the 22nd September, which is worth quoting. It contains, too, an early reference by the Prince to the coming India tour, which had been long anticipated (to the Prince's annoyance) in the Press.

Prince of Wales to Sir Arthur Bigge

MY DEAR BIGGE,—I read your long letter in which you expressed yr. views on the Army Manœuvres with great interest, I am entirely in accord with them all, you have a wonderful facility for writing, which alas I do not possess, otherwise I should have expressed myself in exactly the same way as you have. I shall of course keep yr letter private & have now destroyed it, but I showed it to Francis [Knollys] this morning & he *entirely agrees* with every word you wrote.

I understand that Ld. Curzon has spoken to Lawrence,[1] so Francis tells me, about accompanying me to India, he said that of course he would like to come, but will only do so on the understanding that we accepted or received no presents from the Indian Princes, he laid great stress on that. As I believe Curzon starts for India on 25th inst. I have just telegraphed to you, asking you to go & see him at Walmer Castle, as I think it important that you should see him once more before he sails. . . .

The Geographical Society: Please express to Sir Clements Markham my great regret at not being able to preside or be present on Nov. 7th at the meeting of the R.G. Society when they receive Capt. Scott [2] & his Officers & men. He'd better stick to Nov. 7th, being so full of engagements I could name no other day. Tell him my interest in the expedition has been very great & how pleased I am at their safe return. But my regret at being unable to be present at the Meeting is lessened by the fact that I shall see Capt. Scott here next week, when he comes to stay at Balmoral, from whom I shall hope to have a full account of all his interesting adventures. I believe the King has asked him to bring any slides he may have for a magic lantern & give us a lecture one night in the ball room, which will be far better than the Meeting. . . . I have now killed 18 stags & never felt better or more fit, I can walk on the hill all day without feeling tired. Little Welch [3] is with us, very well considering he is 84. Believe me, Yr. sincere friend, GEORGE.

The reference to Captain Scott is a reminder of a very salient characteristic of the Prince, constantly in evidence during his life—his love of manliness and his enthusiasm for

---

[1] Sir Walter Lawrence, to whom a reference follows immediately.

[2] On his return from his first Antarctic journey.

[3] Captain Sir David Welch, R.N., who lived at Virginia Water. He had commanded royal yachts between 1848 and 1878 and lived to the age of 92. He was a great favourite with the Royal Family.

all forms of adventure which entailed endurance and great courage. Such tales attracted him as a magnet a needle. His interest was keenly and instantly aroused by any oblique reference to heroic feats, and it was never satisfied until he had drawn forth, with expert questions and obvious knowledge of conditions, the fullest details of adventure by sea or on glaciers or mountain tops.

§ 3

The Prince was in London on the 11th December on which day he received Sir Walter Lawrence at Marlborough House and had his first interview with him, formally offering to him the post of Chief of Staff for the tour of India fixed for the Autumn of 1905.

No better man could have been chosen for that important post. Lawrence had brilliantly entered the I.C.S. in 1877 and was Assistant Commissioner in Afghanistan in 1880, afterwards transferring his political service to Rajputana. From 1884 to 1886 he was Under-Secretary to the Punjab Government, and to the Government of India from 1887 to 1889. For the next six years he was Settlement Commissioner in Kashmir. In those years he acquired a vast store of knowledge concerning India, its peoples and problems. He became Private Secretary to Lord Curzon during his important Viceroyalty, between 1898 and 1903, and during those years, when constitutional events of the greatest moment were taking place, he gained invaluable sidelights on the characters of the chief figures concerned with them. A man of strong character and decided views on Indian affairs, Sir Walter, with his wide experience, was well fitted not only to direct the tour, but to educate the Prince in the complex history of the vast country he was to visit and in all matters of which he should have cognisance. At that first interview with the Prince and Princess when he spoke at length to them of India and of all the implications of the tour, they hung on his words and asked him scores of questions. He was able to remind the Princess that it would be the first time in history that India had seen a Princess of Wales.

There is a note in the Prince's diary of the 23rd January 1905, that he had a second and long interview with Lawrence at Windsor when the projected Indian tour was again discussed in considerable detail.

Soon afterwards the Prince left Windsor for Ireland, where he paid a visit to Lord Ardilaun in Galway, and had some notable woodcock shooting.[1] He stayed a day or two at the Castle, Dublin, with Lord and Lady Dudley and was present at a largely attended Levée on one of those days.

Early in April he underwent a minor operation at Marlborough House, and when the royal children arrived in London from Sandringham in the middle of the month, he noted in his diary that he had not seen them for three months.

§ 4

The events of the Summer which preceded the Prince's departure for India may be summarised very shortly. The season's fixtures which he carried out were very much of the same kind as those of other years, but the unadvertised work which he put in in his office with Bigge and with Lawrence in preparation for the tour kept him much busier than ever before. He was already a man of habit. He liked to order his life in an unchanging routine, and among such habits a daily walk to Buckingham Palace to consult with the King was one which he was least likely to forgo.

This Summer the Princess, who was expecting the birth of another child, was much at the Cottage, and the Prince went there whenever he was able to snatch a day. His recreation at Sandringham at that time was golf, which he played with Mr. Hansell and any available Equerry or neighbour. He was keen enough and with his wonderful eye might have become a good player (as he might have become at billiards), but somehow he never managed to give his undivided attention to the game, which he abandoned on his accession. For the sake of his boys he revived also his interest in cricket, taking them to the Oval to see Hayward batting and engaging with them in games on the lawn at Marlborough House.

[1] He records getting a right and left at woodcock, to his great delight, adding that another gun had achieved the feat three times.

The King of Spain paid an official visit to England during the Summer. The usual functions followed and the Prince played his customary part in meeting the royal visitor and driving with him through London. The weather was abominable and marred some of the pageantry, but King Alfonzo made a good impression with a speech in English at the Guildhall, while the gala banquet and opera and the Aldershot Review were as successful as usual. The Prince was at Windsor in June for the marriage of Princess Margaret of Connaught to Crown Prince Gustav Adolf of Sweden. " It makes me feel very old," he wrote, " when I remember her parents' wedding in 1879 which also took place here."

On the 5th July Lawrence brought with him to Marlborough House a young Indian Army Officer whose services for the royal tour he had specially requested. This was Captain Clive Wigram, who was destined to be most intimately associated with the Prince throughout his reign.

The Prince left London next day for the Cottage to await the birth of his child and to enjoy the " delight of peace and quiet after London." On the 12th their youngest son, Prince John, was born, and once more the Prince fell into the routine which he had made customary following the births of all his younger children at the Cottage. He gave the Princess her breakfast at nine o'clock each morning and spent much available time reading to her during the day. The Princess made her usual rapid recovery and Sir John Williams, the doctor in attendance, left the Cottage on the 20th. " I shall miss him very much," the Prince noted in his diary, " a charming man."

He went down to Cowes, and lived on board the royal yacht for the Regatta and for functions attending the visit that Summer of a French Fleet. During his Autumn holiday that year he broke new ground, staying with the Mackintosh at Moy, a visit which later became a regular fixture of his shooting year. This small moor held a big stock of grouse, but the weather was throughout deplorable. The Prince was very happy and comfortable at Moy, and the guns included Highland friends, Lord Tullibardine and Lord Lovat among them. In September he passed two or three weeks at Abergeldie, stalking for the most part, and then with the Princess returned to London for the last busy days of packing, shopping and putting away, of interviews and farewells. On the 19th October, the Prince and Princess left London for Genoa, there to join the *Renown* which slipped her moorings on Trafalgar Day.

CHAPTER VIII

The India Tour. 1905-6

§ 1

THE India tour of 1905–6 brought him that close understanding of the problems and that deep sympathy with the peoples of India which his grandmother somehow acquired by instinct; but, of transcending importance here, it gave him besides, by many vivid proofs and experiences, a notion which was to grow in strength until it dominated his life, of what must henceforth be expected of the man or woman called to wear the Imperial Crown and to stand ever in the white light as the symbol of Empire. If he never learned (to satisfy Sir Arthur) the meaning of the British Constitution, he was thenceforth in no doubt about the importance of the Monarchy and the heavy responsibilities of a democratic Sovereign, and the purpose and policy of his life were founded from these days on that knowledge. He saw then the extent to which the whole Empire might stand or fall by the personal example set from the Throne, and to assure the integrity of that example he was to sacrifice much that men hold dear, much that makes life sweet.

The programme in its original form was enough to daunt the boldest heart; the statistics of business done, of mileage covered, States visited, functions carried out, speeches made and addresses received, evoke admiration even when judged by present-day standards. From Bombay to Peshawar, Peshawar to Rangoon, Rangoon to Mandalay, Mandalay to Mysore, Mysore to Benares, Benares to Chaman, there was hardly a major State or a principal city which the Prince and Princess did not visit, with innumerable stops at lesser places on the route. The Prince enjoyed examining the statistical summaries and carried the figures long in his head. What immediate and permanent good came to India as a result of the tour is for historians to assess. What remains of present importance is the effect which the visit had on the characters of the Prince and Princess and the excellent impression they made on the peoples in the length and breadth of India, on their own Staff and British official circles, and at home.

The long tour was a crowning success, marred by no major mishaps, interrupted by no failure of efficiency. Anticipated dangers vanished, in the hot-beds of sedition the Prince moved about freely, and wherever he went it was his constant aim and practice to get as close as he could into the lives and thoughts of the people of all sorts and conditions whom he met. In a memorandum which he supplied, Lawrence gives a hint that the unadvertised and unplanned contacts made by the Prince and Princess during their progress played quite as important a part in the general success as did their conduct of the listed functions.

§ 2

Sir Walter wrote:

. . . It was my duty to write replies to addresses and drafts for speeches at the various functions, and I always had to submit my drafts to the Prince. He would read them very carefully, and often would say, " That is too high-faluting. Everyone would know those were not my words." Invariably the words he substituted were an improvement, and certainly on two occasions they won his audience far more than my stilted sentences would have done. He had a splendid voice, clear and carrying. In Calcutta, when he was laying the Foundation Stone of the noble Memorial to Queen Victoria, he told me that he hated speaking in the open air, and that it would be impossible for the crowd to hear him. Before he began to speak I left the dais and went to the outside of the crowd. I could hear every word distinctly. When we drove away—by King Edward's order I always had to be with them whenever they went out—the Prince said, " I know they could not hear me." I ventured to dissent. " How could you know ? " he said. " Because I was on the outside of the crowd. The fact is, Sir, you were a great loss to the Church." He was what might be called a strong Churchman. It did not matter where we were on Sundays, whether in the train or on the road, he would always pull up at eleven o'clock, and there would be a service, sometimes in a tent, sometimes in a convenient house near the railway. On board ship there was always the daily service. The Indians noticed this characteristic of the Prince, and it impressed them most favourably.

. . . The Prince had a great dislike to being surrounded by the police. The ferment in India was working when we arrived, and I had been warned by telegrams from persons I did not know in England, against taking the Prince to Peshawar or Calcutta. I used to receive alarming letters about plots against the Prince's life, and, although I felt morally sure that there would be no attempt on his life, I thought it my duty to consider every communication, however fantastic. I know that the Prince's desire to mix with the huge crowds without a police cordon was greatly appreciated by the Indians, but it was a little hard on the police officials, and they used to plead with me that if anything happened they would be blamed. But mercifully nothing did happen, and in spite of detailed warnings from men of great experience, every item of the programme was carried out as it had originally been planned.

During that long and very exhausting tour the Prince and Princess kept every engagement and never showed any sign of weariness or boredom. It was a marvellous achievement, and I know that the one thing that made it possible was his strong sense of duty. He was only absent from one function during the whole of that tour, and that was due to a slight indisposition caused by a chill. He was a man of most abstemious habits. He drank very little, smoked very little, and ate very little.

We spent twenty-four nights in the train, and usually on arrival at our destination the functions began. In Northern India the climate was delightful, but there was always dust. In Southern India, as in Bombay, it was often unpleasantly hot, but all day long until late at night ceremonies, receptions, and banquets were incessant, and I fear that, in spite of the delightful variety of scenery, races, dress, and language, there was considerable monotony. The various Provinces vied with one another in preparing great spectacles. The Prince would never use a car when he was entering the various cities and capitals we visited. He always drove in a carriage, and the orders were to go very slow, in order that he could have a good look at the enormous crowds who lined the roads and, as we entered the cities, the windows and roofs of the bazaars and the streets. In front of these great crowds sat the children, who gazed with intent eyes on their future King-Emperor and his radiant and smiling Princess. Fortunately, the arrangements made in the Provinces of British India and in the Indian States were perfect. Looking back on this tour, I can remember nothing untoward; and the Prince and Princess never tired in their words of appreciation. They noticed everything, and if anything had gone wrong they would at once have seen it.

I had noticed before we left England how sorry they were to leave many of their servants, how they talked about them and wondered what they would be doing in their absence. They had very kind hearts for the lowly and obscure, and they had intense sympathy for the peoples of India. One thing struck the Prince at once, and that was the social cleavage between the British and the Indians. He was greatly astonished to find that Indians could not be members of British clubs. I pointed out that there was a reason for this, the reason of space, that the clubs would be overcrowded if Indians were admitted, also that, after their long day's work with the Indians, unfettered conversation in the club was essential to the British. But he waived all my objections aside, and when he returned to England, he made a speech at the Guildhall, in which he pleaded for greater sympathy in the Indian administration. Since that speech there has been a great speeding up in this direction. One of the most striking things I remember in India was the mourning in Calcutta for the death of Queen Victoria. All classes in India looked upon her as their real friend, and I am delighted to think, indeed to know, that her mantle fell on her grandson, and that the vast crowds of India, as they gazed on his kindly presence and comprehending eyes, felt that he, too, was their friend. His interest in the welfare of the Indian peoples, much increased from day to day on that long tour, never flagged in after years, and I was witness on many occasions to the special kindness shown by Their Royal Highnesses when they became King and Queen to their Indian subjects. Just as the Prince had inherited his grandmother's love and sympathy for India, so he had inherited his father's intense dislike for unkind remarks or spiteful criticisms of persons he had known.

85

§ 3

Following established precedent, the Prince, soon after his great welcome home, went to deliver in the City of London an official report on his tour. His Guildhall speech of the 17th May was a clear and competent survey, well delivered and received, and couched in picturesque language which suited the occasion. Sir Arthur had adopted a prose style of more than usual imagery, though there was a good deal of the Prince in the speech besides the method of delivery. It was nearly five years since he had risen to address the same audience at the end of the *Ophir* tour.

The chief points which he made included a tribute to the remarkable efficiency of the Government of India in the arrangements of his complicated journeys. He told how vividly remembered still in India was his father's tour of thirty years before; of the loyalty and splendours of the many Feudatory States which he had visited and of the fine troops maintained by the Princes for the service of the Empire. He laid stress on the grand administration of India by the Civil Service, and described the important manœuvres which he had watched from Lord Kitchener's camp at Rawal Pindi; he remarked on the increasing efforts to provide for all classes a liberal education, with special reference to the great Mohammedan College at Aligarh; and he concluded that part of his speech with a plea for a clearer understanding of the nature and problems of India which, he said, could not be regarded as one country, but demanded a wider element of sympathy and understanding in those who governed the diverse races, which made up a population of 300 millions in a territory comparable in size with Europe. And then he summarised in a picture (whose imagery owed no little debt to Macaulay) the memories which remained most vivid with him. Of that first contact with India at Bombay, of the Union Jack floating over the fortress of Jamrud and, not less significant symbol of the British Raj, the Outpost of Landi Kotal, garrisoned by five British officers commanding a regiment of Afridis, only recently redeemed from rebellion. He drew a sharp contrast between the historic stronghold of

Ali Masjid, whither came to him with offerings the leading Khans from its wild and lonely areas, and the culture of Delhi and Agra, the preservation of whose priceless treasures of art and monuments of antiquity owed so much to the taste and zeal of Lord Curzon. And he spoke of Gwalior and Benares and of the splendid processions on elephants, and how the Ridge of Delhi and the ruins of the Residency at Lucknow stirred again the undying memories of heroism and suffering in the Mutiny. The new year (he continued) found them in Calcutta, the second largest city of the Empire, whence they journeyed on to Burma which revealed to students of India completely different conditions and offered a new set of problems. He carried his audience along to Madras and its historic associations with the founding of the Empire, to Benares the stronghold of Hindooism, to the frosts and snows of Quetta, the remote outpost of Chaman, and so, through the burning plains of Sind, to Karachi at last.

And he ended by offering a word of advice to all Englishmen who could profit by it—to visit India for themselves and to learn her problems by observation and at first hand.

I cannot but think that every Briton who treads the soil of India is assisting towards a better understanding with the Mother Country, helping to break down prejudice, to dispel misapprehension and to foster sympathy and brotherhood. Thus, he will not only strengthen the old ties but create new ones, and so, please God!, secure a better understanding and a closer union of hearts between the Mother Country and her Indian Empire.

None who heard the speech that day doubted that the Prince spoke straight from his heart. Those who best knew him and studied him most closely realised how deeply this experience was impressed on his mind, and how much it had already affected him.

CHAPTER IX

Widening Interest in Politics—Visits to Madrid and to Quebec. 1906-8

§ 1

THERE was no long holiday for the Prince and Princess. Princess Ena of Battenberg's marriage to the King of Spain was to take place at the end of the month, and on the 24th May she left for Madrid with her mother, Princess Beatrice. The Prince and Princess were to represent the King and Queen at the wedding after the briefest opportunity in which to take up family life again. The 26th May was the Princess's thirty-ninth birthday and there is a pleasant intimacy in the Prince's diary reference to that day (a reference marked by one or two lapses from his improved standard of spelling): " Darling May's birthday (39th) . . . children all recited their poems. David did it quite extraordinarily well. He said Wolseley's farewell (Sheakspeare) without a mistake. ... ." The same evening they left for Spain. " Our party consists of Alice and Alge [1] (who are going on their own hook), the Shaftesburys, Carington, Derek and Lord Fincastle [2] (Major, 16th Lancers, Alfonzo's regiment), and Mr. W. Erskine [3] of the Foreign Office." They spent a day in Paris, where " we went to the Salon and saw some ghastly pictures," and arrived in Madrid on the afternoon of the 29th.

The Prince's note on the wedding day (31st May) is of unusual interest:

THE PALACE, MADRID.—Beautiful day but very hot sun. Breakfast at 8.30. At 9.15 we assembled in a room in the Palace and started in procession in 19 beautiful state carriages

---

[1] Prince Alexander of Teck, now Earl of Athlone, had married Princess Alice of Albany in February 1904.
[2] Now Earl of Dunmore, V.C.　　[3] Now Sir William Erskine.

drawn by 6 or 8 horses for the Church of San Jeronimo, the streets all decorated, crowded with people and lined by troops. The service in the Church was very fine, the music and singing splendid, it lasted from 11 till 1. Alfonzo and Ena were married at 12. She looked very well and went through a trying ordeal with a great dignity. We all left the Church in procession and returned to the Palace.

Our carriage was just in front of the one in which Queen Christina and Aunt Beatrice were driving and they were just ahead of Alfonzo and Ena who were at the end of the procession. Just before our carriage reached the Palace, we heard a loud report and thought it was the first gun of a salute. We soon learned however that when about 200 yards from the Palace in a narrow street, the Calle Mayor, close to the Italian Embassy, a bomb was thrown from an upper window at the King and Queen's carriage. It burst between the wheel horses and the front of the carriage, killing about 20 people and wounding about 50 or 60, mostly officers and soldiers. Thank God! Alfonzo and Ena were not touched although covered with glass from the broken windows. The Marquesa Torlosa and her niece were killed. They were standing on a balcony just below the window from which the bomb was thrown. The two wheelers were killed and another horse, the carriage however went on about 30 yards. Sir M. de Bunsen, Morgan, Lowther and the 4 officers of the 16th Lancers who were in a house close by, rushed out, stood round the carriage and assisted Ena out of the carriage, both she and Alfonza showed great courage and presence of mind. They got into another carriage at once and drove off to the Palace amid frantic cheering. Am most sorry for poor Aunt Beatrice who feels the shock very much.

Of course the bomb was thrown by an anarchist, supposed to be a Spaniard and of course they let him escape. I believe the Spanish police and detectives are about the worst in the world. No precautions whatever had been taken, they are most happy go lucky people here. Naturally, on their return, both Alfonzo and Ena broke down, no wonder after such an awful experience. Eventually we had lunch about 3. I proposed their healths, not easy after the emotions caused by this terrible affair. . . .

The Prince does not exaggerate the emotions of the day or the difficulties of his particular duties.

The next day, in the course of a tour of the Art Galleries, the Prince had occasion to interview the coachman and some of the officers of the 16th Lancers and saw the wounded horses and the damage done to the State Coach. And on his birthday, Sunday, the 3rd June, he was able to record the suicide of the anarchist.

My birthday (41). The Palace, Madrid.

A man in a village close to Madrid yesterday evening shot a Garde Civile and then shot himself. He has been identified as the swine that threw the bomb. . . . The name of the Anarchist is Mateo Moral as proved by the Anarchists at Barcelona who sent Queen Christina his photo & a letter today. The dead man & photo are the same.

After a big military review and a great number of ceremonial calls, the State visit ended on the 7th June and the Prince and Princess returned from a gruelling experience to Marlborough House by way of Paris. They resumed the duties that fell to them during the London Season, and went to Norway later in June to attend the Coronation of the King and Queen of Norway (the Prince's sister Maud) at Trondheim, the Prince representing King Edward.

§ 2

King Edward's was a short reign, judged at least by those immediately before and after it. Middle-aged men (of the privileged class), looking backward across the years of trouble which succeeded it, sadly remember how swiftly passed those last years of the old order. *Pereunt et imputantur*. When the Prince returned from India, his father's reign was more than half over, and a few who had the power to see ahead well knew that the days of that false sense of security in which a majority of the human race still lived were numbered. There was reason enough for disillusionment and little ground for confidence in the future. Bitterness was growing in Europe as the propagandists of the German Press redoubled the cry of Encirclement, and tension grew with growing armaments.

During the months which the Prince spent in India the breach between King Edward and his nephew, the Kaiser, had widened. Day after day he had been pilloried in the German Press as the declared encircler of Germany and the Machiavelli of European politics, and all those friendly visits to foreign Courts to which he was addicted were unjustly coloured with sinister political designs. Tolerable relations between uncle and nephew were re-established late in 1906, though these were again strained by King Edward's visit to the King of Italy in 1907. Europe was tinder for a chance spark, and the student of history to-day marvels to catch a breath of the atmosphere of the easy, luxurious Edwardian Age during which England advanced, so little prepared, to the crater's edge.

In those years the lives of the King and the Prince sped along on regular, well-established lines. The King continued his habit of passing a quarter of the year abroad. Visits to Paris, Biarritz, Marienbad, Homburg, a yachting cruise in Mediterranean or Scandinavian waters, would annually bring him in touch with some or other of the Sovereigns of Europe, many of whom were nearly related to him. He was alive to the dangers of Europe—for both Sir John Fisher and Lord Roberts had his ear—but it was not in his character to arrogate to himself the functions of his chief ministers, and his visits to foreign Courts were indeed, what they purported to be, occasions for friendly contacts, family reunions and social recreation. Thus between 1906 and 1908 he visited the Courts of Spain, Austria, Italy, Norway, Sweden and Denmark, and faithfully maintained, with one more bitter interlude, tolerable relations with his German nephew. And every year the Sovereign of one or more countries paid an official visit to London.

At home he performed his functions as Sovereign to general admiration. In his constitutional duties, within the limits which he had set for himself, he did not spare himself and in ceremonial his energy knew no bounds. His relations with his Liberal ministers were easy and he was most careful to conceal from the more advanced among them his innate distrust of violent changes. He had faith in Mr. Haldane and worked hard for the success of his great scheme for an efficient Territorial Army,[1] exerting all his influence through his County Lieutenants and encouraging the scheme by every means in his power. He was in close touch with Sir John Fisher, and insisted that the Prince should be kept constantly informed of the developments of the Naval programme of 1905. In October 1906 Sir John, with the King's approval, was writing fully to the Prince, " giving the absolute facts of the case." [2] The King wholeheartedly supported Sir John, though many retired Admirals and Civil Servants still shook their heads, and the Prince, rather to the King's annoyance, was himself in opposition to the scheme.

The King's genius and power of inspiration found their most fruitful field in the promotion of scientific and medical research and welfare and in philanthropic schemes generally. He still led Society and dictated fashions. With all his old zeal he encouraged opera and the theatre, racing and yachting, and his appetite for stimulating conversation and constant diversion showed no signs of waning. His health was reasonably good, save for an increasing proneness to bronchitis which sometimes brought on disturbing fits of choking, and his vitality remained extraordinary.

To carry the brief survey on to the Spring of 1908; the King left in March of that year for his visit to Biarritz knowing that he had seen the last of a Prime Minister with whom his relations had been consistently easy. He said good-bye to Sir Henry Campbell-Bannerman and a month later sent for Mr. Asquith to come out to him—a departure from precedent for which he was much criticised—and entrusted to him the formation of a new Liberal Government. In that Cabinet sat Mr. Lloyd George as Chancellor of the Exchequer and Mr. Churchill. It was Mr. Lloyd George's first Budget—a bitter pill to King Edward—which was to precipitate the great House of Lords controversy, still raging when the reign ended.

No less firmly established by custom were the lines of the

---

[1] The Army Bill of 1907 embodied drastic proposals for reorganising in a single Defence Force the old auxiliary forces.
[2] Sidney Lee: *Life of Edward VII.*

Prince's life during those years. The New Year always found him at the Cottage. In February and March he was usually in London working on his many committees and in his office with Sir Arthur Bigge, interviewing visitors from India and the Empire, listening to debates in Parliament, attending and speaking at public banquets and other functions. In April he would go to Frogmore and Windsor [1] and Sandringham, and his days at Windsor usually coincided with the visit of some foreign Royalty. He was at Marlborough House on and off throughout the Season, busy with functions specially allocated to him. Among these, visits to Aldershot and to one or other of the Naval bases were habitual, and when in London he kept in close touch with all Naval questions.

He never missed the chief sporting events of the year in the racing world, and would go usually to Frogmore for Ascot. He generally separated from the Princess (who often went abroad) in July, and would go to Goodwood House with the King for the Meeting and on to Cowes, where he lived in the *Victoria and Albert*, and would divide his time between sailing the old *Britannia* and looking into such Naval matters as offered. By the 12th he was at Bolton or Studley, and, in the changeless order, went on to Tulchan and so to Abergeldie where, with a fishing visit to Gordon Castle usually sandwiched in, he remained into October stalking or shooting, when the move was made to the Cottage to begin partridge shooting over the wide acreage of Sandringham and Castle Rising.

In November there might be a State visit to Windsor and other business which brought him down to London and Frogmore, and shooting visits—already time-honoured and regular—kept him on the move between Sandringham and London until it was time to buy his Christmas presents and return home for the Christmas festivities. Such was his year, varied or interrupted only by the necessity which sent him, reluctant but dutiful, abroad to pay a visit of ceremony or friendship to one or other of the foreign Courts.

---

[1] His recreations in these years while at Windsor included a daily ride, a round of golf, and sometimes a cruise on the river in the electric launch given him by Sir Whittaker Ellis.

§ 3

The Prince wrote in his diary on the 18th February, 1907: " David went up before a Committee and was examined to see if the Admiralty would give him a nomination for the Navy, I am glad to say he did remarkably well, they said he is the best boy they had examined, which is very gratifying."

The change in the matter of the diary is constantly to be observed in these years. More and more, political events tend to shoulder out the more trivial items of the Prince's life. Considerable space is given to Navy matters in his account of his visit to Devonport in February for the opening of the new Prince of Wales' Basin. Early in March he notes with particular interest the successes of the Moderates in the L.C.C. Elections. During these weeks, too, he was assiduous in his attendance at the House of Commons and House of Lords for important debates on Defence and the Colonies, and received several ministers with whom he held long conversations. Lord Esher at this time was bringing him in touch with the leading politicians and Service heads of the day, and discussions over the dinner-table were kept up late. On the 7th March his aunt, the Dowager Empress of Russia, paid her first visit to England for thirty-four years, an occasion for a family reunion.

Towards the end of April the Prince visited Blythswood for an official visit to Glasgow, and while he was there took the opportunity to look over the new *Lusitania*, " the largest ship in the world, built and fitted out on the Clyde: will make her first voyage to New York in Aug. or Sept. 1907." He pasted into his diary some statistical features, records and dimensions of the great Cunarder of tragic fame.

That summer the chief public functions which fell to him were in connection with the State visits of Prince Fushimi of Japan in May and the King of Denmark in June. Early in July he was in Edinburgh on an official visit, staying at Dalkeith and seeing a good deal of his old friend of *Britannia* days, John Scott, now Lord Dalkeith. He travelled north by day and notes that he beguiled the journey with Elinor Glyn's *Three Weeks*, " an extraordinary book." At the end of the month the Princess went to Dresden and the Prince followed his usual programme for Goodwood and Cowes. While at Goodwood House,[1] he recorded that " dear David, looking thinner but wonderfully well, came from Osborne, his holidays having just begun, it is just 3 months since I have seen him."

The autumn in Scotland and at Sandringham passed as usual, and in November the Kaiser and Kaiserin paid a State visit to Windsor. The Prince went on board the *Hohenzollern* and took the visitors through London, which gave them a rousing welcome, and on to Windsor for the customary shoots and entertainments.

" William & Dona very kind & looking well," was his comment on their first meeting. There was a wonderful rally of Royalties at Windsor during this visit, and at a luncheon on the 17th November among others who sat down were the King and Queen, the German Emperor and Empress, the King and Queen of Spain, the Queens of Portugal and Norway, the Prince and Princess of Wales, the Grand Duke and Duchess Vladimir, and the Duchess of Aosta.

§ 4

A pleasant light on his relations with his secretary and on his own generous nature is given in a letter which he wrote at this time to Sir Arthur Bigge:

YORK COTTAGE, SANDRINGHAM, *Xmas Day* 1907.

MY DEAR BIGGE,—I was much touched by your kind letter recevd. this morning. The Princess & I heartily reciprocate your good wishes, but I fear yr. Xmas must under the circumstances be a sad one. Fancy, how quickly time flies, it is nearly 7 years already since you came to me. You have nothing to thank us for, it is all the other way, & we have indeed much to thank you for. As for myself during these 7 years you have made my life comparatively an easy one, by your kind help & assistance & untiring devotion to work connected with me. What would have happened to me if

---

[1] His habits at Goodwood were already firmly established. He invariably rode in the Park before breakfast with Lord Lonsdale and perhaps one other guest.

you had not been there to prepare & help me with my speeches, I can hardly write a letter of any importance without your assistance. I fear some times I have lost my temper with you & often been very rude, but I am sure you know me well enough by now to know that I did not mean it. Among the thousands of things you have done for me, none I know gave you so much trouble as the Bill for the Hospital Fund, thanks mostly to you it passed satisfactorily for us & I rejoice to think that you are now a member of my Council. For all these many past services, I offer you my thanks from the bottom of my heart. I am a bad hand at saying what I feel, but I thank God I have a friend like you, in whom I have the fullest confidence & from whom I know on all occasions I shall get the best & soundest advice whenever I seek it. . . .

My two eldest sons enjoyed their first day's shooting, the eldest got 12 rabbits & the 2nd. got 3.

Always yr. grateful & sincere friend, GEORGE.

§ 5

Sunday, 2nd Feb. 1908.—Horrified to hear that yesterday evening Carlos & the Crown Prince were both assassinated by rifle bullets as they were driving into Lisbon with Amélie & their second son Emmanuel,[1] the latter was slightly wounded but thank God dear Amélie was not touched. Too horrible. The crime was evidently committed by Republicans or Revolutionaries, three of whom were at once shot by the police. Portugal has been a disturbed State for some time.

The murders profoundly shocked the King and Queen who heard details a day or two later from M. de Soveral on his return from Portugal. During the early days of mourning the Prince was several times at the House of Lords and heard " Curzon make a speech of $1\frac{1}{2}$ hours on the Convention with Russia, a fine speech but unfortunate, & will do no good."

At the end of March he went with the Princess to Cologne to inspect his own and other Cuirassier Regiments. He was very well received in Germany and went on to Darmstadt, returning home by Paris. " Went with Derek & Hua to the Nouveautés & saw *Occupe-toi d'Amélie*, amusing but the hottest thing I have ever seen on the stage. At 12 went with Derek,

[1] Later King Manoel of Portugal.

Lowther & Johnson (of Embassy) to Montmartre. Paid a short visit to Bal Tabarin & the Abbaye Restaurant & went to some other places. Bed at 3.30."

The Prince and Princess remained in Paris until the 13th April, made many contacts and revived memories of earlier days. The Prince saw Chantilly again and recalled a former visit to the Duc d'Aumale with his parents in 1885. M. Fallières gave an official banquet in their honour, which was attended by a great number of notable and representative people then in Paris, and there were discussions on the coming Franco-British Exhibition to be held in London.

Soon after his return, the King came back from Biarritz and father and son were much together at Windsor. The political skies were stormy. Controversy was raging round the Licensing Bill introduced on the 27th February. Mr. Asquith's Cabinet had not been formed without difficulties and shaking of heads. There is a note in the Prince's diary under date the 24th April, which gives a hint of the interest which the Royal Family were taking in the political drama: "We were all very excited when we heard that Winston Churchill (President, Board of Trade) had been beaten by Mr. Joynson-Hicks for N.W. Manchester by a majority of 429." Very soon after his successor had taken office, Sir Henry Campbell-Bannerman died, and the Prince attended the Memorial Service in the Abbey at the end of April.

§ 6

His London Season was this year to be curtailed. Arrangements had been made for him to pay another (his sixth) visit to Canada in the middle of July. The occasion was the Tercentenary of the founding of Quebec and the visit was to extend no farther than that Province.

Before he left, he carried out one or two ceremonial functions of some importance. On the 14th May, in lamentable weather, he opened the Franco-British Exhibition at Shepherd's Bush. The arrangements were as bad as the weather and the Prince was frank in his criticism. In a sea of mud he and the French representatives waded through the grounds and his national pride was wounded.

Before going to Aldershot for his usual troop inspections, he snatched a couple of days to go down to Osborne to see Prince Edward, who was playing cricket when his father arrived. The Prince stayed at Barton Manor and entertained some of his son's cadet friends. On the 25th May M. Fallières paid his State visit, the Prince carrying out his usual rôles in the reception and entertainment of the visitor. The President of course visited the Exhibition and under much happier conditions.

On the 15th July he sailed for Quebec.

15th July.—Said goodbye to my beloved May and sweet children and left for Portsmouth, H.M.S. *Indomitable*, for Quebec. My staff [1] Annaly, Sir F. Hopwood [2] & Godfrey.[3] Eddy Dudley is coming with me as a guest. He represents Australia at Quebec and goes on to Australia as Governor-General.

A special significance attached to the choice of the *Indomitable*. She was of the latest type of cruiser which the neck-and-neck Naval Armament race, forced on us by Germany and now temporarily held in check by Mr. McKenna, had brought into being. Driven by turbine engines and of 17,250 tons displacement, she mounted eight 12-in. guns. She was little inferior in efficiency to a battleship and had a speed potential which the fastest liner in the Atlantic service might envy. The royal visit—it was an open secret—was to include an unofficial endurance and speed trial of the new cruiser, which would be watched with interest outside the British Empire.

The Prince had always made a good impression in Canada. At Quebec he was enthusiastically received as he landed at King's Wharf from his beloved green Barge which had been carried in the *Renown*. He was met by Lord and Lady Grey, by the Premier, Sir Wilfrid Laurier, by the Empire and United States representatives, by Lord Roberts and by many Admirals from attendant squadrons. At the Citadel he spoke in French and English and his delivery was praised. He

---

[1] Sir Arthur Bigge, of course, was also on board. Commodore Herbert King-Hall commanded the *Indomitable*.
[2] Now Lord Southborough.   [3] Commander Godfrey-Faussett.

put in a week of ceremonial which he admitted to have been as strenuous as any he had yet undertaken. There were banquets, garden-parties, receptions, a naval and military tournament, a pageant, the laying of wreaths on the famous shrines and statues, and a great review of 14,000 Canadian troops under General Otter on the Plains of Abraham. At the end of it he handed over to Lord Grey the title to the Plains themselves, together with a fund of nearly £100,000 for their endowment as a public park for the peoples of Canada. His visit went without a hitch of any kind, and when on the 29th July the *Indomitable* weighed anchor, the Prince had good grounds for the hope he expressed " that the visit has done good in improving relations between French and English Canadians, never better than today."

Then the *Indomitable* went out for records under very unfavourable conditions. Late as it was in the season, dense fogs and enormous icebergs slowed down progress. Nevertheless, high and hopeful speeds were maintained and by the third day speed-mania seized all on board.

31st July.—I went down in Engine room & into one of the stoke holds with the Engineer Commander, very interesting but distinctly dirty and disagreeable on account of forced draught.

1st Aug.—Great excitement on board trying to break record, the officers and everyone going down & working in stoke-holds. I went down with King-Hall at 6 & shovelled coal for half an hour, getting pretty dirty, fine exercise, quite good fun, all the Staff were down including Bigge & McCarthy, the detective I am bringing home.

The Prince emerged as black as a nigger and was loudly cheered by the stokers.

4th Aug. "Indomitable" at Cowes.—We averaged 25·13 knots from Straits of Belleisle to the Fastnets, so we have practically beaten the record from land to land across the Atlantic.[1] The *Lusitania* & *Mauretania* only did 25·08, which is really a magnificent performance for a man-of-war.

[1] This average was later corrected to just below 25 knots and the record remained with the *Lusitania*.

A day or two later he was sailing the *Britannia* with Prince Edward and showing him the ropes.

§ 7

He was not in London again for more than a night or two until the middle of November. But he came down from Abergeldie to attend on the 11th October at Buckingham Palace a big dinner-party given by the King to M. Isvolsky, Russian Foreign Minister, at which most of the Cabinet were present.

There is a note in his diary on the 7th November: " Bertie [1] went up before the Interviewing Board to pass into the Navy & did well. Fawkes was the Chairman of it."

The political skies meanwhile were as stormy as ever. Militant Suffragettes, at the height of their campaign, suffered for their convictions and made ministers and the public suffer and there were bitter demonstrations against the Licensing Bill, again tabled for the Session. To the general surprise, the House of Lords, whose antipathy to the Bill had been from the first extreme, settled its own and the Bill's fate without the formality of a debate upon it. At a meeting held at Lansdowne House on the 24th November it was resolved to reject the Bill when it came up. That decision was a challenge which put beyond doubt in the minds of a majority of the country that the powers which the Upper House could exercise were no longer consonant with modern Democracy. Mr. Lloyd George was even now at work on his People's Budget, seeking the means to finance his Old Age Pensions and the ever-growing expenditure on the Naval programme, and before that Budget became law the challenge of the House of Lords had been taken up and the ancient powers of the Second Chamber had been doomed to curtailment.

[1] Now King George VI.

CHAPTER X

The Prince as a Game-shot—The Political Crisis— Illness and Death of King Edward. 1909-10

§ 1

DURING the last full year of King Edward's life the Prince's engagements continued to increase in number and importance, and he was kept busy during February when the King and Queen paid a visit to Berlin, and all through March. He managed, however, to attend many debates in the House of Lords, to dine out with his friends and to discuss Service matters with several leading Naval officers. At this time, too, he began with some regularity to attend important football matches.

The King and Queen were abroad again in April, cruising in the Mediterranean, and the Prince and Princess among other duties paid an official visit to Sheffield. Whenever he could spare the time, he went down to see his sons at Osborne and in May he took Prince Edward to Dartmouth, travelling down with all the other cadets of the year. He went over the old *Britannia*, of course, and revived many happy memories of the two years (1877–79) he had spent on board her. The Prince went as usual in May to stay at Government House, Farnborough, where General Smith-Dorrien then held sway, to watch troop exercises. He was saddened at this time by the death of his old French tutor, M. Hua, who had taught him in the *Britannia* and had never lost touch— even during the interlude when he acted as French master at Eton—with the Royal Family. Towards the end of his life M. Hua became Librarian to the Prince and taught some French to Prince Edward and Prince Albert.

Derby Day fell this year on the Princess's birthday. It was a great day for the Royal Family. Minoru, carrying the King's colours, won a thrilling race, a neck in front of Louviers. The Prince wrote:

Minoru belongs to Hall Walker but papa leased it from him as a yearling for his racing career.

The enthusiasm on papa winning was tremendous, everyone went mad, and cheered like anything. I went down with papa on the course & he led the horse in which was beautifully ridden by Jones. Minoru was perfectly trained by Marsh, he & Marcus [1] are delighted.

In June the Prince devoted much time to Duchy affairs both in Cornwall and Somerset; in the course of his tours he stayed at Longleat [2] and attended the Millenary Service at Wells [3] Cathedral. He was back in London in time to attend Shackleton's lecture on his great Antarctic journey. He made a brief speech and presented medals to those who took part in it. Something has already been said of his deep interest in heroic adventure and of his admiration for feats of endurance. Last among the events of that Summer in London, he showed practical interest in the South African Union and Defence Conferences.

He went to Goodwood House as usual with the King and Queen for the races, and records that during the meeting he " laid £300 on Lemberg to win. It came off." The Cowes Regatta of 1909 was very much a Naval occasion, honoured by the presence of the Tzar and Tzaritza. Sir John Fisher was on board the Royal Yacht and there was an important Review at Spithead on the 31st July.

" Home Fleet under Sir W. May & Atlantic under Louis Battenberg, all fully manned ships were present, 24 Battleships, 16 armoured cruisers, 8 other cruisers, 4 Scouts, 48 destroyers, 47 submarines, auxiliaries 8. Total 150."

On the 6th August, the Prince whose memory was always stirred by visits to Cowes, wrote in his diary: " Today 30 years ago Eddy & I joined the *Bacchante* at Cowes. It seems like Yesterday." He was not called on again for any important duty until the middle of November, when he went to Windsor to entertain the new King of Portugal.

During a shooting visit to Powis Castle, on the 24th November, there is an entry in his diary: " Read Lord Lansdowne's

[1] Lord Marcus Beresford, Manager of the King's Racing Establishment.
[2] Lord Bath's.   [3] Wells became an episcopal see in 910.

speech to May on rejecting the Finance Bill in the House of Lords." It was for him the last of the untroubled years in which he could view the bitter political controversies of the day as a spectator, and pursue, almost as a private citizen, the regular order of his life without reference to such issues. It was the last year of peace that he was to know for many years; by comparison with his life thenceforth, the last he would ever know. He was turning the final pages of the second phase of his career.

§ 2

The Prince was now at the height of his fame and skill as a game-shot, and this may be as good a place as any in which to consider his place among the crack shots of his day. No serious estimate is attempted. The present age is not in tune with solemn discussions of the records and achievements of the Victorian and Edwardian cracks. The heyday of the " crack shot " virtually closed with the war which ended, save on a few favoured estates, the days of enormous bags and the era of keen rivalry in statistical records.

Probably that day at the end of the last shooting season before the war when King George fired 1,760 cartridges from his guns in a single day at Hall Barn,[1] represented the high-water mark of superabundance in his sporting career. To be sure he never regretted its passing not to return, if so it was. He constantly killed very heavy bags at home and on the estates of his friends when sport raised its head after the war. In the great season of 1922 and others King George had his

---

[1] The record bag of pheasants is believed to have been made at Hall Barn, Beaconsfield, on the 18th December, 1913, the seven guns being King George, the Prince of Wales, Lord Charles Fitzmaurice, Lord Ilchester, Lord Dalhousie, Lord Herbert Vane-Tempest and Mr. H. Stonor. 3,937 pheasants were killed. Lord Justice MacKinnon has recalled that just after that event he spoke to Major Britten, then agent to Lord Burnham. In answer to a question about the King's reputation as a shot, Major Britten said: " I will tell you what I saw myself. After lunch they were in Dorney Bottom. The birds were coming over very fast and very high. I watched the King and kept count. He brought down thirty-nine birds with thirty-nine consecutive cartridges and only with the fortieth did he miss." Lord Justice MacKinnon made a note of the conversation in his diary.

share of plenty with grouse and he had many good years with partridges.

With his increase in opportunities his zest for shooting continually grew (and lasted undimmed until he could no longer raise his gun to his shoulder). And his skill kept pace with his zest. Joining forces with Sir Horace (afterwards Lord) Farquhar at Castle Rising, and with his own shoot added to the already extensive Sandringham acreage, he had access to something like 30,000 acres of shooting for many years, almost eight continuous miles uninterrupted of various types of sporting country between Little Massingham and Grimston Carr.

By 1898 he had already won ranking among the dozen best shots of the day and his quickness and efficiency did not, as in the case of Lord Ripon, markedly decline. The latter was an " aimer," King George " snap-shot " with both eyes open.[1] One or two of the cracks with whom he now constantly shot (admittedly in keen though friendly rivalry) were trained marksmen and nothing else. With perfectly drilled loaders who knew their every characteristic and with constant practice which the firing of 30,000 or more cartridges in a year gave, they killed their birds to admiration, but when the drive or stand was over, were sometimes inclined to lose interest in the proceedings until the " trouble began again." King George was not one of these cracks. He had the instincts of the " marauder " or fowler, for he had been trained by Norfolk sportsmen. He loved the marshes more than the covert side, and was never happier than when he could go out on them with a single Equerry to take what might come. He chose high and difficult birds when covert shooting and seldom concentrated, even in " competitive " shoots, on birds at one particular angle that came most easily to him. Indeed, his love of shooting woodcock all his life did little service to the covert shooting at Sandringham. For " stops " in front of the guns who would have got the pheasants well up over the line would have sent the woodcock back, and so it was

[1] Oddly enough, he shot big game as he shot hares. He took with him to India a rifle built as nearly as possible on the pattern of his hammer guns and his success astonished the Princes and other experts in India who witnessed it.

that during his rule the quality of the pheasant shooting was sacrificed to the sporting possibilities of the woodcock.

In estimating his place among the front-rank shots of his time many factors must be considered. He began to shoot regularly much later in life than his " rivals," and his period of maximum efficiency was shortened by his accident in France. His physical qualities favoured him. He was long-sighted and clear-sighted, wearing glasses at the end of his life only for reading. He was spare and quick on his feet. His hearing also was very good until a slight deafness—worse in the right ear—developed in the last decade of his life. He was always fit. It is astonishing how little his weight varied between 1889 and 1933. Except in the years 1898–1900, when he appears to have put on half a stone, he seldom varied as much as a pound over or under 10 stone 5. He would turn out at Bolton Abbey, Studley or Abbeystead on the 12th after a busy season in London, and without having had an hour of practice with his loaders, as drilled, as fit, as accurate as at the end of the season.

Set against these natural advantages were certain handicaps, self-imposed. He had not the professional's make-up. Again, his veneration for tradition required that all his life he should continue to shoot with hammer guns. He had shot with them as a boy, *ergo* he must shoot with them in middle and old age. On occasions when he was using three guns that sacrifice to tradition (and personal preference) mattered less. Amos (or whoever it might be) would load, Howlett his valet cocked the guns and handed them to the King. No time need therefore have been wasted. When shooting with two guns, it was another matter.

As a stylist he was unexceptionable. The straightness of his left arm, far out along the barrel, was no photographic pose. All evidence shows that he consistently shot as he was so often pictured with a straight left arm fully extended. The conclusion reached is that, had he been a mere " professional " (and not at heart a " marauder "), and had he employed the full advantage of the hammerless gun, he would in his heyday have had no superior among the first shots of his day. As things were, if he had not perhaps quite the mechanical certainty of Lord Ripon or the perfect grace and science of Sir Harry Stonor in their heyday, he was certainly among the first ten game-shots of his day at grouse and pheasants (when he was in competitive mood), and a very notable driven-partridge shot.

For a long day in the marshes the Prince and King asked no better companion than one of his farmer neighbours. Right to the end of his life Mr. Brereton, Mr. Stanton, Mr. Bullard and others of them shot with him. Mr. Brereton had some recollections of King George out shooting at Sandringham. "The keenest man on a woodcock I ever knew," he called him. "Our rivalry was a good joke between us. If I missed a woodcock, the King wouldn't fail to tell me of it. If he missed one . . . well, he wouldn't tell me. And once he said to Mr. Jones: 'I wish I could kill driven partridges like George Brereton, but I think I can beat him at pheasants.'" As has been said, King George loved Norfolk frankness and Norfolk men and he loved old friends because they were *old* friends. So much indeed that when his sons grew up, they sometimes found that loyalty of his made things a little dull for them. There were so many old friends who must not be forgotten that the claims of the young could not always be met.

§ 3

The political crisis of 1909–1910 arising out of Mr. Lloyd George's People's Budget had raised an issue larger and more important than the passage of the Finance Bill. The Lansdowne House decision had been taken up as a challenge which was to decide at last an issue raised a generation before by Liberal Governments, the veto powers of the Second Chamber. Mr. Lloyd George's Budget rightly or wrongly was regarded by the Opposition as first of all a political device to bring the bigger issue to a head—a budget so devised that the Opposition in the Lords and in the Commons could not but oppose its passage. The chief criticism of the Bill centred of course on the land tax and the increased direct taxation of the rich, with their implications of class prejudice. In recent years the Lords had passed a dozen Bills

marking radical advances in social reform and their rejection
of the Finance Bill, though the legality of the step was not in
question, was yet without precedent.

Mr. Asquith appealed to the country. In the General
Election of January 1910 the Liberals returned to power with
their allies, not less firm of purpose if their majority was
reduced. Secure in the passage of his Finance Bill, Mr.
Asquith that Spring prepared the ground for forcing the major
issue. In April 1910 he introduced Resolutions preliminary
to a Parliament Bill to regulate relations between the two
Houses, and in his speeches he used phrases which made it
clear even then that if the Lords refused to accept the Bill
(for which in his view the new mandate had been given him
by the electors) he would advise the King to create the number
of peers necessary to secure its passing.

The King was fully alive to the ultimate constitutional issue.
With great anxiety he watched every phase of the battle and
on one occasion threw his influence—in vain—into the scales.
He sent for Lord Lansdowne and Mr. Balfour and discussed
the possibilities of averting the disaster he foresaw.[1] So the
issue stood on the King's return from his last visit to the Continent in April 1910. He viewed the possibilities immediately
ahead with profound anxiety and distaste, anxiety for the
Constitution and distaste for the part which he might be
invited to play in an issue which he distrusted.

§ 4

While the " Budget " election of January 1910 went its
noisy way the Prince, as has been said, remained at Sandringham, removing to Marlborough House as usual at the beginning of February. The Spring in London, always a busy
time for him, was more than usually so that year. The King
opened Parliament on the 21st February, and the debates
in both Houses, which the Prince often attended,[2] were

---

[1] " The King is quite clear that he will not assent to any request to
make peers."—ESHER: *Journals*, 25th January, 1910.

[2] He sat on the cross-benches in the House of Lords and in the gallery
behind the clock in the House of Commons. He usually walked to and
from Westminster.

important and highly controversial, though the King's Speech had been of the briefest.

The Prince continued regularly to attend important football matches and for exercise [1] appears to have taken up squash racquets, which he played every week with Lord Charles Fitzmaurice, who had now for some time been a member of his Household, and with Mr. Keppel in the court he had had built in a corner of Marlborough House garden. At this time the Prince and Princess dined out constantly, and his diary is filled with the lists of guests invited to meet him in private houses; the King also gave a number of large dinner-parties to the leading men of the day, which the Prince attended. He was at Knowsley again in March for the ceremonial opening of the great Liverpool Reservoir at Lake Vyrnwy, which had been under construction for a quarter of a century, and to attend the Grand National at Aintree, a meeting which he enjoyed. Thence he went down to Dartmouth to see Prince Edward and spent a couple of days sight-seeing there, reviving as usual old memories.

There was now a project for a visit to South Africa, and he was deep in discussion of the broad outlines with his old ship-mate " Rosy " Wemyss,[2] during March and April.

The King went off as usual to Biarritz and the Princess went on a visit to Strelitz in April, while the Prince was kept busy in and near London. On the 27th April he met his father at Victoria on his return from his holiday and was delighted to find him looking very well. That evening the King, Prince and the two young Princes went together to the Opera to hear Tetrazzini sing in *Rigoletto*, but her performance greatly disappointed the Prince. Father and son were together again at the private view of the Academy. On the 30th April the King, restless as ever, left London for a week-end at Sandringham. It was chilly weather and he returned to the Palace with a cold. He had looked his last on the home he had made and loved so dearly. The Prince walked over to the Palace on the 3rd May to see him and found him ill and feverish.

---

[1] Before his accession he walked constantly about London, sometimes covering the four-mile circuit of Hyde Park. In crossing streets he gave great anxiety to his Equerry. As King, he rarely went on foot outside the Palace garden.   [2] Afterwards Lord Wester-Wemyss.

The next morning Sir Francis Laking brought a much worse report and the Prince returned with him to his father's bedside. Bronchitis had set in, " his colour was bad and his breathing fast." The Prince did not stay for more than a few minutes.

The Queen and Princess Victoria, ignorant of the turn of events, were on their way home from Corfu, and the Prince wrote letters to catch them at Calais,[1] where they were due next day. On the 5th May he became very anxious. The King had had little sleep for three nights, his colour was worse and the shortness of breath was distressing to see. He was definitely weaker and the strain on his heart was severe. The Prince, in the course of a busy and worried day, met on their return the Queen and Princess Victoria, who were profoundly shocked by the King's condition. In the evening he had interviews with the four doctors attending the King. Early on Friday, the 6th May, Sir Francis Laking telephoned an encouraging report. The King had had a better night; and the Prince went across after breakfast in more hopeful spirits. But by the time he arrived the situation had changed for the worse. The King had had a bad fainting fit and was sinking.

The end is best told in the Prince's own words, taken verbatim from his diary written that evening.

A terrible day for us all. We hardly left him all day, he knew us and talked to us between his attacks up till 4.30. The last thing he understood was when I told him his horse Witch of the Air had won at Kempton today & he said he was pleased. It was terrible to see him fighting for his life, but thank God he did not suffer at all. Mother-dear, Toria, Louise, May, Aunt Louise, MacDuff & I, four doctors, Douglas Powell, Laking, Reid & Dawson, & the two nurses, Fletcher & Harlock, were in the room. The Archbishop of Canterbury said prayers, we kneeling round his bed. At 11.45 beloved Papa passed peacefully away & I have lost my best friend & the best of fathers. I never had a word with him in my life. I am heartbroken and overwhelmed with grief but God will help me in my great responsibilities & darling May will be my comfort as she has always been.

---

[1] The letter he wrote to the Queen was not alarmist.

May God give me strength & guidance in the heavy task which has fallen upon me.

So began, in bitter sorrow and in times already dark and dangerous, his reign of ceaseless anxiety. But his innate humility of mind did not lack support. He was fortified by his simple faith in God's help, by his devotion to and his belief in his wife and, not least, by his consciousness of duty done. If he had lost the best of fathers, he had proved every day of his life the best, the most dutiful, son who ever sweetened a father's life. That simple faith in God, that devotion given to and received from Queen Mary, that clear conscience, were to sustain and guide him for the rest of his life.

MARLBOROUGH HOUSE,

" I shall journey through this world but once. Any good thing, therefore that I can do, or any kindness that I can show any human being, let me do it now; let me not neglect nor defer it, for I shall not pass this way again"

The above well-known lines, in King George's handwriting, were always kept on his writing-table.

CHAPTER XI

The New King's Burdens—Estimate of King Edward —King George and the Political Crisis. 1910

[Mr. Asquith, Premier]

§ 1

IN the days which followed King Edward's death the new King had need of all the support which his faith could give him and of all his reserves of endurance. A full fortnight elapsed between the death and the burial of his father. The events of those days are set down by King George very simply in his diary, and the passages give an idea of the strain which those fourteen days must have imposed on his body and nervous system. On many of them there was a service round the bed or in the Throne Room round the coffin of the late King. On almost every day the new King was engaged for long periods in discussions with the Earl Marshal, the Primate and other officials as to the procedure of the funeral ceremonies.

King Edward died on the 6th May. On the afternoon of the 7th King George drove to St. James's Palace to hold his first Council. He " made a short speech to all the Privy Councillors standing round me; the most trying ordeal I have ever had to go through; they then all took the Oath of Allegiance and kissed my hand." On the 8th the inevitable reaction had set in and he felt very seedy, but there was no chance of any relaxation from the strain of business. The work thrown on Sir Arthur Bigge and the Secretariat was enormous, and the King was constantly engaged with his secretary. Some idea of the immense burden of work is indicated by a statistical table pasted into the diary. The number of telegrams dealt with by the Buckingham Palace Post Office alone during the period was 12,297.

The King, too, saw his mother and sister, Princess Victoria, almost every day and many others of the Royal Family. He received members of the Cabinet and practically every foreign ambassador and minister. He had business interviews in connection with the late King's will. He received deputations and addresses from both Houses of Parliament. On the 12th May the foreign Royalties began to arrive, and the King in person met many of them on their arrival at Victoria. On the 17th the late King's coffin was moved to Westminster Hall, the King walking in the procession with some of the Princes then assembled in London. On the 18th, at 11 o'clock in the morning, he gave an historic audience to Mr. Asquith.[1] For although the late King was still unburied, the political situation remained so critical that there could be no delay in endeavouring to bring about a truce.

It will be well to set down briefly at this point the constitutional and political problems which faced the new King in the first year of his reign. After the refusal of the Lords in 1909 to pass the Budget, the election of January 1910 had given Mr. Asquith's Government a large majority with Labour and Irish Nationalist support. That Government the new King inherited[2] in May 1910. The Parliament Bill was now the vital issue and much sympathy was felt for the King in his difficult position. He had many discussions with Mr. Asquith, and attempts were made to bring Liberals and Conservatives together by convening a Conference of both parties. But they were poles apart and nothing came of it. Mr. Asquith therefore approached the King to secure his agreement to the swamping of the House of Lords by the creation of peers sufficient to carry the Parliament Bill, and he assured the King

---

[1] When King Edward died, Mr. Asquith was abroad. It was perhaps the only occasion in history when the chief Minister was absent from England at the death of a Sovereign.

[2] For the reader's convenience, a list of the Prime Ministers of King George's reign with the dates of their administrations is appended.

Until 7th Dec., 1916	Mr. Asquith (2).
7th Dec., 1916–23rd Oct., 1922 .	Mr. Lloyd George.
23rd Oct., 1922–22nd May, 1923 .	Mr. Bonar Law.
22nd May, 1923–22nd Jan., 1924 .	Mr. Baldwin.
22nd Jan., 1924–4th Nov., 1924 .	Mr. MacDonald.
4th Nov., 1924–8th June, 1929 .	Mr. Baldwin.
8th June, 1929–7th June, 1935 .	Mr. MacDonald (2).
7th June, 1935–End	Mr. Baldwin (2).

that such was the policy which King Edward would have followed. King George was in a difficult position and could only answer that he could not assent without another election. If that election gave a clear mandate for the Bill, he, the King, might be relied on to act constitutionally on his Premier's advice. Consequently a second election within a year took place (December 1910) and the Government was again returned with an ample combined majority. The Parliament Bill then passed the Commons and a Coronation truce followed. After it, the Bill came up in the Lords, and the dog-fight began in earnest. Towards the end of the battle Mr. Asquith announced that the Cabinet would advise the King to exercise his prerogative to the extent necessary to pass the measure and that the King would assent to that advice. Eventually the Lords gave way and the Bill became law in August 1911. In the course of the bitter struggle King George was attacked for giving contingent guarantees—described by Mr. Asquith as being rather " hypothetical suggestions." It will be made clear in the narrative that follows in what precise particulars the King was at variance with his Government in its method of extracting from him those guarantees.

The King's own diary reference to the interview of the 18th May above mentioned is of sufficient interest to set down:

At 11.0 I gave an audience to the Prime Minister, we had a long talk, we discussed the Oath of Declaration, the Regency Bill, and the present political situation and he said he would endeavour to come to some understanding with the Opposition to prevent a general Election and he would not pay attention to what Mr Redmond said.

From this interview the King hurried to the Funeral Arrangements Committee, and before tea-time had visited King Alfonso and met King Manoel. Late that night he was " working at boxes with Bigge." On the 19th May he met the Kaiser at Victoria and took him to Westminster Hall. Later he met the King of Bulgaria, and in the evening gave a dinner-party to sixty of the Foreign Princes and representatives at the Palace. Friday, the 20th May, was the day of the funeral: " a very long & trying day for me & one I shall never forget as long as I live." He was up before seven, and when at last he went to bed " dead tired," he had been on his feet for the best part of sixteen hours. The funeral of King Edward has been often described and is indeed fresh still in the memory of middle-aged men. King George wrote down in his diary his heartfelt thankfulness that the arrangements so elaborately planned had gone off without a hitch and that the last ceremonies had lacked nothing of beauty and dignity.

During the next few days, while the foreign representatives were dispersing, the King remained in London, constantly busy in his office and with duties of State and ceremonial. It was not until the end of the month that the tension relaxed.

§ 2

King Edward's death evoked tributes to his qualities from leading men and humble folk all over the world. Time no doubt corrects the judgments and modifies the superlatives expressed in the days which immediately follow the deaths of Princes. Extravagant praise of a dead King must often increase the natural diffidence of his successor, yet Time has not corrected the contemporary verdict that King Edward proved himself a great King for the times in which he lived.

Certain rare gifts and a vast experience of human nature gained in many lands enabled him to shine in his difficult rôle. He did not delve deep into questions of his day and he read very little. Among his chief gifts of kingcraft were a unique power to charm which could instantly dispel antagonism, and the wit to recognise the essential truth concerning a current problem contained in a borrowed phrase, which, shrewdly employed in conversation with statesmen, won their admiration for his statecraft. " This was the greatest man that I ever had speech with," had been the verdict of Sir William Harcourt, a Radical and a man of very independent character, and in that judgment the new King, at any rate, would have concurred. Perhaps no estimate written down at the time would have struck King George as more just than that of Lord Esher:

The King is dead. . . . Towards politicians, even towards those who worried him, I never knew him to be unjust.

. . . He had an instinct for statecraft which carried him straight to the core of a great problem without deep or profound knowledge of the subject. He had one supreme gift, and this was his unerring judgment of men—and women. . . .

To his own son he was a charming and generous father. He always wished the Prince to be informed of everything. . . . Jealousy was a word he could not understand and a thing he could not tolerate in man or woman. . . . I have known all the great men of my time in this land of ours and many beyond it. He was the most kingly of them all.

That is no doubt a just estimate, covering most of the essentials.

It is the new King's own estimate of his father which is relevant here. He admired him whole-heartedly. Trained up to love and venerate him, he had made it the habit of his life which no action of his father had ever shaken. Family life had been an idyll of affection, warmth, gaiety, colour. In his life of forty-five years, the son had never given his parents a moment's anxiety except when he was ill. And when at last the father had the power to initiate the son into the mysteries of State affairs, mutual trust and a total absence of jealousy had marked their relations. Yet this warmth of affection never succeeded in banishing a certain diffidence in the son's approaches to the father—a condition of mind inspired by the character of King Edward. The biggest men who came in contact with him felt it from the first, and increasingly as the years of his reign passed. It was small wonder if King George felt keenly the loss he had sustained in the death of a father to whom he had always turned for advice, whose word he had always accepted as law and wisdom and whose qualities and genius could not in his view be too highly estimated. And it was small wonder if he felt that to succeed such a man and adequately to carry on his work in times so critical might well be beyond his power and might lead to disappointment and failure.

§ 3

To this pessimistic view not a little colour was supplied by gossip and ill-nature in Society and among the public. In modern times the nation has no very good record in the encouragement which it has given to those called to assume the terrible responsibilities of kingship. Too often the accession of a new King has been the signal for the opening of the floodgates of rumour and depreciation; and King George, even while the nation at large sympathised in the difficulties of his position and while not one in a million could have had a doubt as to the integrity of his private life, was not spared.

Two "scandals" once more raised their already hoary heads. Two lies concerning King George, both of which had widely circulated at the time of his marriage and since, were disseminated again and came to his ears before his father was laid in the grave. There would be no purpose in giving a mention to them—for there was no scintilla of evidence to justify the faintest belief in the truth of either—if it were not that one of these lies was finally nailed down in a Court of Law.

The Malta marriage libel—finally killed in the Spring of 1911—had a long and vigorous life. It was a widely circulated report that the King, during his service with the Mediterranean Fleet, had contracted a marriage in Malta with the daughter of an Admiral. At the last, it was made perfectly clear in Court and confirmed by a categorical denial signed by the King and read by the Attorney-General that no such marriage had taken place; and indeed the Prince and the lady in question had never been together in Malta during the relevant period covered by the libel. The other slander which died a natural death related to a charge of intemperance. It, too, had a long life. The King had heard of it more than once and indeed sometimes joked about it. It was substantially based on two facts—that the new King had a loud voice and a hearty laugh—how many people in Society had heard both ring out from the top of the great staircase at Stafford House and elsewhere—and that his colour was not good. There was truth in that; his complexion never recovered its healthy condition after his serious attack of typhoid fever. He may well have felt, with some bitterness, that at least he might have been spared this pinprick in 1910.

These were rumours circulating widely. But in the inner

ring of Edwardian Society, too, malice was not wanting. There were many in or on the fringe of the circle of King Edward who felt that his death was the death-knell of the good times and marked the end of the " great days " or the " happy days " of Society. In a narrow sense perhaps they were right. Some of them were inclined to vent their spleen on the new King and Queen. In many an Edwardian drawing-room and stronghold lampoons were soon enough circulating. The new Court was to be dull and decorous, lights would be turned low and colour banished from the doings of Society. A drab and puritanical régime, with economy and convention as its watchwords, would succeed to the brilliance and initiative of Edwardian social life. The King disapproved of racing, for example, and it was certain that he would never attend a meeting[1] . . . and so on. These also were pinpricks which he might have been spared. He had already a full measure of diffidence as to his ability and experience for the great tasks before him and the special difficulties gathering round him.

A letter written by him at this time to his old friend, Lord Dalkeith, afterwards Duke of Buccleuch, gives some indication of his sense of loss and loneliness.

King George to Lord Dalkeith

MARLBOROUGH HOUSE, 7th June 1910.

MY DEAR JOHN,—I was much touched by yr kind letter and thank you warmly for it & all your sympathetic words in my irreparable loss. Yes, as you say, even in the old *Bacchante* days there was great affection between my beloved father & myself & in later years this grew stronger & stronger. I was simply devoted to him & consulted him in everything, we were more like brothers, he was my best friend. So you can understand how terribly I miss him & long for his advice in the new life which I am now beginning with its many heavy responsibilities.

But I pray to God that He may give me wisdom & strength to try to follow in my dear father's footsteps & to work for

[1] The few excerpts from his diary concerning racing, selected from scores of such references, clearly prove how much interest and pleasure he always derived from the sport.

the welfare of our Great Empire. I can assure you, my dear John, that I have always valued your friendship & I know that I can count on it in the future as I have in the past. . . . Believe me, always most sincerely yours, GEORGE R.I.

He was well aware that his education as a sailor had ill fitted him for many of his new responsibilities. It had been only during his father's reign, nine swiftly moving years, that under the influence of Sir Arthur Bigge he had done something to repair the gaps in his knowledge of English and Constitutional History and to attain to the normal educational standard of the average public schoolboy at the leaving age.[1] These gaps had not yet been repaired, that standard not reached, when he came to the Throne. They had been busy years, much interrupted by official duties overseas. He was still methodically plodding on with his education when his reign was half over. He felt his handicaps, no man was ever more honest with himself and with the world. And it was in part due to that sense of educational inferiority that he developed as King a tendency to monopolise the conversation in his interviews with his ministers. It was perhaps a defensive expedient, perhaps he underrated his own sound common sense which, brought to bear on problems and questions of the day, proved often more effective than profound historical knowledge and higher education.

§ 4

The accession of a new King involves an immense amount of State business demanding the constant personal attention of the Sovereign. It is unnecessary to catalogue the innumerable acts, whose origins in some cases are lost in the mists of antiquity, which required to be done, the documents to be signed, the Missions to be despatched, the representatives of

---

[1] There is a memory of him in later years which illustrates this point:
Enter King George, reading from a paper. " Sandringham-cum-Appleton, Sandringham-cum- . . . What's this ' cum,' what does ' cum ' mean ? Here, you," turning to one of his Household, " you ought to know." On hearing the explanation, " Oh, it means ' with.' Then why can't they say so. They never taught me Latin. They taught me a lot of trigonometry and such stuff when I was a boy."

foreign Powers to be received in audience, the new institutions to be set going, the composition of the Household, the discussions on the Civil List, the thousand-and-one urgent duties which fell to be carried out for the new reign.

He was at work all day long. For several months his diary daily contains the brief note " Busy with boxes with Bigge." This reference was henceforth superfluous. The business of State was now a part, and a large part, of his day's work year in and year out. It mattered not if he were on a private visit, if he were at Balmoral, if it were a public holiday, if he were shooting. The official boxes came regularly wherever he might be, and must be got through punctually. He must rise early and go late to bed if recreation interfered with a full day's work. No recurring references will be made henceforth to this daily routine of office hours. Later on his regularity, his punctuality and the meticulous pains which he gave to it will be described and considered. But the broad fact that a King of England under modern conditions performs, year in and year out, a regular office routine of many hours a day must be accepted as read.[1]

Amid the urgent claims of State business he had a mass of private matters to attend to. There is no need to refer again to his loyalty to his father's memory. None who knew him doubted that he would prove that loyalty in his treatment of his father's old servants of every rank. He regarded it as an urgent and sacred trust, and none was disappointed. He carried out the trust to the limits of quixotism and in one or two notable instances perhaps with the sacrifice of efficiency. Under King Edward's will Sandringham House and grounds had been left to Queen Alexandra for her life. The new King was perfectly satisfied with the arrangement. He was largely charged with keeping up the big house for his mother, and he was more than contented with the cottage for himself. If some of his Household regarded it as quite unsuited to the hospitality needs of a King, he did not share their view. The

[1] An attempt has been made to give an idea of the range, complexity and weight of the official duties affecting the Constitution and the life of the nation which the Sovereign alone can, and must, punctually and regularly perform. This is set down on pages 272–4.

Park House [1] became his property and he proposed to use it as a guest house for the cottage.

One of his first visits after the funeral was made to Mr. Chamberlain at his London house. The great statesman was paralysed, but his brain remained clear and the King had a long and interesting talk with him. It was a characteristically thoughtful act.

§ 5

The new King's Household included many old and tried friends, but places were found in it for several of the late King's servants. Thus, Lord Knollys shared with Sir Arthur Bigge the duties of Private Secretary. Although their relations had always been and remained harmonious and loyal, the plan did not long work well. Lord Knollys was more politically minded than suited Sir Arthur, or indeed the King, and the arrangement soon came to an end. Sir William Carington remained in charge of the Privy Purse, with Sir Frederick Ponsonby,[2] one of the Assistant Private Secretaries, as his understudy. Major Clive Wigram was the other Assistant Secretary. Lord Spencer was Lord Chamberlain, and all the King's former Equerries remained with him, while more old friends were among his Lords and Grooms-in-Waiting.

The Queen's Household also was made up largely of old friends. The Duchess of Devonshire was Mistress of the Robes, Lady Shaftesbury and Lady Airlie were among her ladies, and Lady Eva Dugdale, Lady Mary Trefusis, Lady Katharine Coke and Lady Bertha Dawkins were the Bedchamber Women.

§ 6

In June the Court moved to Frogmore. The new Prince of Wales (so created that day) celebrated his sixteenth birthday at Windsor on the 23rd and was confirmed next day.

[1] The Park House, which has no architectural features of interest, had been lived in by General Knollys, father of Lord Knollys, and latterly by Sir Dighton Probyn, who at this time moved into Sandringham House.

[2] A son of Queen Victoria's great Private Secretary, Sir Henry Ponsonby; created Lord Sysonby in 1935 and died in the same year.

In July the King and Queen spent a week at the Royal
Pavilion at Aldershot, days which he thoroughly enjoyed
among the troops of the Command. He was agreeably
surprised by the comfort of the Pavilion. On the 21st July
the Proclamation of the Coronation was read, and next day
the King and Queen joined the *Victoria and Albert* at Cowes
and sailed in her to Torbay for important Fleet Exercises.
During his visit to Torbay he received all the Admirals and
Captains of the Home, Atlantic and Mediterranean Fleets
assembled and went out in Admiral May's flagship, the
Dreadnought, to watch the tactical exercises off the Devonshire
coast, the Prince of Wales and the Duke of Connaught being
with him. He went back to Marlborough House after the
exercises were over, and notes in his diary that, in the intervals
of business, he engaged his two elder sons daily at squash
racquets.

They went up to Balmoral for the 12th. The King was
delighted to be there again and the weather was glorious. It
was the Prince's first taste of grouse shooting, and the King
took him out to initiate him under a gruelling sun into the
business of walking up grouse. They returned exhausted but
triumphant, the Prince having killed seven birds. A letter
which the King wrote at this time to his mother gives a good
picture of the new life at Balmoral:

BALMORAL CASTLE, 29*th August* 1910.

MY OWN DARLING MOTHER DEAR,—I can't tell you how
deeply touched I am by all the dear & kind things you say
about me in the blessed letter I have just received for which
I thank you from the bottom of my heart. I know indeed
the terrible strain you have gone through during these last
awful months of sorrow & I quite understand that you now
feel as if you were beginning to recover from a severe illness,
the shock has been so great & now you realize all you have
lost in beloved Papa & you must miss him terribly at dear
Sandringham which he created & where you have spent so
many happy years of yr life. Only time can soften the hard
feeling in your heart when all the world seems cold &
miserable. . . .

You are quite right when you say we have never had any

misunderstandings, you know darling Mother dear how devoted I am to you & have always told you everything since I was a little child, we have never had any secrets. My great object is to try & help & comfort you in any way I can & make your life easier & your sorrow lighter to bear. I have always loved you deeply & shall take care that nobody or anything ever comes between us. . . .

David has gone out stalking, he has already shot two stags, the only two he has fired at, so I hope he will make a good shot, he is certainly very keen. . . . We have had Sir Edward Grey & the Lord Chancellor. The Prime Minister comes this evening & next week Mr. Lloyd George, I think it will do good his coming here, he has a large number of admirers in the country & he is certainly an agreeable man. Others are coming later including Mr Balfour & Rosebery. . . .

He was still at Balmoral in October, and on the 4th heard with sorrow of the Revolution in Portugal and learned that King Manoel, though unharmed, was temporarily a prisoner.

The Court moved to London, and the King took leave of the Duke of Connaught and his family who were leaving for South Africa. The Duke was to open the United Parliament in the King's name, a duty which King George himself would have performed if his father had not died. The Queen's brother, Prince Francis of Teck, died at this time. His death was a great grief to the Queen and to the King also, who had always been on the most affectionate terms with his brothers-in-law. A few days later the ex-King of Portugal and his mother took refuge in England and went to Wood Norton, where the Orléans family were living and at the end of the month King George and Queen Mary visited them there and heard the story of the Revolution.

§ 7

Queen Alexandra had been on a visit to Denmark, and the King came to London to meet her on her return on the 5th November. On the 7th he spent his last night in "dear old Marlborough House where I have lived for 35 years." Buckingham Palace had now been made ready for their reception and on the return of the Court to London they intended to go there.

He spent the sixty-ninth anniversary of his father's birth at the Cottage and passed a fortnight at Windsor in the middle of the month. " My rooms lovely, they are dear papa's, but we miss papa & Mother dear dreadfully." Before he left Windsor he held a Council in the Castle to dissolve Parliament. The dissolution arose from the rejection on the 23rd November by the Lords of Mr. Asquith's Parliament Bill. On the 21st Lord Lansdowne had carried the adjournment of the Second Reading of the Bill in favour of a Debate on his own Resolutions for Second Chamber Reform. The Conciliation Conference had broken up and the great constitutional issue, which was arousing so much bitterness, had to be faced. For the King it remained intermittently the sharpest trial and continuously the heaviest responsibility which he had experienced hitherto, right through to the Autumn of the year following. Never was the trial sharper than in November of 1910 when the question of contingent guarantees became insistent.

It was the demand for contingent guarantees which most nearly affected the King. Because he was still untried and little known to his ministers, he was the more likely to be wounded by any ministerial doubts that, if and when the occasion demanded it, he would do his duty as a constitutional King. He was not at variance with his ministers on the Constitutional principle which might be involved; what he sought to shake was their opinion of the juncture when his assent to the exercise of his prerogative (to create peers) should be extracted and announced; and in the event his assent was secured in advance for a contingency which never arose. At that time he was advised by two secretaries, both of great experience, and the weakness of a dual Secretariat was clearly proved. The King was strongly opposed to giving contingent guarantees at that juncture and had so informed Mr. Asquith on the 14th November through Lord Knollys. Sir Arthur Bigge was of the King's opinion; but when the crisis was at its sharpest, Lord Knollys advised that the King should give way. The issue is common knowledge and has been elsewhere referred to.

A reply which Sir Arthur [1] made to Mrs. Asquith, who on

---

[1] Sir Arthur was in 1911 raised to the peerage as Lord Stamfordham.

the 7th August, 1911, wrote to him glorifying Mr. Asquith's fine speech on that afternoon, and pointing out how greatly its terms must redound to the credit of the King's conduct throughout the crisis, is (without commentary or further commendation) an adequate and admirable note on the part played by the King:

I can quite understand your delight at the Prime Minister's speech. But you will not mind, I know, my saying that even Mr. Asquith's power and eloquence cannot make me forget that the King, on the 16th November [1910], was induced to do what was contrary to his nature and that he did it with much reluctance.

Had the Prime Minister and the Cabinet known His Majesty as well as I do they could have trusted him to act rightly and constitutionally whenever the circumstances might make it necessary for him to do so. They would thus have saved him from being obliged to enter into a secret understanding as to his course of action in what at that time was a mere hypothetical contingency. This is in no way the opinion of an " old Tory," but of one who, like you, loves the King and admires his absolute straightness. Yrs. very sincerely, S.

At the end of 1910 a new outbreak of militancy by the Suffragettes worse confounded the confusion of the stormy scene. But the King was at Sandringham when the election fever was at its height, and heard many of the results as they came in during a shooting visit to Elveden.

CHAPTER XII

The Coronation—Political Crisis—Durbar Visit
1911-12
[Mr. Asquith, Premier]

§ 1

A YEAR which included the Coronation, the Durbar visit to India, the Agadir Incident and a political crisis involving a vital decision as to the exercise of the King's Prerogative, could not at first sight be described as a quiet year in a King's life. The year 1911 was indeed not much less memorable than 1910 for both the King and Queen, who in the course of it performed for the first time many important functions of State which were to grow familiar with use. Nevertheless, important happenings in 1911, closely affecting the King, lacked quantity if not quality. The Agadir crisis, if sharp, was short, and to-day, judging it coolly by modern experience, one may perhaps feel that its intensity has been exaggerated. As for the Parliament Bill, some of the fiercest flames had died down by 1911 and the end was less sensational than had been anticipated.

It was the Coronation—as great a draw, if not so rare a spectacle and portent as King Edward's—which overshadowed other events in the year and kept the King busy. All through the Spring and early Summer he was constantly occupied with Committees and in discussions on Coronation and Durbar matters and plans.[1] Before the Court left Norfolk he had several talks on Sandringham affairs with his Agent, Mr. Frank Beck, and saw most of his tenants there. He went on to Windsor and entertained a succession of guests, ministers, politicians and others, and had some preliminary discussion of the Durbar visit with Lord Crewe.

[1] In Windsor Castle grounds a plan of the Durbar was staked out with flags in its actual size from details received from India.

He was still at Windsor when the trial of Mylius for the Malta marriage libel came up for hearing, and his own comment on the verdict and sentence was in these words:

Bigge returned from London where he had attended the trial of Edward Mylius for libelling me, saying that I had married Miss Culme Seymour (Mrs. Napier) in Malta in 1890. The Admiral and his daughter were present & gave evidence. The Lord Chief Justice sentenced him to 12 months' imprisonment, the maximum. The whole story is a damnable lie and has been in existence for over 20 years & I trust now that this will settle it once and for all.

His hopes were justified. The trial of course was front-page news, and some of the lengthy and elaborately reasoned refutations which appeared in the Press at the time make sorry reading to-day. But when the orgy was over, the damnable lie was killed, and never again was the voice of malice raised against a King the integrity of whose life should for ever have preserved him from slander.

On the 6th February, the King and Queen opened Parliament.

At 1.30 May & I started in state in the old Gold Coach for Westminster to open Parliament. There were very large crowds in the streets who gave us an enthusiastic reception both going & returning. I wore Admiral of the Fleet's uniform. As soon as we reached Westminster we went to the Robing room to put on the robes. Then we walked in procession hand in hand to the House of Lords, it was indeed a terrible ordeal, as the House was crowded in every part & I felt horribly shy & nervous. I first read the Declaration & then the Speech, my voice was somewhat husky but I believe was fairly well heard. I also felt very emotioné & thought of beloved Papa & Mama whom I had seen do the same thing so often. It was a great relief when we got back to the Robing room. . . .

It is right to reflect a moment on the nervous strain which such functions may impose on highly strung men and women whose destinies raise them to a throne. People are inclined easily to assume that it is the *métier* of Royalties and that such ordeals call in their case for none of the nerve discipline which ordinary people must exercise. Such State functions, less or more important, are fixed months ahead, immense and elaborate preparations precede them, and when the hour strikes the whole success or failure rests on the punctual appearance and the conduct of the central figure. King George was highly strung, always his emotions were near the surface, tears came easily to his eyes, and, when much moved, his voice would sometimes fail him. Magnify the function to the fearful importance of a Coronation, and it will be admitted that it may be possible to define too loosely the word *métier* in its application to men and women who wear crowns.

The King and Queen moved about this time into the rooms in the Palace which King Edward and Queen Alexandra had used, and they spent many hours arranging the furniture and pictures. That month and the next the King gave four important dinner-parties to representative men, at each of which forty to fifty sat down. These dinners gave him an opportunity to converse with nearly 200 of the leaders of thought in various spheres of national life. The Queen and he dined out often with their friends, thus making wider contacts. It was Lord Stamfordham's earnest wish that they should do so. He had long realised how much King Edward's statecraft owed to his constant contacts with men in public life and with intelligent men and women in general, and it was ever his aim to overcome King George's preference for dining *en famille*.

That Spring, also, the King made a point of paying visits to many national institutions, among them the General Post Office, the British Museum and the new Radium Institute; and in the middle of May with all the Royal Family he opened the Festival of Empire at the Crystal Palace. From Windsor in April he " showed the rogues they lied," satisfying his lifelong interest in racing by paying one of many visits to Newmarket, where he stayed at the Jockey Club rooms. He always loved these visits and greatly enjoyed his habitual morning ride on the Heath. On the journey to and fro every village turned out in force to cheer him.

The 16th May had been fixed for the ceremony of unveiling the memorial to Queen Victoria in the Mall, and, on the day before, the King met the German Emperor and Empress who came over for the occasion. At noon on the 16th he performed the ceremony and in the evening gave a banquet in honour of his chief guests. A State Ball followed, and before the visit ended the King and Kaiser had a long and friendly conversation on important questions during a walk in the Palace garden. (It was barely six weeks later that the German gunboat *Panther* put in her unwelcome appearance at the Port of Agadir in Morocco.) On the last day of May the King gave his first dinner to sixty members of the Jockey Club, following the victory of Mr. Joel's Sunstar in the Derby.

§ 2

The day fixed for the Coronation drew near and June was a busy month for the King. He was at Aldershot for several days, living in the Pavilion now modernised with electric light and bathrooms, and daily inspecting troops and witnessing exercises. The Court was at Windsor again on the 10th, on which day at a Garter Chapel the King invested the Prince and walked in a procession of Knights to St. George's Chapel for the service which followed. As the royal party drove down the course for the Ascot meeting, they received a great welcome; " very kind," the King called it.

Then followed the last rehearsals and trial robings before the tremendous ceremony. By the 18th June most of the royal representatives had arrived. On the 20th the German Crown Prince at the Palace handed to King George the baton of Field-Marshal of the German Army, and in the afternoon the King showed himself to the crowds assembled in London, driving with the Queen, the Prince and Princess Mary through the Parks. An enormous banquet followed; nearly six hundred royalties and other representatives of Missions and Deputations, ministers, ambassadors, Suites and the Household sat down to dine in two great rooms in the Palace, and the King shook hands with every guest. On the Coronation Eve he received the Empire Premiers and their wives.

Thursday, 22nd June. Our Coronation Day. Buckingham Palace.—It was overcast and cloudy with slight showers, & a strongish cool breeze, but better for the people than great heat. Today was indeed a great & memorable day in our lives & one we can never forget, but it brought back to me many sad memories of 9 years ago when the parents were crowned. . . . There were over 50,000 troops lining the streets under the command of Lord Kitchener. There were hundreds of thousands of people who gave us a magnificent reception. The Service in the Abbey was most beautiful & impressive but it was a terrible ordeal. It was grand yet simple & most dignified & went without a hitch. I nearly broke down when dear David came to do homage to me, as it reminded me so much when I did the same thing to beloved Papa; he did it so well. Darling May looked so lovely & it was indeed a comfort to me to have her by my side as she has been ever to me during these last 18 years. . . .

The King went on to describe in his diary how he and the Queen twice during the day showed themselves to the people from a balcony of the Palace.

The next day was the Prince's birthday, and after giving him his presents; " At 11.0 May & I started on our wonderful drive through London, over 7 miles in length through the most beautifully decorated streets which were crowded with people from top to bottom who cheered in a way I have never heard before." In the days which followed, he carried out constant functions and ceremonies between long hours in his office. On the 24th June they went on board the yacht for the great Spithead Review. " The largest fleet ever got together & not one commissioned for the occasion."

Back at the Palace on the 27th, they gave a big garden-party and attended a Gala Performance at His Majesty's, and at the end of it took leave in the theatre of all the representatives. Next day, too, was long and tiring. As President of the Royal Agricultural Show, the King visited the Show Grounds at Norwich and received the welcome of all Norfolk. During the following days came the Thanksgiving Service at St. Paul's and the Guildhall luncheon, a great inspection of the Empire contingents, a visit to the 100,000 children who were the King's guests at the Crystal Palace, a dinner with the Prime Minister—and then the scene shifted to Windsor, and the ceremonies and everlasting labours continued unabated. Only for a few hours was the tension relaxed. There is a characteristically simple entry on Sunday, 2nd July; " Took it easy, as I am rather tired." On this day the *Panther* made her appearance at the Port of Agadir, but the King made no special reference in his diary to the critical negotiations which succeeded the incident.

On the 7th July the King and Queen left for Holyhead on a State visit to Dublin, and one of the first sights in Kingstown Harbour which impressed the King was his " little old gunboat *Thrush* " doing fishery work. Various ceremonies had been arranged for him by Lord Aberdeen; there were addresses received and replied to, visits to Phœnix Park and other popular centres, talks with Mr. Birrell. Everywhere their reception was warm, even enthusiastic. They crossed again to Wales for that famous ceremony at Carnarvon on the 13th July:

I invested David with the insignia of the Prince of Wales & Earl of Chester. . . . I put a mantle or robe on his shoulders, a coronet on his head, a ring on his finger, & a gold rod in his hand, he kneeling before me all the time, then he took the oath of allegiance, & [I] raised him up kissing him on both cheeks. . . . The dear boy did it all remarkably well & looked so nice. . . .

Days of ceremonies in Wales followed, the King and Queen staying at Plas Machynlleth,[1] and then the scene was Edinburgh, while the Court stayed in Holyroodhouse. There was a spell of hot weather at the time, and the King returned exhausted to London on the 21st July to face further days of worry and hard work.

§ 3

On the 22nd July the thermometer rose to 93° in the shade, and the heat of the political crisis sympathetically increased in intensity.

[1] Lord H. Vane-Tempest's.

The King's own words may be set down;

Directly after breakfast had a long talk with Francis [Knollys] & Bigge about the situation. At 11.30 I received the Prime Minister and I only promised to allow him to create a sufficient number of Peers in event of House of Lords throwing out Parliament Bill, to pass the Bill & no more. All this worries me very much & I fear the Unionists will be sore but I have only acted constitutionally, as a General Election at this moment is out of the question.

It was the King's expressed wish that his decision should be made known to the leaders of the Opposition without loss of time. On the 24th there is another reference to the political crisis. On that day the King received Lord Lansdowne and Mr. Balfour and later the Prime Minister. " We discussed the political situation, it worries me very much." The bitter issue, uncertain to the last, was settled on the night of the 10th August, after Lord Morley had announced the King's assent to the exercise of his prerogative if the Parliament Bill were thrown out. The Bill was passed by the House of Lords with a narrow majority.

The intense heat continued and the King was kept at work until 29th July, when the Royal Family got away at last to the yacht and found relief in the cooler sea breezes. The King and Queen of Spain were at Osborne Cottage, but formalities were few and the King could bathe and sail his beloved *Britannia* and enjoy his first real holiday after a long spell of hard work and anxiety.

He returned to London from Sandringham during the first week of November, for some particularly busy days devoted to affairs of State and the final preparations for departure to India. On the 8th he received Mr. Balfour, who had resigned the leadership of the Conservative and Unionist Party. " He will be a terrible loss," he noted, " but of course will remain a member of Parliament." Mr. Balfour's opinion of the King's ability, given to Lord Esher before accession, has been quoted. Their relations had always been easy and mutually helpful. Mr. Balfour had judged him " really clever." A man with a big brain and mind may well have set a high value on such qualities as simplicity, naturalness, modesty, frankness and good sense in those with whom he had official dealings. They were qualities which the King possessed in marked degree.

§ 4

The 11th November was the day of departure to India. Queen Alexandra and some of the children and members of the Royal Family travelled down to Portsmouth with the King and Queen. Rear-Admiral Sir Colin Keppel received them on board H.M.S. *Medina* in which they were to take passage, and presented the ship's officers. Soon afterwards the last farewells were said—as " horrible to say " as ever— and the *Medina* slipped her moorings. At Spithead the escort of four cruisers took station astern and the coast of England vanished across an angry sea.

The weather got worse and worse, and the King and Queen moved to cabins amidships. The heat of Port Said, where coaling took place and where the King received the Khedive in state and had conversations with Lord Kitchener and Generals Wingate and Maxwell, came almost as a relief. The long voyage across the Indian Ocean was trying, and it was in heat " damp and awful " that the *Medina* cast anchor off Bombay on the 2nd December.

The royal party disembarked on the 5th and, after official ceremonies in Bombay, left that night for Delhi, travelling in their old train which they had found so comfortable six years before. Arrived at Delhi, they were received with great pomp in a tent in the fort where a hundred and nineteen Princes and Maharajahs were presented to the King. A procession was then formed to the King-Emperor's camp and passed " through large but not demonstrative crowds."

The King's comment on this early contact with the people of India is interesting. Those who best knew him are gener- ally agreed that the Indian Durbar visit greatly influenced the King's character. They consider that that tremendous experience, the magnificent ceremonial among those millions of his subjects many of whom felt for him and hailed him almost as a god, convinced him finally and for his life of the majesty of his office and of the magnitude of his responsibilities.

The Durbar Camp was probably the largest ever pitched, and the extent of it, statistically indicated, held the King's interest. It contained something approaching " 40,000 tents with 300,000 people living in them." The programme of ceremonial began at once. The King laid the first stone of the plinth on which was to stand the equestrian statue of King Edward. The finals of polo and football matches were played off before him. On the 10th December there was a full rehearsal of the Durbar.

That tremendous ceremony was performed on the 12th December. It has often been described and illustrated. The King's own words will best serve here:

Today we held the Coronation Durbar, the most beautiful and wonderful sight I ever saw, & one which I shall never forget. All the arrangements were perfect and everything went without a hitch. After breakfast I was busy seeing people. I held a Council at ten to approve the Proclamation at which the Governor-General [Lord Hardinge], Crewe, & Bigge were present, Wigram acting as clerk.
The weather was all that could be wished, hot sun, hardly any wind, no clouds. May & I were photographed before we started in our robes, I wore the same clothes and robes as at the Coronation with a new Crown made for India which cost £60,000 which the Indian Government is going to pay for. We left the camp at 11.30 with escorts . . . in an open carriage with 4 horses, the whole way to the Amphitheatre lined with troops. The Amphitheatre contained about 12,000 people, there were some 18,000 troops inside it & over 50,000 people on the Mound. On our arrival we took our seats on the thrones facing the centre of the crescent. I first made a speech giving the reasons for holding the Durbar. Then the Governor-General did homage to me followed by all the Ruling Chiefs, Governors, Lieut.-Governors and members of the different Councils. We then walked in procession, I holding May's hand, our trains being held by young Maharajahs . . . to two other silver thrones raised up on a platform facing the troops & the Mound. The Heralds rode into the Amphitheatre & the Chief Herald, Gen. Peyton, read the Proclamation (which the Assistant Herald read in

Urdu). Then the Governor-General read a paper announcing the boons. Then all the troops presented arms & a salute of 101 Guns was fired & a feu de joi. . . . We returned in procession to the first thrones when I announced that the Capital will be transferred from Calcutta to Delhi, the ancient Capital, & that a Governorship would be created for the Presidency of Bengal, the same as Madras & Bombay, which was received with cheers; the secret had been well kept.

The whole of the people present then sung the National Anthem & the most wonderful Durbar ever held was closed. . . .

Reached the Camp at 3.0. Rather tired after wearing the Crown for 3½ hours, it hurt my head, as it is pretty heavy. . . .

Afterwards we held a reception in the large tent, about 5,000 people came, the heat was simply awful. Bed at 11.0 & quite tired.

Certainly the King was not given to exaggeration in his diary.

There followed the great review of 50,000 troops under command of Sir O'Moore Creagh, and a number of other engagements which kept both the King and Queen very busy in rather cooler weather. There were banquets and big functions almost every night, and constant investitures and the giving of presents. On the 18th December they separated, the King going to Nepal for a week's sport. Shortly before he left he received news of the wreck off Cape Spartel of the *Delhi* in which the Princess Royal and the Duke of Fife and their daughters were travelling to Egypt. The King was anxious, but went off in the belief that all the family were safe at Tangier. A wonderful week's sport followed. For months before, in anticipation of the King-Emperor's visit, the Maharajah Chandra Shamshere Jung had borne the heavy burdens of compensation while the tigers were preserved as sacred animals, to ensure a plentiful supply. The King used a ·450 rifle for rhino and his old ·400 for tiger. With the latter weapon he shot as a man shoots hares in a drive, and his prowess astonished the Princes and natives. He started by stopping two charging tigers, the first killed stone dead; and soon after had a right and left at rhino. During the week the party's bag was 31 tigers, 14 rhinos and

4 bears; and even the Maharajah expressed himself as delighted and surprised.[1]

The King and Queen were separated for Christmas Day and met again for the journey to Calcutta. Received by Lord Hardinge, they steamed down the Hooghly and landed at Prinsep Ghaut within a few hours of the time when they had landed there six years before. And at Calcutta another momentous year ended, giving occasion for another characteristic tailpiece in the King's diary: "This has been a heavy & anxious year for me, I am thankful to God for the way He has watched over me & given me health to carry out all my numerous duties & responsibilities. Goodbye, dear old 1911, the most momentous year of my life."

§ 5

The chief event of the full Calcutta programme was perhaps the Pageant, a marvel of colour and organisation. It was the centrepiece of a great variety of lesser functions, some of them onerous. There were visits to a number of institutions, and many banquets and investitures and receptions. A more restful occasion, much appreciated, was a luncheon at Barrackpore under the famous banyan tree. They reached Bombay at last, and on the evening of the 10th January, after a round of farewells and amid great enthusiasm, the King and Queen left India in the *Medina*, to steam the 2,353 miles to Port Sudan.

In his diary note of the 11th January the King briefly set down his reflections on the tour. The passage is notable for its confidence, and suggests that the importance of the Durbar visit in the development of the King's character has not been exaggerated.

Our second visit to India is now over and we can thank

[1] The lasting impression made by the King-Emperor's personality on the people of Nepal is evidenced in a most interesting and significant fact. Twenty-eight years, filled with tremendous happenings and world changes, have elapsed since his visit, but still to-day he and the details of his visit are gratefully and vividly remembered there, and not a year passes but his surviving secretary receives letters from the Maharajah and members of his family which breathe the goodwill and loyalty and affection to the Throne engendered by that visit.

God that it has been an unqualified success from first to last. It was entirely my own idea to hold the Coronation Durbar at Delhi in person, & at first I met with much opposition but the result has I hope been more than satisfactory & has surpassed all expectations. I am vain enough to think that our visit will have done good in India. We have been fully repaid for our long journey.

Something of the same thought he expressed to Queen Alexandra in a letter he wrote her from Malta :

This will actually be my last letter to you, what joy, there are only 9 days before we meet. I shall then feel proud that our historical visit to India has been accomplished successfully I hope & that I have done my duty before God & this great Empire, & last but not least that I have gained the approval of my beloved Motherdear.

During the voyage home he had conversations with Lord Crewe on the political situation, and for recreation played many rubbers of bridge. In the Mediterranean on the 29th January the King and Queen heard of the serious condition of the Duke of Fife.[1] They passed Cape Spartel, but too far out to distinguish the wrecked *Delhi*. On the 5th February in bitter weather they landed at Portsmouth to be reunited with their family. They had a great reception both there and on arriving in London, and at the end of the day showed themselves to the people on the balcony of the Palace, receiving " splendid cheers." Next day they attended a Thanksgiving Service at St. Paul's for the success of the visit to India, and then the King was once more deep in affairs of State.

[1] He died that day at Assouan.

CHAPTER XIII

Visits to Industrial Centres—Their Majesties' Initiative—Political Anxieties—Berlin. 1912-13

[Mr. Asquith, Premier]

§ 1

ABRIEF summary[1] of the Home Rule Crisis 1912–14 will make clearer the extracts and allusions which are contained in the narrative of the last years before the War.

The King had had a " lull " after the passage of the Parliament Bill in which, as has been told, he went to India for the Coronation Durbar. Parliament during that time was occupied with the Welsh Disestablishment Bill and, among other matters, with the Marconi Affair. But at the date of the King's return from India, the atmosphere again became charged, with the passionate preliminaries of the Home Rule Bill. Ulster set up a Provisional Government under Sir Edward Carson and the probability of the Army being drawn in was made apparent. The King was soon in the thick of another raging political tempest. He was bombarded with letters and suggestions from all sorts of people, ranging from Elder Statesmen to militant women, who advised a variety of expedients ; and the bombardment and the bitterness did not decrease in intensity until the middle of 1914. He listened patiently and remained perfectly cool. He would sometimes remind his ministers that whereas in due course the Government would disappear, he would remain and his actions be remembered.

He made every possible effort to bridge the gulf and to compose contending passions. During the Autumn of 1913

---

[1] For this and several more summaries of political crises and events of the reign I have had the great advantage of studying Lord Wigram's private notes.

Lord Crewe and Mr. Bonar Law were often seen playing golf on the Balmoral Links, and Mr. Asquith, who was there in October 1913, was persuaded by the King to meet Mr. Bonar Law privately and Sir Edward Carson also. The Army became restless, the deadlock continued and on the 24th July, 1914, the King summoned the party leaders to an historical Conference at Buckingham Palace. That Conference failed, but civil war did not follow. The Great War came to close the ranks.

To return. There are notes in the King's diary of February 1912 of many important interviews and discussions. Among them he had a long talk on Navy matters with Prince Louis of Battenberg and saw both Lord Curzon and Lord Londonderry. Lord Curzon did not conceal his opposition to the changes announced at the Durbar; the latter dealt at length with the latest political crisis, the hoary and thorny question of Home Rule.

It was little wonder that the King was overworked and constantly anxious. Every year between 1908 and 1914 the chance of war breaking out was not much less real than during 1939. It must be remembered also that he had still an immense amount of ground to make up in his education for kingship. He knew little beyond the elementaries of many of the political questions which now occupied him. He was discovering all the time new aspects of the problems on which his ministers were consulting him daily, and learning details of the procedure which governed his own constitutional functions; and within his limitations he spared no effort to comprehend the full implications of all these matters.

Since the election of December 1910 the Liberal Government had been kept in power solely by the whim of the Irish Nationalists. That favour helped to secure at last the passage of the Parliament Bill and, through the House of Commons, measures for the disestablishment and partial disendowment of the Church in Wales and for Home Rule in Ireland; by virtue of the Parliament Act, the House of Lords would only be able to delay the passage of these Bills for two years. The Home Rule Bill, in its inoperative state, set Ulster afire. The six Protestant counties were resolved to resist by force any attempt to coerce them into union with Southern Ireland, and they found many stalwart allies in the British Parliament. The Great War was to bring a truce to the unsolved problem, but in the two years before it Ulster was brought to the verge of armed rebellion.

Meanwhile the Suffragettes continued relentlessly their violent campaign of embarrassment, and outrages were frequent. Labour was in ferment, too. Since 1907 strikes had been constant, and culminated in a disastrous coal-strike in the Spring of 1912, when Industry was brought almost to a standstill and the Premier was forced to use dictatorial powers. And if these things were not enough (to convince Germany that Britain had plenty of trouble at home), the Marconi Affair threw suspicion on members of the Government at a very unfortunate juncture and for some time to come tarnished the high reputation for integrity of English public life.

§ 2

Overworked and worried as the King was, he had with the Queen's constant help struck out a line for himself and begun already to put into practice a new conception of the responsibilities of Constitutional Monarchy in times of rapid social changes and grave danger. Mr. D. C. Somervell makes the point clearly and fairly:

About this time people began to realise that the King and Queen were striking out on a line of their own. They took tea with a miner's wife in South Wales; they visited the mines and industries of Yorkshire, and soon afterwards the Railway Works at Crewe and the potteries of the " Five Towns " near by.

These visits, one felt, were no mere sight-seeing; they were less expressions of pride in the triumphs of Industry than of homely friendliness for the simple folk on whose daily work the triumphs of Industry depended. If the politicians were out of touch with the things that really mattered, were not the King and Queen doing what they could to redress the balance?

The Great War was to win for the King the proud title of Father of his People. It is interesting to observe how early in his reign he began to earn his right to it. Not seldom before the war was well in progress, had the London public called him out to the balcony of the Palace, there to receive the acclamation of the Capital.

In February 1912 the Miners' Strike seemed imminent, and the King was constantly in touch with his ministers. Mr. Asquith took a very cheerless view of the prospects of settlement, and before the beginning of March this disastrous stoppage, affecting a million men, was in progress. The King stayed in London throughout March, seldom leaving the Palace except for functions. For exercise he relied on tennis in the Palace Court [1] and played whenever he could with the Prince, who left for Paris with Mr. Hansell at the end of the month after an operation for the removal of tonsils. The King had seen a good deal of his eldest son in the past weeks. Two old friends died at this time, and he felt their loss deeply—Mr. Arthur Sassoon and Mr. Willie James. The majority of his work during March was in his office. He had a long talk on Navy affairs with Mr. Churchill and many conversations with the Premier. There are several pleasant references in his diary to his younger sons at their private school, St. Peter's Court, Broadstairs. However busy, however anxious, he might be, he never neglected their letters to him. Wherever he might be, he answered by return their childish reports of small, important school events, and always recorded on their return home his impressions of their health and development.

The first important function of the Season took the King to Portland for a great review of the Fleet which much impressed him. "Very fine sight, 12 Admirals' flags flying, 35, 610 officers and men present, 908 guns with Fleet including 20 13·5″ and 160 12″." On this occasion he went out, in the company of Prince Albert, Mr. Churchill, Captain Roger

---

[1] The King revived his interest in the game at this time, Lord Willingdon and Sir Frederick Ponsonby playing regularly with him, while Major Wigram, an expert on this variety of tennis, was often called in to coach and to play.

Keyes and others in Submarine D4 (Lieutenant Nasmith).[1] The vessel dived about 27 feet for a run of three miles and the King commented: " perfectly safe unless they are run into." He later went on board the *Neptune*, flagship of Sir George Callaghan, to watch the 1st Battle Squadron of Super-Dread-noughts at battle practice, but hazy weather curtailed the programme. The Army's turn came next, and he spent several days at the Pavilion, watching exercises directed by Sir Douglas Haig.

The Court was again in London on the 21st May, and at the Palace on the 23rd the King and Queen entertained at luncheon the Arch-Duke Franz Ferdinand of Austria and his wife, the Duchess of Hohenberg. Tagalie, a grey mare, won the Derby that year, and the King afterwards entertained a Jockey Club membership of fifty-five at the usual banquet. But he was tired and depressed and his comment was brief: " Talked to most of them: very tiring."

In the middle of June Mr. Asquith came back from a holiday spent in the Mediterranean, and the King heard from him his impressions of the situation at home and abroad. Lord Loreburn resigned the Great Seal and the King offered it to Mr. Haldane, whose worth he had always appreciated. Colonel Seely [2] filled the vacant post at the War Office.

After the Trooping of the Colour and the regular Court functions, the King and Queen went to Windsor for Ascot, paying one day a visit to Harrow, an item in a programme of public-school visits. Then they cut adrift from tradition and carried out an important visit to South Wales. They lived for a few days on board the *Victoria and Albert*, whence they inspected the docks at Cardiff, and the King laid the foundation-stone of the National Museum and visited the University of Wales. They went on to the Pontypridd district to visit the coal-mine area, entering one or two houses of the workers and showing the greatest interest and sympathy wherever they went. The tour continued to Dowlais, where they saw over the great steel-works, and then to Bristol. In July

---

[1] Admiral of the Fleet Sir Roger Keyes. Admiral Sir M. E. Dunbar Nasmith, V.C., famous for his exploits in command of Submarine E11.
[2] Lord Mottistone.

they left London again for Yorkshire. During their visit the disaster at the Cadeby Colliery occurred and, within a few hours of it, the miners and their families were astonished and touched by the sight of the King and Queen moving among the mourners at the pit-head. They visited also several of the big mills at Halifax and talked with the weavers with an informality and friendliness which was then something of a novelty.

"Thank Goodness," the King wrote on the 19th July, "the last Court function this year." The comment perhaps was an indication of his opinion that in times so grave at home and abroad the more fashionable functions of the Sovereign were unusually hard to bear. After visits to Bolton Abbey and Abbeystead,[1] the King joined the Queen at Balmoral at the end of August. It was at Balmoral that he entertained in succession his ministers and other leaders in Church and State. Among them came regularly Dr. Lang, then Archbishop of York, who would often go out with the King when he was stalking, and shared a frugal luncheon while they discussed a score of subjects of major and of minor importance. The Prince of Wales was now preparing to go to Magdalen College, Oxford, and the King had several talks with Major William Cadogan, who was to go there with him in the capacity of Equerry and adviser.

The big-scale Manœuvres in the Cambridge area that year interrupted his Scottish holiday. The King had decided long before to attend them, and he stayed at Trinity College for a few days, watching the Manœuvres and having conversations with all the foreign Attachés present. He saw again after twenty-eight years his brother's old rooms in Nevile's Court. At the end of October he went as usual to his rooms at the Jockey Club, Newmarket. On this occasion the weather was bad, and he spent an afternoon and evening alone, reading. The stress of his days is evidenced by his entry: "First time I've had any peace for a long time. 4.15 to bedtime reading alone."

The November visit to Windsor that year was busy and anxious. Ministers came and went; Sir Edward Grey spoke

[1] Lord Sefton's.

much on foreign affairs, Mr. Churchill on Navy matters; Mr. Walter Long and Mr. Burns and other political leaders were included in the usual parties, and Prince Lichnowsky, the new German Ambassador, presented his letters. After a visit to Welbeck the Court returned to the Palace, and from 13th December the King was much engaged with his ministers and gave interviews to many Naval men. Before leaving for the Christmas holidays, he received the Peace delegates who were conferring on the Turkish-Balkan terms of settlement.

He was at Sandringham when the news came of the attempt to assassinate Lord Hardinge at Delhi and he sat down instantly to write to his old friend. And so " another year comes to an end and it has been a hard one for me. I have tried to do my duty."

§ 3

King George's first letter of the new year was to his secretary:

YORK COTTAGE, SANDRINGHAM, 1st January 1913.

MY DEAR BIGGE,[1]—Thanks for your two letters recevd. today. Bonar Law can certainly trust me, anything he mentions to you to tell me I shall keep to myself. All he told you is not very satisfactory, I am sure it will be fatal if he resigns the leadership, there is simply no one to take his place. I am certain that the whole party is loyal to him. They ought to have a meeting of the party and thrash the whole question of food taxes out, much better now than on the eve of an election & surely they could solve this question satisfactorily & thereby keep the party united. We hope to be at Windsor on two Sundays, Jan 26th & Feb 2nd., I should like to ask the Archbishop & Mrs Davidson for one Sunday & Canon Hensley Henson for the other.

You might come here on Saturday or Monday whichever you like. Mary [2] is dying to hunt & has no one to go out with. I entirely disagree with Churchill about the 1st Sea Lord [3] only giving advice to 1st Lord about the high commands, I am

---

[1] The King continued to call his secretary by his surname long after the latter became Lord Stamfordham (1911).

[2] Princess Mary.

[3] Sir F. Bridgeman, First Sea Lord, soon afterwards resigned.

sure he is wrong. Of course *he* is responsible but surely the Senior Naval Officer is the person to give advice; what can a civilian know about the different Admls.' professional abilities? . . . Yr Sincere friend, G.R.I.

In the middle of January Prince Albert left Sandringham for a cruise: " Said goodbye to dear Bertie, tomorrow he joins the *Cumberland* and sails with the other Cadets of his term to the West Indies."

During the January visit of the Court to Windsor [1] he notes in his diary that he " Wrote a memo on the present political situation & how it affects the Sovereign." The clouds were lowering, and only the Premier among his ministers remained at this time an optimist. On the 5th February the King went to Portsmouth to inspect the great cruiser *New Zealand*, given by the people of New Zealand. On the 11th he heard of the fate of Captain Scott and his polar party, and a few days later he attended a Memorial Service to the five heroic men in St. Paul's.

An unpleasant duty came next to be performed. The arrangement of a dual secretaryship had for some time proved unsatisfactory and the King forced himself to break it to Lord Knollys that it must end. Lord Knollys did what he could to make the task easier and remained a friend and trusted adviser for the rest of his life.

The King was at Windsor again when on the 18th March news came of the assassination of the King of Greece : " Beloved Uncle Willie has been assassinated at Salonica, while walking in the streets. . . . Too horrible, I was devoted to him & he will be a great loss to Greece. Motherdear is fearfully upset by this fresh sorrow." He went up at once to London to comfort her. It was his habit henceforth when at Windsor in the early Spring to pay a visit with some members of his family to Madame d'Hautpoul at Turville Heath. In the garden there almost every tree was planted by some member of the Royal Family, and it was noted on these visits how invariably the King's cares and anxieties fell away from him and how he renewed his youth and high spirits as he

[1] Up to the War the Court usually paid four visits a year to Windsor.

talked of old times with one of his first and closest women friends.

§ 4

In April he was back in London facing new crises. Superimposed upon them was the Marconi scandal which naturally added greatly to the King's worries while it called in question the good name of some of his ministers. That month the Queen and he made an important tour of the Potteries from Crewe Hall, taking the greatest pains to get into contact with the workers throughout the Five Towns. On his return at the end of April he inspected the Guards Brigade and had anxious conversations with Sir Edward Grey: " This crisis about Scutari is the worst we have had yet and may be the most dangerous." Certainly Europe was in ferment. Turkey, forced to an armistice, was still bargaining in London over Bulgaria's claims to new territory. Soon enough, as generally prophesied, war broke out again in the Balkans, the individual states turning one on another while Turkey slipped out once more with a whole skin. The long Conference in London, over which Sir Edward Grey presided jealously watched by the Great Powers, was concerned with the delimitation of frontiers between an enlarged Servia backed by Russia, and a new state of Albania protected by Austria and Italy, with Germany behind them.

The Aldershot inspections that May had special significance, and the King was daily engaged with Sir John French and Sir Douglas Haig watching exercises. It was the turn of Territorial units and he was indefatigable in his inspections of barracks and quarters. But still Lord Roberts cried out for National Service to the deaf ears of the Government and a vast majority of the nation.

It was a disagreeable moment for an official visit to Berlin. The Kaiser's daughter was to be married at the end of May and the King and Queen had long been committed to attending the ceremonies. As it turned out, the visit was not only a successful but an agreeable one. As he drove beside the Kaiser through the streets of Berlin on the 21st May between lines of troops from the Garrison, he received a very warm welcome. There was a most harmonious family banquet that evening, after which the King had speech with the Chancellor, Bethmann-Hollweg, who was "most friendly." And small wonder, for now Germans made common cause in their efforts to secure Britain's friendship—and neutrality. Next day the Tzar arrived and there was an enormous State Banquet and "Circle." On the 24th, the Wedding Day, it was all smiles and sentiment. The Kaiser (the King notes) made a most touching speech taking leave of his daughter, and Tzar and King of England supported the bride, one on either hand, during a part of the elaborate ceremonies. "Most interesting," was the King's comment. And so, in the giving of and responding to toasts and healths, the ruling Houses of Europe agreed for a few hours to forget the dangers and to sink the differences of the day. But no opportunity was given for private conversation between the Tzar and King George. The Kaiser saw to that. "We have," was the King's *envoi*, "enjoyed our visit very much, & I can't say how kind William & Victoria have been." Always fair to the Kaiser in his private references, King George clearly was predisposed to friendship with him. Perhaps, if the autocrat had been an autocrat in deed, last-minute appeals from one royal House to another before the great tragedy burst would have been more potent to avert it. The King returned to London shortly before the Balkan Treaty of Peace was signed at St. James's Palace. "Greatly due to Sir E. Grey. I trust now that the allies may not fight among themselves." It was too large a hope.

M. Poincaré, the French President, came on a State visit on the 24th June, and the usual functions, banquet and State ball, followed, with a visit to the Horse Show at Olympia. There were comparatively few important London engagements during the rest of the Season. The King went to Portsmouth to inspect H.M.S. *Australia*, to Bristol for the Royal Show, and on the 7th July the Queen and he went off to Knowsley for one of the most comprehensive of their tours of the industrial areas. They passed from Colne through a chain of towns to Rochdale, from Wigan to Chorley—where they had luncheon at Hoghton Tower,[1] "sitting at the same table

[1] Sir James de Hoghton's.

that James 1st sat at when he knighted the loin of beef ": from Bolton to Liverpool. There they went on board the *Galatea* and reviewed a hundred ships of 225,000 gross tonnage in the Mersey, were shown over the *Mauretania* and christened the new Gladstone Dock. For a week they were so engaged, passing " tiring but very successful days." The King observed : " We have now practically visited every town of importance in Lancashire & motored 220 miles & seen several million people, it has been all marvellously arranged by Eddy Derby."

There were busy days in London, whither they returned on the 14th July. Among the minor ceremonies which the King performed were the reinauguration of Henry VII's Chapel as the Chapel of the Order of the Bath—" a lovely service," the laying of the foundation-stone of the new Commonwealth building in the Strand and the presentation of Antarctic medals to survivors of the Scott Expedition. They paid a visit to their sons' private school at Broadstairs, watched cricket and found " Harry and George looking very well."

At the end of July, the King got away as usual to Goodwood House and after the races enjoyed as much as ever sailing the *Britannia* in the Solent. At Cowes on the 3rd August, " the *Cumberland* arrived & Bertie came on board, he has now become a midshipman & is very proud of his patches." The King was at Studley for the 12th. It was to prove his last season of grouse shooting for some years. Balmoral followed, interrupted, as the year before, by the Manœuvres. On this occasion he stayed at Althorp with Lord Spencer, the exercises being based on Northampton.

In the middle of October the Queen and he returned to London for the marriage of Prince Arthur of Connaught and Princess Alexandra, daughter of the Princess Royal and the late Duke of Fife, and he supported the bride at the Chapel Royal ceremony. Soon afterwards he saw the Premier, who told him of the meeting with Mr. Bonar Law. " It is a beginning," he wrote, " but neither of them are at all sanguine that any compromise with regard to Ireland can be come to."

During the November visit to Windsor, the Queen and he received the Arch-Duke Franz Ferdinand and his wife once more. The ill-fated heir to the throne of the Habsburgs was in cheerful mood and " shot quite well, but he uses 16 bores and a light load."

That year one of the last, as the first, of his letters was written to his faithful secretary :

YORK COTTAGE, SANDRINGHAM, 29*th December* 1913.

. . . I am sending you various letters (1). *George Buchanan*, which please answer for me & tell him I am glad Sazonov now realises that we are ready to give him support as far as possible. And that I am glad that M. Karostovitz, the new Russian Minister in Tehran, is animated with the best intentions & will work loyally with England for the good of Persia. I am sorry that the Cesarevitch after getting so much better at Livadia should have hurt his good leg & been laid up again, it is really most unfortunate & upsets the Empress so much. When he sees the Emperor on New Year's Day I hope he will tell him how keen I am that the relations between our two Countries should become more friendly every day & that we shall always be able to overcome any little differences which may occur from time to time. . . .

. . . I don't know what I should have done without your kind help and advice. I have indeed had worries & anxieties (& also they are not over yet) but I have been able to overcome them solely with your help as I have absolute confidence in you & your judgement, which I know is unbiased & I know you always tell me the truth however unpleasant it may be. Please God 1914 may be a brighter year for my Country & that anyhow peace may be maintained. When the time comes I trust I may be able to do the right thing & my duty, but I do feel that the responsibility now on my shoulders is great, but I put my trust in God & I feel that British commonsense which has saved us in the past will do so again now. . . .

CHAPTER XIV

The Home Rule Bill and Ulster—The Outbreak of War. 1914

[Mr. Asquith, Premier]

§ 1

AN icy dawn ushered in the year of fate which was to be the end of the world's security for generations. The King shot on New Year's Day in fine, frosty weather at Anmer: " more pheasants than I have ever seen there, we got 2,831 without pick-up." The old world had a few months more to run before Armageddon broke out. For a short time longer the old life went on for the King, the regularly ordained moves of the Court, the shooting holidays and race meetings, the fixed routine of office and ceremonial duties.

It is not in human nature to accept as inevitable an unspeakably terrible prospect. In common with most of his Government and ninety-nine per cent. of the nation, he lived in hopes with both feet planted still in the old world. The issues of the Turkish-Balkan War did not, as feared, directly bring about world war, but the crisis remained and England was ill-prepared to face it. The armaments still piled up. The German Army grew ever larger, and France, as best she could, countered each increase and anxiously speculated about the attitude of England in certain contingencies. But the British Government economised in words and promises, and Lord Roberts continued his cry for National Service to deaf ears. Only the Navy was ready and adequate for the tasks ahead.

Meanwhile in England political events combined to discourage France and to encourage Germany. On the 9th March Mr. Asquith in the House made his offer to Ulster that the nine counties should ballot, each for itself, whether or not to be excluded from the Home Rule Bill. Sir Edward

Carson indignantly rejected the offer. Three days later came the news that most of the British officers in the Cavalry Brigade at the Curragh had announced that they would resign their commissions rather than risk fighting against Ulster. It was an impulsive gesture based on misunderstandings and the resignations never took effect. But in the result Colonel Seely, the Minister for War, resigned and the Premier himself took over his department. There followed, in April, the Larne gun-running incident. Contrary to the new restrictions, Ulster secretly imported and disposed of a particularly important consignment of munitions of war from German firms. In May the Home Rule Bill passed the Commons and Nationalist Ireland in her turn enrolled her thousands of volunteers and imported what arms she could. On the 23rd June came the Amending Bill, which proposed to restore to the Measure what Sir Edward Carson had rejected, the right to exclusion of the nine counties.

Baron Franckenstein [1] of the Austrian Embassy has described the English scene as observed by a foreigner in those last brilliant and dangerous days of the old order :

The brilliance of social life in London contrasted strongly with the dark and confused situation in home politics. The rejection of the Women's Franchise Bill resulted in repeated demonstrations by the suffragettes, who conducted their campaign of Votes for Women by arson and other violent methods. Many London museums and picture galleries had to be closed as a precaution against these Amazons.

Far graver still was the Parliamentary situation, when the Irish Home Rule Bill, after passing the Commons, was thrown out by the House of Lords. Under the strong leadership of Sir Edward Carson, the Ulstermen had won strong support. In April 1914 a big demonstration in favour of Ulster took place in Hyde Park. I suggested to Count Mensdorff that I should visit Ireland in search of first-hand information on the question. . . . Ulster's grim determination to offer armed resistance was brought home to me in Belfast, where I saw Protestant clergy in full canonicals bless the colours of the volunteers to the accompaniment of prayers and hymns.

Many thousands of these volunteers (there were 104,000 in

[1] Now Sir George Franckenstein: *Facts and Features of my Life.*

all Ulster) marched by with a detachment of nurses, while Carson, his face hewn out of granite, looked the very symbol of unbending resolve, as he towered above the crowd and spoke of their determination to stop at nothing rather than be forced out of the Union. The extraordinary character which marked this whole crisis was especially emphasised on this occasion by the loud cheers for the King, against whose Government the men of Ulster were arming.

§ 2

The King and Queen went into residence at Windsor, and by the end of January many ministers and foreign Ambassadors had been guests at the Castle and the King had had long talks with M. Cambon, Count Benckendorff and Mr. Page, United States Ambassador. He found the Russian Ambassador's appreciation of the European situation the clearest and most pessimistic of all which were offered him by British and foreign observers. Mr. Page has set on record how human and friendly a man he found the King, how charming and simple a host; and how full of common sense and shrewdness were his often forcible references to political questions at home and abroad. On the 2nd February, the day on which the King notes that " David had his first day out with the hounds at Oxford," Gustav Hamel paid his postponed flying visit to the Castle and " looped the loop " many times in view of the King and a crowd of Eton boys and Windsor residents.[1]

On the 10th the King opened Parliament for a momentous session. A mistake by the Lord Chancellor caused him a needless embarrassment. It was his rule that his speeches should be printed in large type.[2] " My speech was rather long and unfortunately the Lord Chancellor gave the paper in small print instead of in the large type which is specially

---

[1] The King's interest in flying never induced him to go up in an aeroplane.

[2] Years later he told Lady Cromer that the chief reason for this rule was his inability to control the shaking of his hand as a result of unconquerable nervousness. But no doubt the ever-increasing size of the type demanded for these speeches kept pace with the natural decline of his eyesight. He did not wish to be compelled to use pince-nez while wearing uniform. At the end of his life, the type was enormous.

printed for me to read from, which put me out. I laid great stress on the paragraph about Home Rule, in which I appealed for a peaceful settlement."

During the rest of the month, he gave a number of dinner-parties, including several to leaders of the Government and Opposition, and in the course of conversation at these dinners never ceased to work for a settlement of the Irish Question. On the 9th March Mr. Asquith announced in the House his proposals in regard to the Home Rule impasse. " I fear," the King commented, " the Unionists will not accept them." On the 30th Colonel Seely's resignation was announced and the King agreed to the Premier's proposal to assume the vacant office in person.

After another short visit to Windsor, the King and Queen left London on a State Visit to Paris; Sir Edward Grey, with Sir William Tyrrell (his official private secretary), went with them. The customary reception and banquet at the Elysée was followed by a great review at Vincennes and a visit to the races at Auteuil. The King found time to have discussions with no fewer than five French ex-Foreign Ministers and returned home in the belief that the visit had done good and succeeded in its objects. " Everyone from the President downwards was most kind, we shall never forget the wonderful reception which has been given to us by the people of Paris."

After a brief visit to Newmarket he was back at work in London by the end of April, and on the 1st May he sent for the Speaker and laid before him his own proposal for " calling at my house " a conference on the Home Rule impasse between the Prime Minister, Sir Edward Carson, Mr. Redmond, Mr. Bonar Law and Lord Lansdowne.

On the 8th May he notes that " Henry of Prussia came to breakfast." Prince Henry, as it chanced, paid a visit to England of considerable length during the critical weeks before the Great War broke out. In the course of it he had two or three conversations with the King, and inevitably they discussed, as between relations, the anxieties which predominantly occupied their minds. It would have been strange indeed if they had not done so, strange if the King had not sought by every means in his power constitutionally and as a man of honour to communicate, through the brother,[1] with a nearly related Sovereign who, rightly or wrongly he believed, might still do something to avert the impending catastrophe. If he held an exaggerated belief in the Kaiser's power to stem the current, his relations with him, so constantly friendly, so little critical, justified, favoured, indeed loudly called for an unsparing effort to that end. It was a " diplomatic channel " which, often effective in the past, was favoured by the King's Prime Minister, at whose urgent request it was employed again in a last-minute appeal to the Tzar from the King personally and directly.

Meanwhile, he had daily interviews with his ministers, and his diary contains many approving comments on their calmness, good sense and desire for appeasement. With Mr. Churchill he spoke at length on Navy matters and on Ireland, and Mr. Lloyd George was " most sensible in working for peace." On the 16th May Mr. Asquith was a guest at the Pavilion at Aldershot. The King inspected mobilisation equipment and watched troop exercises daily. The 27th was Derby Day and as usual the King attended the meeting and gave his customary dinner to the Jockey Club. The routine went on unchanged. There was a Court on the 4th June. " One girl, Miss Bloomfield, I suppose a Suffragette, went down on her knees and shouted ' For God's sake, Your Majesty,' and then she was led away. I don't know what we are coming to."

The scene changed to Windsor for the Ascot races. The Russian and Austrian Ambassadors were again among the guests at the Castle, and the King was able to adjust his views on the situation by further conversations with the two men in England who saw most clearly the trend of events. Late in the afternoon of the 28th June the King received the news of the Sarajevo murder. The brief comment on the event recorded in his diary—" Terrible shock for the dear old Emperor "—confirms the view that the significance of the crime did not instantly strike him or the Government and the nation, though it was otherwise with many of the European

[1] Prince Henry's simple and frank nature resembled King George's, and his admiration for England and things English was still strong at this time.

Embassies in London. Of the British Press only two dailies recognised the assassination as the match of Fate which would set Europe ablaze.

July came in. On the 2nd the great Imperialist, Mr. Joseph Chamberlain, died, happy perhaps to have been spared a survival beyond his era. On the 3rd the King put in a long and tiring day at the Royal Agricultural Show at Shrewsbury and on the 6th left with the Queen for Edinburgh. From Holyroodhouse they paid a State visit to Glasgow, in the course of which the King was able, by means of his hearty laugh, to repair an unfortunate mistake of Mr. Mackinnon Wood, who had handed him the wrong answer to an address which the King had proceeded to read out. Amid constant interruptions by Suffragettes, the Scottish programme continued in Edinburgh, and in Dundee which provided the warmest welcome of all.

From Scotland they travelled to Portsmouth, and on Sunday, the 19th July, the King steamed between the lines of the great British fleet, fully mobilised and stretching from Spithead nearly to Cowes. It was a thrilling and heartening experience for him. Later he visited the *Collingwood* in which Prince Albert was serving, and after the presentation of all her officers and midshipmen he returned to London for the Conference he had himself convened in an endeavour to secure at the eleventh hour a settlement of the Home Rule crisis.

Three days later he knew to his infinite sorrow that his effort had failed. The Conference broke up.

I spoke [he wrote down] to each member alone for nearly a quarter of an hour, both Mr Redmond and Mr Dillon were very reasonable and only wished they could have settled the question. Sir E. Carson said the same but they were each frightened of their followers. . . . I am greatly worried by the political situation which is turning very grave.

On the 25th July, after an interview with Sir Edward Grey, he knew that Count Benckendorff had rightly interpreted the implications of the Arch-Duke's murder. " It looks as if we were on the verge of a European War caused by sending an

ultimatum to Servia by Austria." Early next morning Prince
Henry of Prussia called to say good-bye before returning to
Germany. From this interview there was built up during
the war (and more than once subsequently revived) a legend
which has been held to impugn the King's good faith. That
legend was examined and disposed of in a letter [1] of the 1st
June, 1938, from Lord Wigram published in *The Times*. The
only reference in the King's diary to the interview with Prince
Henry is in these words: " Henry of Prussia came to see me
early, he returns at once to Germany." From this interview
the King turned to deal with a constant stream of telegrams
which came in all day long.

[1] " ' THE WORD OF A KING '
" *To the Editor of ' The Times.'*
" Sir,—In the *Deutsche Allgemeine Zeitung* Captain Erich von Müller,
German Naval Attaché in London in 1914, has recently revived the
allegation that King George V told Prince Henry of Prussia, on the 26th
July, 1914, that, in the event of a European war, England would remain
neutral. This story was promptly denied, upon its first publication 21
years ago, in the following circumstances:

" Mr. James W. Gerard, American Ambassador in Berlin at the outbreak
of War, published in 1917 a book entitled *My Four Years in Germany*, in which
he printed the text of a telegram sent by the German Emperor to President
Wilson on the 10th August, 1914, reporting the alleged statement by King
George to Prince Henry. In August, 1917, Mr. Gerard's book was appear-
ing in serial form in the *Daily Telegraph*, and the portion containing the
Kaiser's telegram was due to be published in the issue of Monday, the 6th
August. Lord Stamfordham, then Private Secretary to the King, having
been warned of this the evening before, obtained from his Majesty a
categorical denial, which was issued to the Press in the following form:

" ' With reference to a telegram sent by the German Emperor to President
Wilson, the 10th August, 1914, which we understand appears in the *Daily
Telegraph* to-morrow (Monday), we have the highest authority to declare
that the statements alleged by the Emperor to have been made to Prince
Henry of Prussia by his Majesty the King are absolutely without any
foundation.

" I was Assistant Private Secretary to the King in 1914, and His Majesty
often talked to me about this conversation with Prince Henry of Prussia.

" ' The word of a King ' never varied from what it was in 1912. On the
8th December of that year King George wrote to Sir E. Grey, after a similar
interview with Prince Henry:

" ' He asked me point blank, whether in the event of Germany and
Austria going to war with Russia and France, England would come to the
assistance of the two latter Powers. I answered undoubtedly yes under
certain circumstances.'
" I am, Sir, your obedient servant,
" WIGRAM, *Keeper of the King's Archives.*
" WINDSOR CASTLE, 1st June, 1938."

§ 3

Of the critical days which followed, one or two brief notes from the King's diary may document without commentary an oft-told tale.

July 29*th.*—Austria has declared War on Servia. Where will it end? . . . Winston Churchill came to see me, the Navy is all ready for War, but please God it will not come. These are very anxious days for me to live in.

July 30*th.*—Foreign telegrams coming in all day, we are doing all we can for peace and to prevent a European War but things look very black. . . .The debate in H. of C. on Irish question today has been postponed on account of gravity of European situation.

July 31*st.*— The Prime Minister came to see me and we discussed the European situation which he thinks is more grave. . . . Lord Kitchener came to see me, he returns to Egypt on Monday. He is most anxious to go to India as Viceroy when Hardinge's time is up. . . . Very tired, bed at 11.30. Colin [Keppel] came and woke me up at 12.45 saying the Prime Minister wanted to see me. I got up and saw him in Audience Room & he showed me a draft of a telegram he wanted me to send to Nicky as a last resort to try and prevent War, which of course I did. Went to bed again at 1.40.

August 1*st.*—Saw Sir Edward Grey. Germany declared War on Russia at 7.30 this evening & German Ambassador left Petersburg. Whether we shall be dragged into it God only knows, but we shall not send Expeditionary Force of the Army now. France is begging us to come to their assistance. At this moment public opinion here is dead against our joining in the war but I think it will be impossible to keep out of it as we cannot allow France to be smashed.

August 2*nd.*—We issued orders to mobilise the Fleet last night. . . . Worked all the evening, masses of telegrams and papers to read. At 10.30 a crowd of about 6,000 people collected outside the Palace, cheering & singing, May & I went out on the balcony, they gave us a great ovation.

August 3*rd.*—Saw Winston Churchill who told me the Navy was absolutely ready for war & all the ships mobilised. . . . Crewe came to see me to tell me what had taken place at the last Cabinet. John Burns has resigned. Morley, Beauchamp

& Sir John Simon probably will do so. May & I went for a short drive in Russian carriage down the Mall to Trafalgar Square through the Park & back by Constitution Hill. Large crowds all the way who cheered tremendously. . . . We were forced to go & show ourselves on the balcony three different times, at 8.15, 9.0 & 9.45, tremendous cheering. Public opinion since Grey made his statement in the House today, that we should not allow Germany to pass through English Channel & that we should not allow her troops to pass through Belgium, has entirely changed public opinion, & now everyone is for war & our helping our friends. Orders for mobilisation of the army will be issued at once.

August 4th.—Warm, showers & windy. At work all day. Winston Churchill came to report at 1.0 that at the meeting of Cabinet this morning we had sent an ultimatum to Germany that if by midnight tonight she did not give satisfactory answer about her troops passing through Belgium, Goschen would ask for his passports. Held a Council at 4.0. Lord Morley & John Burns have resigned & have left the Cabinet. . . . I held a Council at 10.45 to declare War with Germany, it is a terrible catastrophe but it is not our fault. . . . When they heard that War had been declared the excitement [of the crowds outside the Palace] increased & it was a never to be forgotten sight when May & I with David went on to the balcony, the cheering was terrific. Please God it may soon be over & that He will protect dear Bertie's life.

CHAPTER XV

The War Years. *1914-16*

[*Mr. Asquith, Premier*]

§ 1

THERE is justification for according a rather different treatment to the details of King George's life during the years of war. To call the Great War an isolated episode is not to underrate its importance in his life. When it began, his qualities of kingship and leadership were still but half proved. When it ended, the Empire over which he ruled had acclaimed him a great leader and a great King. Nevertheless, for him as for many a man who went through those years as an adult, the War was an excrescence, a slice of years cut from his life, albeit an experience which marked him and brought him permanent physical disability.

As soon as he had adjusted his mind to the new conditions which the War brought about, the whole plan of his life was remade. The rotation of his year to which he was habituated was abandoned, and he created a new order of his days which indeed differed little from the routine of a Commander at the seat of war. For him the business of State and ceremonial functions took the place of the Commander's tactical plannings and strategical conferences, but most of his innumerable duties of inspection were very much on the lines—though many times multiplied—of those of a Commander-in-Chief in the field. His whole year was mortgaged to business. His holidays were cut down to a minimum. During the course of the War he never saw Balmoral, and used a gun during his short holidays at Sandringham or Windsor only to kill game for the use of hospitals and for the benefit of the farmers. For months at a time and nearly always through August he lived at the Palace, rarely leaving his office save for tours of inspection and other functions and perhaps a short constitutional in the garden. The one recreation which he seems to have allowed himself was an occasional hour with his stamp collections.[1]

The statistics of business done during these years are sufficiently impressive. It is difficult to see how the available hours of those four years could have been stretched so far as to take in some 450 inspections of troops and investitures held at the Palace and elsewhere, 300 or more visits to hospitals all over the country, not to speak of those paid to soldiers' and working-men's clubs, ambulance units and a dozen other uncatalogued organisations of life in war-time. And not to speak of his contant visits to the Fleet at many Naval bases and to the troops at the front. Impressive enough is the figure of War Decorations personally conferred by him—50,000 and more.

Many of the duties imposed on him, or self-imposed, took far too much out of him. He was not broadly a sentimentalist, but he was always emotional and acutely sensitive and sympathetic. Reading through his diary of the early part of the War, one realises how hardly it hit him, how bitter was the experience. He loathed war for what it was in all its hateful implications. He had none of his grandmother's robust Victorian outlook on war. He was a man of peace, a very sensitive, highly strung nature. He was compelled to work immensely long hours in his office, and was on his feet far too long at the most tiring of all duties—inspection. With none of his father's power to divert his thoughts into easier channels, with only a little of his father's elasticity and *joie de vivre*, he found doubt and anxiety in half the decisions he was called on to make and he could not shake the anxiety off. Intensely loyal and fair-minded, he was sometimes required to give the congé to superseded commanders whom he trusted and to approve appointments in which he felt no clear confidence. Every visit to a hospital containing wounded and maimed men wrung his heart and required an effort of mind discipline, yet he forced himself several times to watch operations in the War Hospitals and, as the years passed, his

[1] He declared more than once in later years that this hobby helped him to preserve his health and reason in the nightmare of the War years. It is a subject too technical for treatment in this memoir, but its importance in his life as hobby and recreation must not be overlooked.

visits to the wounded and to victims of air-raids took up hours every week.[1] From the very start of the War, he began to use up his reserves of strength and before it was half over it had cost him permanently a substantial measure of his health. He felt continuous anxiety for all that most concerned him, his Country, his Government, the Services, his family, his friends.

§ 2

It is made clear how much he suffered, when one reads between the lines of his simple, restrained narration of events. Of the supersession of Admiral Callaghan, of that sad farewell to the Expeditionary Force at Aldershot, of the Council held to declare war on Austria, with his private sorrow for Count Albert Mensdorff, of General Grierson's death, of the retreat from Mons and the hideous losses. Day by day came news of another friend dead, another relation or intimate gone to the Front. He was worried for his sons: the Prince had early joined the Grenadier Guards and soon enough went out to France. Prince Albert was taken suddenly ill and was operated on for appendicitis at Aberdeen, and his health remained an anxiety to his father for months to come.

Domestic politics were no less bitter and discouraging. Reluctantly he was compelled in that first September to give his assent to the Irish Home Rule and Welsh Disestablishment Bills, to be left inoperative for the duration of the War, the major issues still undetermined. All through those anxious first weeks he remained in London, ceaselessly worried, constantly at work, sometimes unwell. He very soon adopted military or naval service uniform as his normal dress, a sound decision which had a good effect on the country and increased his popularity. It was his own decision, instantly made when the need for example from the top became apparent, to ban alcohol from his table during the War while the munition workers had need of their highest efficiency.

It was not until the 24th September that he got his first day in the country for some desultory shooting. Before the

[1] He once said to a lady of the Court, "You can't conceive what I suffered going round those hospitals in the War."

month was over, his heart was wrung again by the enforced resignation of Prince Louis of Battenberg and the death of Lord Charles Nairne.[1] And day by day the list of losses grew. " All the best officers and our friends," he wrote, " are going in this terrible war." Then came Lord Roberts' gallant death, and in the middle of November the Prince of Wales said good-bye and left for the Front.

§ 3

The King's first visit to France was a gruelling experience. At the end of November 1914 he crossed from Newhaven in a gale, " sick all the time "; the weather was generally bad and the programme immensely heavy. This tour involved like all others a great deal of motoring on bad roads in bad weather. The Indian troops, who received special attention, were widely scattered and efforts were made to ensure that the King should see French units and have discussions with the President, the French Commander-in-Chief and as many French Generals as possible. He saw all he could of the War between Ypres and Béthune, near the Front and in reserve, and visited hospitals and base establishments. He conferred decorations, gave interviews and worked in his lodgings at St. Omer at his ordinary routine. He returned to London on the 5th December. In February 1915 he made from Dalmeny his first visit to the Grand Fleet in the Firth. There is a diary note on the 24th March: " Dined out for the first time since the War began." It was at the Marlborough Club, a small, informal dinner, and he enjoyed it very much, as he always enjoyed men's dinners.

The middle of May brought him another sharp crisis in domestic politics. The growing differences between Mr. Churchill and the First Sea Lord, Lord Fisher, over the Dardanelles and Fisher's Baltic scheme then came to a head and the First Sea Lord resigned. His resignation led Mr. Bonar Law to put a pistol at Mr. Asquith's head—an immediate challenge debate or a Coalition Government. In this decision he had Mr. Lloyd George's support. Mr. Asquith,

[1] Lord Charles Fitzmaurice, who had assumed the surnames of Mercer-Nairne. For many years an Equerry and personal friend.

however, had reached the same conclusion as to the necessity for a Coalition Government. Days of bitter wrangling and manœuvring led up to the final formation of the new Ministry.[1] Lord Kitchener's immense prestige throughout the Empire kept him at his post. The King at any rate still reposed great trust in him and valued his friendship and deplored the efforts, in which Mr. Asquith took no part, made to remove him.

In May, too, came the news of the sinking of the *Lusitania*, and not many weeks after, the King was called on to visit the maimed victims of a Zeppelin raid on London. His comments on the first horror, " a dastardly crime," and on the second, " Simple murder, & the Germans very proud of it," give an indication of his bitter feelings. He was slow to believe in the baseness of human nature, slow to accept the worst implications of war, and the experience of becoming convinced affected him deeply. Colonel House, President Wilson's confidential adviser, came to see him, told him that in his view the *Lusitania* outrage would bring America into the War, and the King heard that " wishful " anticipation without surprise. What else could she do?

In the press of work which the political crisis brought him, his endless round of duty went on. During May he went over the shipbuilding yards of Glasgow and Newcastle, and returned to deal with the heavy business entailed by the new Coalition Government and the exchange of Seals.[2] By the end of the month the War had cost Britain a quarter of a million casualties, and among the mourners was the King's devoted secretary who had lost his only son, John.

In July the King went to Scapa Flow for another visit to the Fleet, and that August went to Windsor for a stay of six weeks. " We went," he wrote one evening at Windsor, " to Evening Service in St. George's. They had that lovely hymn 477 [' The day Thou gavest ']. They sang it divinely." No doubt during these black years he derived strength and comfort from his religious faith, as simple and honest as his nature. The impression gained from reading his diary is of

[1] The first Coalition Government in which some of the Opposition and other party leaders took office.

[2] Mr. Asquith remained Premier. Mr. Balfour replaced Mr. Churchill at the Admiralty. Mr. Bonar Law took the Seals of the Colonial Office.

his difficulty in escaping from his thoughts. The frequent reference to an hour snatched with Mr. Bacon and his stamp collection confirms that it was in this hobby that he found the most effective means of brief forgetfulness. He had need of all his faith. When he attended at St. Paul's the service of humble prayer on the first anniversary of the War, the casualties had risen to 380,000 and the end was no longer " soon to be hoped for."

§ 4

On the 21st October he paid his second visit to France, whence he returned a permanent war casualty. Again the weather was cold, wet or foggy for the most part and during seven busy days he repeated the general programme of his first visit. Wherever he went, his presence obviously heartened the troops who had recognised him. In a letter to Lord Stamfordham at this time he gives an impression of his visit:

CHATEAU DE LA JUMELLE, AIRE, FRANCE, 25*th October* 1915.

Many thanks for all yr. letters & you tell me just the things I want to know. Fritz [1] has written to you, so you will realize what a strenuous time we are having. We motored today *160* miles, which alone is tiring, the most beastly day I ever saw, strong cold East wind with rain & the same old mud. I had a long talk with the President & naturally he talked about the troops for Serbia. I practically gave him the answer that K. suggested, but he said Joffre wanted to talk to me tomorrow when I saw him.

Millerand said nothing, I fear he is going to leave the Govt. & be succeeded by Galliéni (Governor of Paris) & Briand succeeds Delcassé—this Poincaré told me, but that their policy would be the same: stick to the Allies & fight to the end. Joffre's position absolutely secure. He also said they are going to send Russia 200,000 rifles & some million cartridges at once. Of course we can't give ours to Russia, that is impossible. Roumania may not allow her troops to pass through, either. I fear Serbia is done for, none of our troops could arrive in time now. The President asked if we couldn't send some more troops from Gallipoli, I said we had hardly

[1] Sir Frederick Ponsonby.

enough to hold it now. The troops here are all right but I find that several of the most important Genls. have entirely lost confidence in the C. in C. & they assured me that it was universal & that he must go, otherwise we shall never win this war; this has been my opinion for some time. This is of course *secret*. We ought to be represented at the Service on Friday for Miss Cavell. Certainly the papers may say I am in France. Very tired, so excuse very incoherent letter. Always yr. sincere friend, G.R.I.

I don't think I shall be back before Saturday.

On the 27th he had a long interview with General Robertson, who gave him some very frank views on the need for changes in the Higher Command. The diary entry for the 28th October is in another's handwriting:

Then rode to Hesdigneul where I inspected representative troops of the 11th Corps. . . . Lastly I inspected representative troops of the 1st Corps under Gen. Hubert Gough, decorating Capt. Foss with the V.C. in front of the parade. Passing on to the Flying Ground I rode down the lines of the 1st Wing, R.F.C., who gave 3 cheers as all the other troops had done. Unfortunately my horse was only a few yards off them at the time, took fright, reared straight up and fell back on top of me giving me an infernal bad fall which completely knocked the wind out of me.

They picked me up & took me back to Aire in the motor as quickly as possible. I suffered great agonies all the way.

Doctors and two nurses were hurried to his bedside. During the next three days the pain was intense and the shock to his system combined with the pain made sleep impossible. An X-ray examination then revealed that his pelvis was fractured. They got him home on the 1st November; his bruises were terrible to see and, to increase his pain, he was very seasick during a stormy passage. It was not until the 9th November that he was moved to a chair and could sleep without the aid of drugs. On the 10th he began to work again. But ten days later he was still in considerable pain and grew tired very quickly. Another full week passed before he was able to have a real bath and to dress. He spent his leisure hours during that month reading books of an improving kind. Just before Christmas he got away to York Cottage, and at the end of the year was able to go out shooting. Those best qualified to know—keepers, loader, friends—have testified that in efficiency as a shot and in physical powers he was never the same man again after his accident.

§ 5

In the New Year, he wrote to Lord Stamfordham:

YORK COTTAGE, *2nd January* 1916.

MY DEAR BIGGE,—I was greatly touched by your kind letter written on New Year's Eve & thank you most sincerely for all your good wishes for 1916. We have passed through another strenuous and anxious year & I don't deny that I have felt the strain of it, as have most people. It is not possible for me to find words to express how really deeply grateful I am to you for all your kind & helpful advice & the enormous amount of work you have done for me during these last 12 months. For you & Lady Stamfordham it has been a terrible year & I know what your sorrow is. I do indeed feel most deeply for you & have tried to show my sympathy. Only time, alas, can heal a wound like yours. However hard it is to say so, you are really proud that dear John met with a glorious death fighting for his Country. Yes, thank God, my boys are still safe & He spared my life the other day in France. The Country is united & determined to win this war whatever the sacrifices are & please God 1916 may bring us victory & peace once more is the heartfelt prayer of your sincere & grateful friend, G.R.I.

But the War dragged on, bringing its endless duties, its anxieties and sorrows. As the months passed, the calls of the hospitals increased and, as the critical stages of the War came one by one, records of vital interviews and grave discussions with the heads of his own and the French Government fill the pages of his now briefer diary. He was returning from a few days of inspections at Portsmouth when the Battle of Jutland was being fought, and his first report of it is under date the 2nd June at Buckingham Palace:

Heard from Jellicoe that a large naval action took place in North Sea on evening of May 31st, apparently the whole

Grand Fleet took part in it. I regret to say the *Queen Mary*, *Invincible*, *Indefatigable* (Battle Cruisers), *Defence* & *Black Prince* (Armoured Cruisers) & 7 or 8 Destroyers were sunk & various other ships damaged. He believes we sank of the Germans 2 Battleships (*Kaiser* Class) & 1 Battle Cruiser, 1 Light Cruiser, 6 Destroyers & 1 submarine, also severely damaged 2 Battle Cruisers & 2 Light Cruisers & many other ships were hit.

It was not in the most favourable light that Sir John Jellicoe announced his victory to his Sovereign.

And then on the 6th June, during a visit to Felixstowe, the King " got the sad news that Lord Kitchener & his staff on board *Hampshire* had been drowned last night at 8, sunk by an enemy's mine on his way to Russia. . . . It is indeed a heavy blow to me & a great loss to the nation & the Allies. I had every confidence in him & he was a great personal friend. . . . The Prime Minister came to see me, he is much upset, but we shall now redouble our efforts to win this War. . . . That charming Fitzgerald [1] was of course with K. & is lost." He felt the loss deeply, for he had a great affection as well as admiration for Lord Kitchener. For many days after that he was listening to first-hand accounts of the Jutland battle, in which Prince Albert had taken part, and on the 14th June he went once more to Scapa Flow. It was a strenuous visit and he returned with a high temperature, to take to his bed.

Those who may hereafter read King George's diary will perhaps be struck by the effect which that part of it which deals with the War years has upon them. Throughout its length they will be affected by its simplicity, its impartiality, its impersonality, its curious blending of the trivial with the important, above all with its restraint and utter honesty. It is a mirror of simple truth and a model of fair-minded statement (or under-statement). But during the War the journal seems to take on a new virtue. It reveals much more of the character of the writer. A man who had never spoken with King George or known anything of the accepted view

[1] Colonel Oswald Fitzgerald, Military Secretary and close friend of Lord Kitchener, was an officer of the Indian Cavalry.

of his character might well see him emerge clear-cut, convincing, irrefutably the man he was, from these pages of the War diary. His straightness, his frankness, his simplicity, his deep loyalty to country and friends, his silent devotion to duty, his uncomplaining endurance of physical disability and pain, his constant under-emphasis of his difficulties and labours must win the admiration of the reader. From the dictated entry concerning his accident at Hesdigneul onwards to the end of the War, the picture grows, clear and clearer, of a great gentleman and a true Christian whom one cannot but admire, cannot but love (as his intimates admired and loved him greatly).

§ 6

As the weeks passed, he was constantly preoccupied with Cabinet difficulties and the growing demand for further changes in the Higher Command. Sir Douglas Haig had succeeded Sir John French in supreme command of the British Armies in France in December 1915, and it fell therefore to his lot to receive the King on his third visit to France. He left England on the 8th August, and after a very full tour of inspection at Etaples, went on to Advanced Headquarters at Beauquesne. In the course of this visit he saw the work of General Allenby's Army near St. Pol and with the Prince visited the Guards Division. He inspected German trenches two or three miles distant from St. Eloi and saw the British Front Line of the 1st July at a point near Fricourt in the Somme area. He went down a German dug-out and noted on all sides evidences of death and destruction. "All very pathetic, such is war." He went on to General Byng and inspected the Canadian camp at Reninghelst and returned to Cassel. It was as usual a full programme, entailing a great deal of motoring over bad roads. He thought it had been successful and was satisfied with it. It is a view which many soldiers who can clearly remember the heartening effect of his presence in their midst will endorse.

He was back in London on the 17th September and passed nearly all the Autumn at the Palace. To his constant worries was added considerable anxiety, which continued for some time to come, for Prince Albert whose operation had not had the hoped-for results.

On the 6th December he records in his diary:

Mr Bonar Law came at 1.0 and asked me to have a conference here this afternoon, which I agreed to. At 3.0 Mr Asquith, Mr Balfour, Mr Bonar Law, Mr Lloyd George and Mr Henderson came and we held a conference which lasted till 4.30. We discussed the possibility of forming a National Government. It was agreed that Mr Asquith shd inform Mr Bonar Law if he would serve under him, as soon as possible; if he could not do this, then Bonar Law would not become Prime Minister & I should then ask Lloyd George to form a Government. . . . At 7.0 I received Bonar Law who told me he could not form a Govt. as Asquith refused to serve under him. So I sent for Lloyd George & asked him to form a Govt., which he said he would endeavour to do.[1]

On the 18th December the American Ambassador " presented a note from Bethmann-Hollweg making an offer of peace on behalf of Germany & her Allies & that they would be ready to start negotiations, but they did not specify any conditions. The French 4 days ago made a splendid advance at Verdun & took 11,385 prisoners . . . 115 guns & 105 machine guns. That is the best answer to Germany's peace proposals." Altogether, there were reasons enough why the King should remain in close touch with his Ministers, and that Christmas of 1916 was, exceptionally, spent at the Palace.

[1] " The National Government of the 7th December, 1916, under Mr. Lloyd George, included Mr. Bonar Law, Mr. Balfour, Lord Derby, Lord Milner and Lord Curzon. With many changes and exchanges in personnel, it saw out the War, survived a general election and came to an end only in October 1922. It was during the crisis of December 1916 that the King (who was firm in his opinion that a General Election in war-time would be disastrous) instructed Lord Stamfordham to get a legal opinion from Lord Haldane as to the Sovereign's constitutional right to decline on grounds of war expediency a request to dissolve Parliament as a condition of any Minister undertaking to form a Government. Lord Haldane answered that the Sovereign had no such right." (*Haldane*, by Sir F. Maurice.)

CHAPTER XVI

The War Years. 1917-18

§ I

THE Silvertown disaster was one of the first tragedies on the Home Front in 1917. On the 4th February the King walked among the ruins caused by the great explosion of a fortnight before and went on to see and talk with the wounded at the Poplar Hospital. There was yet no abatement of anxiety. In the Army, in the Cabinet, in Russia, in whatever direction he turned his thoughts, difficulties and dangers loomed ahead. The struggle between Poland and the Bolsheviks and the revolution in Petrograd caused him the deepest disquiet. Towards the end of the month of March an informal War Conference was sitting in London and an Army Conference with the French, and the King entertained the delegates of both and had discussions with many of them.

There was better news in April, of progress at Arras and of the Canadian success on Vimy Ridge. The Court moved to Windsor, and the King and some of his family now turned out regularly to plant potatoes at Frogmore. He enjoyed the digging and found it very hard work. He made a note at the time that racing would probably have to stop, as oats could no longer be supplied to training establishments. During his stay at Windsor he received the Imperial Conference delegates and made them an important speech which seemed to foreshadow vital changes to come in the conception of Imperial relations.

In May he made a tour of munitions factories in Cheshire and Lancashire and Cumberland, visiting the war-time settlement at Gretna. He was back in London to receive on the 23rd May " the Prime Minister who brought Prince Sixt of Bourbon [brother of the Empress of Austria] to inform us that the Emperor [Charles] of Austria had written to him to try and arrange a separate peace with the Entente. The difficulty will be with Italy." In the middle of June there was an air-raid on the Liverpool Street area of London; the King went instantly to St. Bartholomew's Hospital to see the wounded and watched an operation on one of the victims. His daily programme was at this time unusually heavy. Before June ended he had carried out inspections in Newcastle and Hull and paid another long visit to the Fleet in Scapa Flow. On the 3rd July he paid his fourth visit to the Front and on this occasion the Queen went with him.

July brought fresh changes in the Ministry. Mr. Churchill took the Ministry of Munitions, Mr. Montagu the India Office, Sir Eric Geddes the Admiralty. At this time the King was much occupied with the proposed changes in the names and designations of members of the Royal Family and with precedence and other questions involved. At the end of the month he paid another long visit to Aldershot, and while there saw the Empress Eugénie who, now ninety-one, was waiting with intense interest for the final victory which was to be her *nunc dimittis*.

In the middle of September the King was in Glasgow and on his return to London was as busy as ever. He attended Prince Christian's funeral at Windsor on the 1st November. Before he left for Sandringham for a much-needed Christmas holiday, he was cheered by the news of the surrender of Jerusalem to General Allenby on the 9th December. But he was now a very tired man.

§ 2

On the 12th January 1918 the King opened Parliament with the shortest speech he had yet made. Politics and the politicians of the time worried him to distraction. His whole heart was set on national unity in the supreme effort to win the War at this most critical stage, and day by day he was made aware of quarrels and intrigue within the Cabinet and in the Army which outraged his loyal spirit. Closer bound to tradition and much more disposed to follow old and tried ways than his father had been, he had tried to adapt himself to political policies and methods which he disliked and distrusted.

He had never shown his feelings, never withheld his sympathy from his ministers of whatever political party; he had given the best that was in him and spent himself in the duty. He was well aware that in the testing time of war men chosen for high posts must sometimes prove unfit for their tasks, but he could not adjust his principles to an era of constant replacements and uncertainty of tenure in key positions. " 16*th Feb*.—The P.M. came to see me, he is in difficulties & I regret to say Robertson is to go & Derby too. Henry Wilson will be the new C.I.G.S." There followed his farewell interview with General Robertson, a trusted friend. It was a hateful necessity. Sir William was transferred to the Eastern Command. " I much regret his going as I have absolute confidence in his judgement." These words are all which the King allowed himself to set down of his feelings.

The number of hospital inspections rose that Spring to new records. March came in, and in the middle of it M. Clemenceau visited London for an Allied Conference and had conversations with the King. The great German attack was expected every day. On the 21st the first news of it filtered across, and for the next three days the King's diary is a reiteration of anxiety. At the most critical phase he offered to go again to the front, expressing his readiness to abide by Sir Douglas Haig's decision.[1] The Commander-in-Chief instantly welcomed the proposal and the King crossed on the 28th March. It was a short but most successful visit and proved a very wise decision. He stayed again at Tramecourt Château; talked to scores of wounded men straight from the Front, inspected many units, some hastily recruited from any and every available source, and wherever he went his presence had an electrifying effect on the troops who saw him, in that hour of confusion, in their midst. " Gawd, *the King*." It is a memory of the War still vivid with many who were in France at that time.

§ 3

He was back again on the 30th, and relieved to be back on this occasion, for he knew that his place was at Headquarters

[1] Lord Stamfordham was not convinced of the advisability of the proposal at that juncture.

in London. There were three days' accumulations of his
" boxes " to be cleared off before he could go to bed " and
pretty tired, too." He went down to Windsor soon afterwards, but by the 9th April was off again on tour, this time
to Lincolnshire to inspect several factories engaged in munition work. The situation in France was intensely grave.
On the 12th he heard that the 2nd Army had been forced
back behind Merville; on the 16th that Bailleul had fallen.

Meanwhile, Cabinet changes came thick and fast and the
King found his position almost unbearable. There was
serious conflict of opinion in the Air Ministry,[1] now under the
direction of Lord Rothermere, and General Trenchard
resigned as Chief-of-Staff, to the King's great sorrow. Lord
Derby, too, came to say good-bye and to hand in the Seals of
the War Office, which were assumed by Lord Milner, Lord
Derby being appointed to the Paris Embassy. A few days
later the King was handing the Seals of the Air Ministry to
one more nominee, Sir William Weir.

The 23rd April, St. George's Day, brought the glorious
episode of Zeebrugge. In the stress of hard work the King
found no time for more than the briefest reference to an
episode which warmed his heart and burned itself on his
memory.

The 6th May, his accession day, supplies a retrospective
note in his diary which reflects his feelings in simple language:
" I don't think any Sovereign of these realms has had a more
difficult or more troublous 8 years than I have had." Somewhere among the records of those innumerable addresses and
messages to his troops which, so admirably composed, were
delivered during the War years, there was a sentence which
appealed with particular force to many young soldiers at the
Front. It was in this sense: " I cannot share your hardships,
but my heart is with you every hour of the day." There
was in the sentence a note of pathos, of regret, of intense
sympathy which seemed to come straight from the King's
heart. Looking back over the years, those who remember
the words to-day may judge that their hardships were shared
in full measure by the King in his Palace in London or his

---

[1] It was created only at the end of 1917.

Castle at Windsor. He endured as much as most of his soldiers were called on to bear.

He was still uncertain of the degree of success attained by the German drive between Rheims and Soissons when on the 29th May he left London for Bolton Abbey for one more, very tiring tour, this time in the munitions areas between Shipley, Huddersfield and Leeds. From that tour he went straight to Aldershot for a short inspection on the 5th July. The 6th was Their Majesties' Silver Wedding Day. It was a lovely summer day and the public tribute was as warm as the sun during their progress to and from St. Paul's for a thanksgiving service. The King and Queen of the Belgians and all available members of the Royal Family were present at a luncheon in the Palace and hundreds of beautiful presents were given them. A day or two later the Commander-in-Chief was in London and had long conversations with the King.

On the 22nd the King left for Dalmeny again, to be received by Admiral Beatty in the Firth and to give special attention to the American Squadron at anchor there. He went over the American Flagship, *New York* (Admiral Rodman)—" a most beautiful, clean ship and they are most efficient "—and later went on board the *Queen Elizabeth*. On the 25th July " May & I attended a service at the Russian Church . . . in memory of dear Nicky who I fear was shot last month by the Bolshevists, we can get no details, it was a foul murder, I was devoted to Nicky who was the kindest of men, a thorough gentleman, loved his country & his people."

And then on the 5th August he went yet again to France. It was a more cheerful visit than any he had paid and from Tramecourt he made long visits to the 2nd Army area. The Commander-in-Chief was now satisfied and confident and M. Poincaré shared his optimism. The King heard the first encouraging news of the great Somme attack. All along the roads to the Headquarters of the 5th Army he was cheered to the echo by triumphant troops and the welcome of the Australians was tremendous. He had " tea with Birdie [General Birdwood]." Then he visited the Canadians and saw something of the jumping-off ground at Villers-Bretonneux, now once more a back-area. Before he left France he was already aware of the huge German losses in the Allied offensive. It was in a much more hopeful frame of mind that he returned to London, having added another eight hundred miles to his grand total of 3,500 covered on the roads of France during his visits to the Front.

§ 4

Throughout August his diary is filled with newspaper cuttings, mostly estimates of the Allies' gains in prisoners and guns; by the end of September the number of prisoners taken on all fronts was placed at over 350,000. Sir Douglas Haig's special " Victory " order of August, in sharp contrast to the more famous " Backs to the wall " order, also finds a place in the diary. And now week by week came evidence that the end was in sight. On the 1st October the King recorded the armistice signed in Macedonia and the unconditional surrender of Bulgaria. He was at Sandringham then, enjoying a little shooting, and the Premier and Sir Henry Wilson came to him with optimistic reports. The Germans would soon be ready for peace. The retreat was rapid. Lille was occupied. . . . On the 1st November came the news from Mudros of an armistice with Turkey. On the 3rd Austria signed the terms. On the 8th the German delegates came in under a white flag to hear the conditions and to be granted seventy-two hours for a decision. Revolutions were reported from many parts of Germany, and from Munich the declaration of a republic.

Nov. 9th, dear papa's (77th) birthday:
News that the German Emperor has abdicated, also the Crown Prince. " How are the mighty fallen." He has been Emperor for just over 30 years, he did great things for his country but his ambition was so great that he wished to dominate the world & created his military machine for that object. No man can dominate the world, it has been tried before, & now he has utterly ruined his Country & himself.

Such, at the time, was the verdict of one who had never prejudged the Kaiser, but on the contrary had always seen the best side of him. Time and greater knowledge of facts may no doubt have modified the opinion held by the King at this time of the Kaiser's responsibility in the tragedy.[1] At the end of the War it was shared by a majority of restrained and honest men in England.

Nov. 11*th.* William arrived in Holland yesterday. Today has indeed been a wonderful day, the greatest in the history of this Country. At dawn the Canadians took Mons which was the place where we first came in contact with the Germans over 4 years ago & from where the retreat began. At 5.0 a.m. this morning the Armistice was signed by Foch, Wemyss & the German delegates, & hostilities ceased at 11.0. . . .

§ 5

It was over at last. The long agony, the nightmare years, the physical and mental torture of humanity which had set its mark permanently even on those who had escaped the bullets, the bursting iron and the diseases of war. It was over, and after the briefest interlude of dignity and silence a madness of relief and wild hopes for a new world order succeeded it. The King and Queen drove through the streets of London, a city in a dream. Londoners crowded the Palace gates in their urgent need to express their relief, thankfulness and gratitude in an intimate and personal form. And a tired, grey-bearded man in khaki, with the wife who had stood by him and helped him to shoulder the grievous burden of those long black years, came out on the balcony and returned time and again to receive the heartfelt, tumultuous tribute they had well deserved. The untried, doubted man who had ascended the throne eight years before was that day acknowledged throughout his Empire as their leader and exemplar, the symbol of their effort and of the victory it brought, the symbol of unity that bound together and would bind a commonwealth of peace-loving nations.

Ample evidence had been furnished to the public of those

---

[1] Certainly the King at one time believed that the Kaiser might, at an earlier stage, have averted the disaster. In after years he sometimes, without bitterness, traced the stages of the Kaiser's attitude to England, from admiration to envy, from envy to hatred. He thought him a man of ability with a fatal irresolution in moments of crisis.

qualities in the King and Queen to which *The Times* referred in its leading article on 13th November. There was another quality, essential in a War leader, which King George revealed consistently throughout the War even in its darkest weeks—the quality of unflinching courage with an unswerving faith in the ultimate triumph of the Allied arms. He would have no croaking, he could not endure headshakers, he repudiated peace talk so long as the issue which had precipitated the tragedy of war remained undecided and the guilty unpunished. It was so that he met the warnings and headshakes and proposals of Colonel House and other such warnings and half-measures. Throughout the four dark years he marched breast forward, never doubting that right would triumph, never turning his back on duty however heavy, or on facts however menacing. With a stern and calm courage and an infinite compassion he saw the dreadful business through to the end.

CHAPTER XVII

The Bitter Aftermath of War—The "Coupon" Election—Peace Day—The King and Americans. 1918-20

[Mr. Lloyd George, Premier]

§ 1

THE War was over, but the peace proved almost immediately as little satisfying as edifying. Only abysmal ignorance or insane optimism could have expected that after four such years the victorious Allies would fold their hands and enjoy the Millennium or take their rest while Germany paid the bills. Most people anticipated that when peace came economic difficulties of unparalleled magnitude must disorganise social life for years to come. A few days of the carnival spirit might be justified, but not a spirit of easy optimism. The *mi-carême* was short indeed.

Perhaps the greatest handicap to an orderly reconstruction was the ill-health of the nation. Long undernourished and overworked, with nerves stretched taut for years, mind and body had become favourable breeding-grounds for poison germs. The casualties from the epidemic of virulent influenza at the end of the War were as severe as battle casualties in the worst phases of the fighting; and lies and half-truths, grievances real and imagined, class bitterness and jealousy and the lusts for pleasure and for revenge, soon drove out from millions of distraught minds those finer feelings which had made possible and sustained a common effort of endurance and restraint, of courage and patriotism.

Vengeance was in the air. It was breathed in and out in high places, and required no fanning from mean streets or public hustings to give it a place in political policy. The

Armistice was not long signed before England was in the throes of a General Election, as bitter and as unedifying as any in her political history. At the juncture an election was probably inevitable under our system of democracy. The nation which had brought into power the Government responsible for the conduct of the War was a changed nation, having few affinities with that which now demanded to have its say in the making of the peace and the resettlement of Europe and English national life. But it was an unfortunate time for an election when minds, educated and uneducated alike, were unbalanced and abnormally deficient in vision and restraint. The " Coupon " election was a Blind Man's Buff, in which wise counsels and high ideals found no place; no Englishman who coolly considered it at the time or afterwards could find in it anything for commendation, if perchance he found something for excuse. The slogan of " Let Germany pay " carried all before it, brought back, before the year ended, Mr. Lloyd George and his Coalition in triumph and greatly lowered British prestige in the eyes of the new world and a part of the old. It is easy to criticise. It is a weakness of history—which is a record of, and a commentary on, the decisions and actions of peoples and their rulers—that it is sometimes written when the passions which provoked those decisions or actions are forgotten or no longer to be easily recaptured.

Of the economic problems of Peace, that most anxiously anticipated proved for a time the least acute. Industry readily absorbed all the labour which the Army released during the short boom of 1919, which came on a wave of spending throughout a world long starved of luxury and necessity. But the demobilisation schemes, hastily prepared and ill thought out, inevitably bred bitterness and even mutiny, and before the middle of the first post-war year the record of strikes in industry was among the blackest ever known. By June 1919 most men who thought at all accepted as just the argument of *The Great Illusion*. Nothing good ever came or could come out of war, which must end not in victory and defeat, but in common distress and bitterness unassuaged. The workers had seen money poured out like water for the

178

conduct of the War. They had handled it and freely spent it. The reservoirs of the nation and of the capitalists alike seemed inexhaustible, and they would see to it that the taps were not turned off while any item in the Charter of Labour remained unsatisfied. And even while the boom continued, the voice of Socialism rose loud and more clamorous against the capitalist system which had already received its due reward in Russia. The Premier was in no mood or posture to tighten up the purse-strings. Public money continued to be poured out like water.

§ 2

If the King's anxieties were not over with the Armistice, neither was his war-work. During the rest of that year and the next, he continued to carry out a programme as heavy as in any of the first three years of the War, and to the sequence of investitures, troop inspections, hospital visits and so forth were now added many more receptions of Allied leaders and addresses to be received and replied to.

The price of victory in human life and health and treasure had been terrible. It had cost Britain over three million casualties, and it was no consolation to know that Germany must have suffered twice as many. It was with a full sense of the continued gravity of the times and of the need for unrelaxed national effort that the King went down to Westminster on the 19th November to deliver to both Houses his message for the people: " During the past four years of national stress and anxiety my support has been faith in God and confidence in my people. . . . For centuries past Britain has led the world along the path of ordered freedom. Leadership may still be hers among the peoples who are seeking to follow that path." His solemn words implied a right understanding of the damage done to our reputation as a nation and to the nation's morale in the few days which had elapsed since the Armistice. He clearly saw whither further relaxation must lead, and his words were a warning. He at least had not lost his head nor his sense of justice and proportion. He was not too busy at this time to remember some of those whose great contributions to the victory had received too little notice. There is a letter, dated the 23rd November, 1918, which his secretary wrote to Lord Haldane: "The King directs me to . . . tell you how deeply he appreciated all you have done to make our victory possible and how silly he thought the outcry against you." The words deserve their place here.

After a visit with the Queen to the Fleet in Scotland and a Thanksgiving Service in St. Giles', Edinburgh, the King with the two elder Princes left for France once more. After a night at Montreuil, the royal party went to Paris to receive a great welcome from the President, the Ministers and the people of Paris. It was a successful visit and a clear manifestation of France's appreciation of the efforts of the British nation. From Paris the King returned to the War area. He stayed at the Château de Sébourg, and visited many old and recent battlegrounds.

On the 10th December he was back in London to find England in the delirium of the Election. Polling day took place on the 14th December and Mr. Lloyd George and his Coalition were returned in triumph with a majority of 249. Among the casualties was Mr. Asquith, who lost the seat he had held for thirty years. His defeat was greatly regretted by the King, who admired him as a great statesman and a great Englishman. There was no chance of getting away for Christmas, which was spent in London.

The next day President Wilson arrived on his State visit. It took in modified form the usual course. The President had a gratifying reception from the public, and after a visit to Manchester was entertained at the Palace. The King had a very warm feeling for America, and in the course of his reign made several close friendships with Americans who came in contact with him officially. If President Wilson was not one of these, the differences in the natures of the two sufficiently explain it. With Mr. Page King George was on intimate and very cordial terms. Few men understood better than he the vital importance to civilisation of close co-operation and understanding between the great English-speaking nations or better appreciated the mighty part played by America in the preservation of the ideals of freedom and humanity and democracy. His was a nature to enjoy and to value the frankness of speech and the directness of approach of individual Americans. They judged him as a man and their verdict was very favourable. Beneath the trappings and ceremonial of British royalty, which attracted and puzzled them, they saw the essentials and the truth—the head of a great nation whose conduct was beyond reproach, whose tastes were simple, whose speech was frank, a great gentleman, a good Christian, a man as straight as he was forthright, a man who stood above politics and outside party and was unable to comprehend class distinctions or jealousies. So much for the man; and for the symbol, one who stood for social and political decency, for respect for the rights of others, for increasing those rights and adding to the benefits enjoyed by the humblest, for truth, humanity, justice, liberty. His ideals were theirs, his speech theirs.

§ 3

He returned to London on the 14th January to hold a Council for the swearing-in of the new ministers. Four days later his youngest son, Prince John, died at the house at Wolferton (Wood Farm), where he had been living of late happily enough. His health had long given anxiety to his parents, he was subject to fits and his normal development had been arrested. But he was dear to his family and some of his funny sayings were treasured among them. On the 21st January " dear little Johnnie was laid in the Churchyard next to brother John." Years (how many years!) before, Mr. Dalton had sent Prince George at sea flowers from the grave of his little brother.

February was a month darkened by strikes and industrial bitterness. There was a family wedding at the end of it. Princess Patricia of Connaught was married in the Abbey to Commander Alexander Ramsay.[1] " No doubt," commented the King, " a most popular match & she is now Lady Patricia Ramsay by her own wish & takes precedence before Marchionesses."

[1] Third son of the 13th Earl of Dalhousie; now Admiral Sir Alexander Ramsay.

The weather was horrible during April at Windsor. The King was not only kept hard at work but constantly apprehensive. All through the Peace negotiations, doubt and anxiety were present in his mind. He had the gravest mistrust of the competence of some of the chief leaders to see beyond the bitterness or the political theories of the day to a future when the redistribution of territory and races would be tested in a very different spirit. He never ceased from the first to shake his head over the Polish Corridor, and often declared that the lessons of history had not been studied with care. He regretted that he was powerless to make his own voice heard at the Peace Conference.

Nevertheless, there were signs not lacking that in some respects the " good old " pre-war world would come back. On the 3rd June the Trooping of the Colour was " better done than before the War," and in the course of the first post-war Epsom meeting, when Grand Parade won the Blue Ribbon, the King received a great reception on winning the Stewards' Handicap. Ascot was glorious, too, and " everyone wore a high hat like old days." At the Palace on the 28th June, " after dinner I received a letter from the Prime Minister telling me peace was signed, brought in an aeroplane [from Paris]." With the Prince, the King went out on to the balcony and each made a short speech. " Today," wrote the King, " is a great one in history & please God this dear old Country will now settle down & work in unity." It was the fifth anniversary of the Serajevo murder.

Peace day was celebrated on the 19th July with the great Victory March. The King stood in the pavilion erected by the Queen Victoria Statue before the Palace gates, and the seven-mile-long procession wound by during two hours of deep emotions. Pershing, Haig, Beatty and the unforgettably dignified figure of Foch passed in turn at the head of units, and each commander fell out as he passed, to take his place beside the King who later entertained them all at the Palace. " The most impressive sight I ever saw," he wrote down that night. Before he went to bed, he walked up to the roof of the Palace to watch the fireworks. His last function of the London Season was a visit to the Guildhall to receive an address of congratulation on the Peace. On the 5th August he went down to Portsmouth to bid farewell to the Prince who was leaving in the new *Renown* for a short tour of Canada. Urgent work kept him in London during a heat wave until the 17th August when he got away to Balmoral.

But his holiday was to be interrupted. The negotiations on the wages of railwaymen, which had been proceeding between Sir Auckland Geddes and Mr. J. H. Thomas as principals, quite suddenly broke down, and at the end of September the national transport system was totally paralysed by a strike. Despite the inconvenience caused to the public, sympathy was not lacking for the case of the railwaymen. On the 2nd October " a mail got through from London [to Balmoral] with 19 boxes which took me all the evening to do with Wigram." The King instantly resolved to go back to London by road, realising that his absence must embarrass the Government. The Queen decided to go with him. The plan of their journey was hastily prepared; they broke it at Lowther,[1] where they spent the night, and covered the 540 miles at an average speed of $33\frac{1}{2}$ miles an hour. Twenty-four hours after their arrival the Premier called to announce a settlement.

He was in London again at the end of the month for the State visit of the Shah, and on the 11th November attended the first ceremony of the " Two Minutes' Silence." " At 11.0," he wrote, " everyone throughout the Empire ceased work & stood still for 2 minutes in memory of the glorious dead. It was most impressive."

In December the Prince returned from Canada. At a dinner on the night of his arrival the King made him a speech of welcome and " dear David, looking very well," replied. The family was reunited at Sandringham for Christmas, Prince Albert and Prince Henry having returned from Cambridge where they were now keeping terms.

§ 4

The old world was in the melting-pot. Three great ruling dynasties—those of Russia, Germany and Austria-Hungary—

[1] Lord Lonsdale's.

had been driven out. Those countries which still preserved orderly forms of government were torn by internal strife and bitter class feeling, evidenced in unparalleled industrial unrest. Most of those which had shed or were about to shed their ancient forms were in the throes of political rebirth. Germany, Hungary, Poland, Turkey, to name a few, were in labour. Russia's old allies were fighting Bolshevism within her borders. International finance was in a pass which clearly presaged the collapse of world trade. Under these unfavourable conditions, with the splendid courage of idealism, the League of Nations created itself by an exchange of ratifications in the first, and held its opening assembly in the last, month of 1920.

There was no chance as yet for a return to normal conditions in England, though sanguine men still dreamed of happier days to come and of an early resumption of sanity and peace and settled prosperity. No man in England had better opportunities than King George of knowing how insecurely based were such hopes, how dangerous were the times and how anxious the future of the Empire and of Europe. If he had the heart and mind of the English squire and most of his tastes and ideals, he was before all things a man of sound common sense with an abnormally developed sense of duty, an intense patriotism and an understanding of the responsibilities of his own lonely position, and he was enough of a realist to know that, for himself as for his country, present conditions required a continuance of abnormal existence. There was as yet only a very gradual return to the manner of life endeared to him by tradition and custom, but 1920 was not, in the public eye, a particularly busy one for the King. His secretaries may have held a different opinion.

On the 3rd June he celebrated his fifty-fifth birthday. In *The Times* on that day a certain novelty crept into the traditional expressions of loyalty and respect which are appropriate on such occasions. In referring to the King's character, the writer set forth its salient features which were now universally accepted throughout the Empire: " A simple dignity, a broad-based sense of duty, and a sympathetic interest in all that concerns every section of the nation, characterise him." Thereafter he drew attention to the marked change which the War had produced in the Imperial conception of the Crown. The King was now the King of each Dominion, not merely the British Sovereign; and each component of the Empire regarded him first and foremost as the King of its own nation, an equal partner with Britain and every other Dominion in the Commonwealth. And then the leader-writer turned to the Heir to the Throne lately returned from Canada, and put in a plea, which contained something of a warning, that his willingness to serve should not be too strenuously exploited, lest in pursuing his innumerable functions he should overtax his strength.

On the 9th June the King opened at the Crystal Palace the Imperial War Museum, and soon afterwards attended in State an Ascot meeting which proved a record for numbers. On the 25th at the Palace the Queen and he gave a garden-party to holders of the Victoria Cross. Three hundred and twenty-three attended with their relatives, the King shaking the hand of each V.C. and speaking a word or two to most of them. At the head of the procession which filed by walked old Sir Dighton Probyn, still the faithful servant of Queen Alexandra. The King considered the party a great success.

After the July visit to Holyroodhouse Their Majesties joined the *Victoria and Albert* at Gourock. The King noted that this was the first time he had been on board a yacht since the Spithead Review of August 1914, six years before. Next day at Rothesay he caught sight of " dear old *Britannia*," and soon he was sailing her again, in dirty weather. After Goodwood, he enjoyed a holiday which recalled old days. At Cowes he sailed the old *Britannia* to his heart's content. It was a happy time. " Never saw the old ship sail better. Everything went right." Victory followed victory. In one notable race *Britannia* easily outsailed *White Heather*. " This year," the King summed up, " I have sailed in *Britannia* in 9 races & won 5 firsts, & 2 seconds, which is a wonderful record." He had earned his holiday and his good fortune.

He broke his journey to Scotland in London for grave discussions of current problems at home and abroad with the Premier and Lord Curzon, and reached Balmoral on the 16th

August. He was not in London again until the 14th October, on which day he received the new German Ambassador who was presenting his credentials. " The first time I have shaken hands with a German for over 6 years," he noted. On Armistice Day he unveiled the Cenotaph, and after the Silence acted as Chief Mourner at the burial in the Abbey of the Unknown Warrior. He was visibly moved and deeply impressed by both these ceremonies. The end of the year found him at Sandringham.

CHAPTER XVIII

Visit to Belfast—Irish Conferences—The King and Yachting—Princess Mary's Engagement. 1921

[*Mr. Lloyd George, Premier*]

§ 1

THE Lloyd George Coalition Government hung on during 1921, the support of the Conservative section showing distinct signs of weakening when ill-health compelled Mr. Bonar Law to resign in the Spring. Industrial unrest continued, and in the Autumn a general strike was averted only at the last minute. Abroad in Europe it was the year of Putsches. There were two in Hungary, the Habsburg Putsches of March and October, and in Berlin there was the Kapp Putsch in March, soon followed by the plebiscite in Upper Silesia. In May came the Allied ulti-matum on reparations and in August the murder of Dr. Erzberger, President of the German Republic. A trade agreement was signed between Britain and Soviet Russia in the Spring, and in the Autumn the League was busy with the financial reconstruction of Austria. All these matters held the attention of the King, most of them added to his anxieties and labours. But it was above all the deplorable state of affairs in Ireland that weighed heaviest on him in 1921. Only the barest and most general references to these problems are here possible, and, as regards Ireland, the diary notes quoted in the narrative that follows must serve as explanation.

．　．　．　．　．　．

On the 15th February the King opened Parliament with a return to the pre-war splendours of uniform and ceremonial. The Queen and he drove to Westminster in the Gold coach. But to one popular pre-war institution there was no return: eight black stallions[1] had replaced " the creams which have

---

[1] In 1923 to the end of the reign eight bay horses replaced the blacks which the King felt were too funereal in appearance. In the present reign the Windsor Greys draw the State coach.

been done away with." A few days later he received Mr. Preston, who had been Consul at Ekaterinburg when the murders of the Russian Royal Family took place there, and from him learned many dreadful details. Early in March the Premier reported to him the failure of the conference with the Germans.

At the end of March, when the Miners' Strike was threatening, the Court moved to Windsor. On the 1st April, the day on which the strike started, the King and Queen went to Hawthorn Hill and had the pleasure, fully shared by the public who saw the happy sight, of congratulating the Prince after his victory in the Welsh Guards' Challenge Cup. The situation at home was now very serious, and the King returned to London on the 8th April. The Rail and Transport Unions seemed likely to support the miners, and the King held a Council to call up the reserves of the three Services. London was full of troops under the command of Lord Cavan and energetic measures were planned to deal with a complete stoppage of essential services. A week later the worst of the crisis passed. The miners' leaders, by a policy of intransigence, forfeited the sympathy of the transport workers, and the weapon of the General Strike was put aside for a few more years. The Season's regular features were duly carried out. The Crown Prince of Japan arrived on a State visit. The King saw Humorist win the Derby, performed his functions at the Trooping of the Colour and looked in at the Australian Test Match at Lord's. He found it full and noted that in the two hours he remained there only 72 runs were scored.

There was the usual party for Ascot at Windsor, the list of invited guests affording a reminder that the younger generation was knocking at the door. The Prince of Wales was now twenty-seven years old and the youngest son, Prince George, was nineteen. It was a departure from precedent that the younger members should insist on dancing after dinner, and new fashions in ball-room dancing were another reminder to the King that times were radically changed and not, in his view, for the better. He was worried at this time by the increasing expense of his racing establishment, and he sent for Lord Marcus Beresford to discuss possible economies.

§ 2

His proposed visit to Ireland to open the Northern Parliament was now taking shape and before the Court left Windsor the Premier came there to discuss the terms of the Speech from the Throne. On the 21st June the King and Queen left for Belfast in the *Victoria and Albert*. They went to Ulster for the one purpose of opening the Northern Parliament and, in all the circumstances, it was a fine decision finely carried out. On the 22nd the yacht steamed up the harbour and the King and Queen drove in state direct to the City Hall, there to open the Parliament. Going and returning a wonderful welcome was given them. The King declared that never in his life had he heard anything to compare with the cheering. His fine speech was prefaced with these words, delivered with much feeling: " For all who love Ireland, as I do with all my heart . . ." He went on to say that the future of Ireland lay in the hands of the Irish people. " May this historic gathering be the prelude to a day in which the Irish people, north and south, under one Parliament or two, as those Parliaments may themselves decide, shall work together in common love for Ireland." That day he wrote in his diary: " I think my speech was appreciated, in it I made an appeal to the whole of Ireland for peace." When the ceremony was over, the Queen and he attended a luncheon of four hundred guests given by the Premier, Sir James Craig,[1] and thereafter returned to the yacht for an enthusiastic send-off.

It has been said that on this occasion he was let down by his Government; was allowed to start in ignorance that before the function was over the Government would have announced in Parliament a decision which must stultify his own words of conciliation and his expressions of hope for peace and unity. *The Times* on the day following the ceremony in Belfast spoke in this sense: The King at least has played the game, but the Government has not played the game towards the King. On the very day he left, it declared its policy of military coercion unless the Southern Parliament consents to be established. (That, in brief, was the immediate crux in the

[1] Now Lord Craigavon.

Irish problem.) It is, *The Times* went on, astounding that such a policy, essential or not, should have been announced on the eve of the King's appeal for peace. It is characteristic of the King that no word of criticism, no mention of his having been let down, occurs in his diary.

. . . . . .

He was at Newmarket on the 30th June. He had had a very unlucky spell as an owner of racehorses and, as has been said, had been worried by the increasing expense of his establishment. Now he had an agreeable change of luck after a dismal sequence of " eight seconds and no wins." His horse Springbuck won the Princess's Stakes, and he was delighted. Back in London the Queen and he received the King and Queen of the Belgians on a State visit on the 4th July, with the usual banquet and State ball, the latter a particularly brilliant affair. Soon after, they paid an official visit to the Channel Islands on board the yacht, attended at St. Helier a royal court and received the homage of the Seigneurs, the King replying in French and English to addresses.

He was concerned now about the Prince's restless energy. The latter was run-down and depressed by a bad cold and had obviously overtaxed his strength. The King and Queen visited him at York House and during the month the King recorded several serious talks with him. He was convinced that his son tried to do too much and he believed that the advice he gave him would bear fruit.

On the 20th July the Premier had brought to him the terms to be submitted to Mr. de Valera. " I must say," he had noted, " they are very generous & I trust will be accepted."

§ 3

The year 1921 was perhaps the happiest, as it was one of the most successful, in King George's yachting history. He continued to enjoy the sport he loved until the end of the season of 1935, indeed to the end of his life, and to derive from these brief holidays the surest relief from the cares and anxieties which continued to gather round him. It may therefore be an apt juncture here to consider his career as a yachtsman.

The sea was in his blood. When at Osborne in childhood,

Prince Eddy and Prince George missed no opportunity to be afloat. Then came at a tender age the years in the *Britannia*, during which, as has been seen, Prince George began to show special aptitude in the handling of boats and sails. Further opportunities came to him during the *Bacchante* cruises, and as a midshipman the command of boats was one of his constant duties and the sailing of boats in the harbours he visited in the Empire one of his favourite diversions. His service in the Navy kept his hand constantly in and his experience ever on the increase. He retired from the Navy not long after the yacht, with whose name his career as a yachtsman is for ever linked, was built. The *Britannia* was no doubt the most famous racing yacht in the world. She was certainly one of the objects dearest to King George's heart. Right at the end of his life, when ill-health had stamped its mark on him and increasing cares had weighed him down, he could still become " a different man," " his old self," when he trod her decks—as those who best knew and loved him have abundantly testified.

Her history accordingly is worth setting on record. She was designed by George Watson and built on the Clyde by D. & W. Henderson's in 1892. Her commissioning was due to the sporting desire of the Prince (Edward VII), awakened by the pleadings of Mr. Willie Jameson,[1] to stimulate interest in big-class racing, then at a low ebb. She was launched in 1893 and came in for a certain amount of criticism from the cognoscenti. Her Viking bow was said to be ugly, her lines above water were condemned. But her critics became her admirers as her career proceeded. Before the end of her first season, 1893, she had made her reputation and won dazzling successes. In that year she beat all rivals, American included, and continued in the same way in 1894. At the end of five years of life she had made 289 starts and won 122 first prizes. Yet she was put up for sale. The Prince had begun to regard her as out-of-date, or, more precisely perhaps, he was bored by the frantic " armaments race " in yachts, which in part

---

[1] Mr. William George Jameson, who died in November 1939, was a personal friend of King Edward and of King George. He handled the *Britannia* in her great years from 1893 with John Carter as skipper. His first wife was a sister of Lord Haig.

resulted from the jealous anxiety of his nephew, the Kaiser, to sweep the board in British waters, a competition which, by constantly stimulating yacht design, turned new yachts into back numbers almost before they were tried out. The *Britannia* passed swiftly through the hands of three owners, and then, with another very sporting gesture, the Prince bought her back to be a pacemaker for Sir Thomas Lipton's *Shamrock*. In 1900 she was again for sale and Sir Richard Williams-Bulkeley became her owner. Two years later King Edward once more acquired the old yacht, now to be regarded purely as a cruiser, and during the rest of his reign he never entered her for a serious race. A wheel was put in in place of the tiller, and the young Princes (King George's sons) were free to clamber about her and learn the ropes.

Her second spell of active life began in 1913. For that season King George, who had succeeded his father as Admiral R.Y.S., had her rigged as a racing cruiser. In that year Major Philip Hunloke [1] became her racing master and so remained for the rest of her successful life. The War years hit yacht-racing hard. It was not until 1920 that Cowes raised its head again. In that year, thanks largely to the enthusiasm of the King, handicap racing for mixed groups of large yachts was revived, and successfully revived. Soon afterwards the *Britannia* was elaborately renewed and the King was well satisfied with her performance. There is a note in his handwriting reproduced in the *R.Y.S. Memorials* which gives her record up to 1924. Between 1893 and the 4th August, 1924, she had won 164 first prizes in 323 starts.

Next year, 1925, there were new alterations of a radical kind which caused more shaking of wise heads. She was Bermuda-rigged. Then the King's illness intervened in her career. After his recovery she was fitted out again, and in 1930 was the largest British yacht, Bermuda-rigged, afloat, and she did well in races, though overshadowed by *Shamrock*. At that time, no doubt, she was outclassed by more modern designs, but nevertheless the King decided to fit her out for the Season of 1935, and he was content with her performance.

On the last day of Cowes Week that year her career ended.

[1] Afterwards Sir Philip Hunloke.

He decided to withdraw her, and his own death followed a few months later. Early in the morning of the 10th July, the old *Britannia* was towed into deep water south of the Isle of Wight in semi-darkness and there was sunk under naval arrangements. It was the end he wished for her. Her wheel and the Admiral's flag were presented to the Squadron. Her history and records will live as long as British yacht-racing survives, and beyond that; as long as the great King who sailed and loved her and knew her every mood is remembered.

It has been said [1] that he was equipped alike by temper and training to qualify as the ideal owner of a racing yacht. Patience to wait, promptness to act, powers of observation, resourcefulness in anything like emergency—with all these qualities he was richly endowed. He possessed an extraordinary knowledge of what yachts in general, and his own in particular, could do. Better, he knew his yacht's and his own limitations. He was sometimes a terror to those who felt responsible for his safety. Nothing would stop him lending a hand. If an emergency arose, the King would not be an onlooker, but—here his great quality had play—if some specially technical difficulty arose, which might lie outside his seamanship, he would cheerfully hand over and take a hand in the working of the yacht. Small wonder if they loved him; he was so slow to blame, so swift to observe and praise good work done.

Those two great Admirals of the R.Y.S., father and son, worked in very different ways. King Edward was indeed the magnificent patron; he was a much more regular figure at the Squadron headquarters than was King George. Loving company, constant change and varied conversation, he was for ever in the rooms and on the lawn during the Regatta. King George, always a little diffident, often truly believing and declaring that " it will bore them all if I go in there," would usually restrict himself to fixed visits and seldom made informal calls. Yet both had the welfare of the Squadron near to their hearts and scores of warm friends in the Roads and ashore with whom, when occasion offered, they loved to talk and joke. King Edward was a patron of yachting, King

[1] *Household Brigade Magazine*, Memorial Number, 1936.

George a " working," and particularly experienced, yachts-man. No doubt at all among King George's chief pleasures yachting came high and perhaps highest, for in the nature of the sport the season was short and during much of it he was too busy to enjoy it. He *might* have grown tired of shooting by having too much of it; of yachting, never.

§ 4

During 1921 he resumed his customary visits for grouse shooting. He was at Bolton Abbey on the 12th, and after a few days at Balmoral went once more to Moy, to the small moor on which he so much enjoyed himself in the company of Mackintosh and other Highland friends. But cares of State interrupted even this brief visit. The Premier, with Sir Edward Grigg,[1] arrived at Moy for vital discussions on the Irish difficulties. A new note to Mr. de Valera was in draft. Some of the Cabinet favoured a firmer tone. The King considered it and strongly urged moderation. At his sug-gestion, Sir Edward Grigg altered the draft on lines firm but conciliatory. That morning a Cabinet meeting was held in Inverness, the Highland capital—a very rare event—and in the evening the King learned to his satisfaction that the amended draft had been agreed to and despatched. He went back to Balmoral soon afterwards and spent several days stalking, with Archbishop Lang as his companion on the hill. The two old friends found many subjects, serious and trivial, to discuss, as they ate their frugal luncheons.

October brought him to London again, for he had many urgent matters to talk over with his ministers, and towards the end of the month he bade farewell to the Prince before he sailed in the *Renown* for his tour of India and Japan. During November the King had several discussions with Lord Curzon and others about " the nice state of foreign affairs all over the world."

Before the month was over, there was a notable event in his family life. To his only daughter, Princess Mary, he was entirely devoted. There was between them an understanding sympathy that needed no expression in words. And now that

[1] Then Private Secretary to the Premier.

she was to find a new happiness in marriage, the King realised how much he would miss her constant companionship. On the 22nd November he was happy to make public his approval of her engagement to Lord Lascelles, and he records in his diary his pleasure at his first visit to Chesterfield House.

There seemed indeed some hope of a happier ending to a grim year. The Irish conferences had been hanging fire. On the 6th December at Sandringham:

I got the joyful news the first thing this morning from the P.M. that at 2.30 this morning articles of agreement were signed between the British representatives and the Irish delegates, involving complete acceptance of the British Government's proposals, allegiance to the Throne and membership of the Empire. . . . It is mostly due to the P.M.'s patience & conciliatory spirit & is a great feather in his cap & I trust that now after seven centuries there may be peace in Ireland. Ulster has got the option of coming in within a year, if they wish, but they will not be coerced.

Cheered by this large hope, the King went out to shoot at Grimston Carr.

Next morning he went up to London to " hold an historic Council to summon Parliament next Wednesday. . . ." All but one of the members of the Cabinet attended, and the King said " a few words of congratulation & thanks on this great event." On the Wednesday following, the 14th December, he was in London again to open Parliament and to ask for the ratification of the settlement, which was secured by big majorities in both Houses. And so an anxious and difficult year ended at Sandringham with a real note of relief and with the traditional festive ceremonies.

CHAPTER XIX

Family Weddings—Mr. Lloyd George's Resignation.
1922-23

[*Mr. Lloyd George, Premier; Mr. Bonar Law, Premier, October 1922; Mr. Baldwin, Premier, May* 1923]

§ 1

ANOTHER " quiet " year—by comparison with some which came before and after—began for the King at Sandringham. It was the year which brought about the fall of Mr. Lloyd George and his Coalition. The great achievements of his administrations need no stressing. It is for political historians to examine the causes of the change and the extent to which it was due to the Government's Near East policy and the " Chanak Crisis." At the Peace Conference the Greek Cause had benefited at the expense of Turkey. But Turkey made a swift and startling recovery. Mustapha Kemal arose and in three years remade the nation, smashed the Greeks, advanced on the Dardanelles and faced the British garrison under Sir Charles Harington in Chanak. It required all the tact of Sir Charles, unsupported by his French and Italian allies, to avert war between Britain and the Kemal Turks and to save the southern shore of the Dardanelles. These events came to a head in the Autumn of 1922, the Turks occupying Smyrna in September. King Constantine of Greece abdicated, and in October the Allies and Turkey signed an armistice at Mudania. In the same month Mr. Bonar Law replaced Mr. Lloyd George.

Other notable events of the year, of which King George took note, were the replacement in January of Poincaré by Briand as French Premier; the occupation of Fiume by the Italian Government in March; the death of the Ex-Emperor Charles of Austria in April; the murder of Rathenau, the German Foreign Minister in June; the Fascist march on Rome in

October, and in December the declaration of default against Germany by the Reparations Committee, the British member voting in a minority.

In King George's post-war life his constant preoccupation with affairs of State and with European and world politics has been taken for granted. Outside his " office hours," the new year was unremarkable for ceremonial functions, but notable for happy occasions in his domestic life. Indeed, 1922 opened cheerfully enough for him. He was now able to see much more of his family. Queen Alexandra and Princess Victoria were constantly at Sandringham, with old Sir Dighton Probyn, now in his ninetieth year, and Miss Knollys still in faithful attendance, and nearly always there during the Court's residence at the Cottage. Queen Maud, too, usually came to her house at Appleton in the Christmas holidays, and King Haakon occasionally joined her, when he could get away from Norway. During this Christmas holiday, naturally, Lord Lascelles came to the Cottage and arrangements for Princess Mary's wedding were discussed at length.

Politically, too, the year opened with hopeful signs. Early in January the Dail in Dublin ratified the treaty by sixty-four votes to fifty-seven. At the end of the month the Court returned to London. The King was at once engaged with his ministers and high officers. Lord Curzon was summoned for further discussions on the thorny problems in foreign affairs and Lord Cavan, who succeeded Sir Henry Wilson as C.I.G.S., put the melancholy case for cutting down Army Estimates before the King. He felt deeply the sadness of seeing so many fine regiments disbanded, while he was convinced of the necessity.

He opened Parliament on the 7th February in a speech of unusual length, and soon after received Mr. Balfour, newly arrived home from the Washington Conference. He offered him an Earldom and the Garter, both of which Mr. Balfour begged for time to consider.[1] A day or two later Lord Allenby, High Commissioner, explained his proposals for Egypt which he expected the Government to accept.

[1] He received the Garter and was knighted on the 3rd March.

Princess Mary's wedding was fixed for the 28th February and the King and Queen were busy with the preparations for it, interested in the arrangement of the splendid presents and in their inspections of the treasures of Chesterfield House.

BUCKINGHAM PALACE. *Feb.* 28*th.*—Today darling Mary married Harry Lascelles. There were enormous crowds in the streets from here to the Abbey. They began taking up their places in the middle of the night. Mary had breakfast with us as usual, she was quite calm & not a bit nervous. She drove with me in my coach to Westminster Abbey where we arrived at 11.30 & I led her by the hand from the West door to the altar steps. The Archbishop of Canterbury married them. Victor Mackenzie was best man. It was a beautiful & most impressive service & I was proud of my darling child, but it was terribly sad to think that she was leaving us. . . . We took them out on the balcony & they got a tremendous ovation from an enormous crowd. Luncheon at 1.45. . . . I went up to Mary's room & took leave of her & quite broke down. They left for Weston[1] at 3.45. . . . They drove with 4 Greys in open carriage with travelling escort to Paddington. Felt very low and depressed now that darling Mary has gone. Worked & read all the evening.

Next day he wrote in his journal (facing a gummed-in facsimile of the royal letter of thanks to the nation for its sympathy and good wishes); "I miss darling Mary too awfully."[2] That day he wrote a letter of great length to the Prince of Wales, describing the wedding in detail.

§ 2

The narrative of events has reached the Spring of 1922.[3]

[1] Lord Bradford's place in Shropshire.

[2] Lady Mary Cambridge, the Queen's niece, soon after began admirably to fill her place, and went about with him, as Princess Mary had been wont to do. Lady Mary married the 10th Duke of Beaufort, then Lord Worcester, in 1923.

[3] It was to this point that the first rough draft of the memoir had been written when the Second World War broke out on 3rd September, 1939. The events of 1939 and 1940 must inevitably cause the troubled reign of King George V to recede a little more quickly into " history " than would otherwise have been the case, albeit the latter years of his reign were the prelude to Septembers 1938 and 1939.

The King's life and preoccupations in affairs of State may be more easily followed by a brief reference to the composition and changes of his Governments during the next few years and to the principal questions at home and abroad which occupied those Governments.

Something has been said of the causes and evidences of industrial unrest. At this time the chief anxiety at home in industry was the alarming rise in unemployment. There was a more or less continuous tale of strikes threatened, averted or carried out with varying degrees of success. The weapon of the General Strike, to which the Government was not blind, was not to be employed for four years to come, and long before then measures had been carried through Parliament to counter it, if it were used.

The chief problems abroad were of course the Peace Settlement and the many difficulties arising out of it. It is vain to throw mud at Versailles and to belittle the statesmanship of those who worried the Treaty out to completion. The spirit of the hour controls the actions of men in political as in social life. The men of Versailles were no blinder or smaller or more vindictive than those who settled the destinies of Europe after other wars. On the contrary, high ideals played a larger part in the world settlement after 1918 than in most settlements which have followed great wars, because, if for no better reason, the sanction of force was then a weakening factor in security.

The vital problems were reparations from Germany, disarmament and security. History clearly proves how strong, how continuous and leading a part Britain played in efforts to secure general disarmament in those years. That was the chief plank in our policy of security and one which King George heartily supported. Infinite labour was expended over the assessing of a " possible " figure of reparations. It is, once more, vain to cry out upon the absurdity of the estimate of Germany's ability to pay. The absurdity lay in trying to harmonise what she ought in bare justice to pay with what she was capable of paying, and, with France and Belgium shattered and bleeding and British vital industrial centres comparatively immune, the British voice of warning was not suffered to dominate the conference table of financial experts.

The end of Mr. Lloyd George's Government came in October 1922, when the Greek tangle was temporarily smoothed out. Mr. Bonar Law succeeded him, but ill-health compelled him to resign in May 1923, and five months later he died. In choosing his successor the King in the interests of the Nation set personal considerations aside. Lord Curzon's claims were overwhelmingly strong and he was a close personal friend. But he was a peer and the Labour Party had no real representation in the Lords. The King sent for Mr. Baldwin, to him an unknown man. There was no necessity for a dissolution.

Mr. Baldwin's first administration was very short. In December of the same year he resolved, to King George's regret, to appeal to the country, and, failing to secure at the General Election an absolute majority, he resigned and the King sent for Mr. Ramsay MacDonald as head of the largest Opposition Party, and thus the first Labour Government came into office, insecurely based on the sufferance of the Liberals. Mr. MacDonald's first Government was nearly as brief as Mr. Baldwin's. The Liberals combined with the Conservatives to defeat him in October 1924.

At the General Election of 1924 the Conservatives swept the board, with a solid majority against all combinations, and the Liberal Party suffered something approaching extinction. Mr. Baldwin came to stay. His Government ran its course, having achieved the Locarno Pact, the one bright diplomatic stroke of these post-war years, and having defeated the General Strike.

§ 3

To return: In that Spring of 1922 the King was assiduous in attending football fixtures. He would sometimes come rather ruefully to the scratch when such engagements came round, but when he was in his place watching the game he was invariably transformed into the enthusiastic schoolboy, gripping his hat with excitement and following every detail with zest and with a sound knowledge of technique.

Early in May the Queen and he paid a State visit to Belgium, the first made by any British sovereign for seventy years. On the 13th he met the Queen at Terlincthun, where General Castelnau and Allied Representatives and relatives of the fallen were assembled for the ceremonies at the Stone of Remembrance and the Cross of Sacrifice. Both the King and the Queen took part, the words of the King's speech on this occasion being among the finest pieces of prose among innumerable examples which he delivered. He himself was deeply moved at " a pretty and touching little ceremony." He came back to carry out his usual Summer visit to Aldershot, and to continue the arranged functions of the Season. Among these was Princess Mary's first dinner-party at Chesterfield House. A dance followed and the King and Queen much enjoyed what was obviously a great success. " Dear Mary," he noted down, " looked charming and wore my sapphires." Next day was his birthday—his fifty-seventh —and he considered the Trooping Ceremony had never been better performed. There is a note recording his horror and detestation of the insensate murder of Sir Henry Wilson on the 22nd June, on which day he was among the first to offer his sympathy to Lady Wilson. It haunted his mind for many months to come.

Before the Season ended he got away to Newmarket on two occasions, staying as usual in the rooms he loved, riding out on the Heath to watch his horses at their gallops, and discussing with Bland, who would come over from Sandringham, the prospects of sport for the Autumn. He liked to chaff his keepers for their sound conservatism, which amounted almost to pessimism, and would often open the discussion with : " Well, Bland, all the partridges drowned, I suppose ? "

In London that Summer his exercise—never very extensive —was confined to rides in the Park and walks and talks in the Palace gardens, with an Equerry, or often with Sister Agnes,[1] who had a key to the Palace gardens and would come over the way from her hospital to discuss professional and

---

[1] Daughter of Mr. Charles Keyser, she founded King Edward VII's hospital for officers in Grosvenor Crescent. She remained a valued friend of the Royal Family.

general topics. At the beginning of July he performed a duty near and dear to his heart. In the royal yacht he sailed to Torbay, in and off which lay the Atlantic Fleet under Admiral Madden. He carried out a very complete inspection of warships and engaged in exercises on board the *Queen Elizabeth*, entertaining most of the senior officers available.

After his usual shooting visits, he settled down at Balmoral, where his holiday was greatly interrupted by the critical situation in the Dardanelles and by the press of telegrams and documents with which he had daily to deal. He had of late been a good deal concerned with the finances of the Privy Purse and had considered various plans for retrenchment and reorganisation which culminated this year in the appointment, at the suggestion of the Treasury, of Mr. Ralph Harwood [1] to carry out the scheme, the details of which had given the King a great deal of trouble.

The prospect of an early dissolution brought him South again on the 10th October. The Coalition Government had been losing ground in popular favour and no one saw the truth more clearly than Mr. Lloyd George. On the 19th October the Conservative leaders held a meeting of the Party. The King had gone to Sandringham, but, feeling that all was not well, returned to the Palace that day. The same evening Mr. Lloyd George tendered his resignation after six years as Premier and the King sent for Mr. Bonar Law. With Mr. Lloyd George went into the wilderness Lord Birkenhead and Mr. Austen Chamberlain. There were certain difficulties to be cleared away. Mr. Lloyd George had resigned, but Mr. Bonar Law felt that, until he had been elected Leader of the Conservative Party, he could not accede to a request to form an administration. Duly elected Leader, he kissed hands on his appointment as Prime Minister and was sworn in as First Lord of the Treasury on the 23rd October. A Conservative Government could not be formed from that in being, as the ministers had been elected upon a Coalition vote and a dissolution was therefore asked for and granted by the King. Mr. Lloyd George came to the Palace to say good-bye. " I

[1] Afterwards Sir Ralph Harwood, Deputy Treasurer and later Financial Secretary to the King from 1922 to 1937.

am sorry he is going," wrote the King, " but he will be P.M. again." At the elections the Conservatives were returned with a clear over-all majority. Early in December the King approved the constitution of the " new Dominion of the Free State of Southern Ireland."

§ 4

The King's diary grows shorter at this point. One volume does the duty of two or more of earlier days. Partly no doubt this was due to his increasing preoccupation with affairs of State, in part perhaps to the fact that his year's round was once more established firmly in a rotation of Court moves and annual fixtures which varied very little with the years.

The next few were troubled and anxious enough, and certain salient events, affecting his public and private life, deserve mention. On the 15th January, 1923, at Sandringham, he wrote : " Bertie with Greig [1] arrived after tea and informed us that he was engaged to Elizabeth Bowes Lyon, to which we gladly gave our consent. I trust they will be very happy." On the 20th Lady Elizabeth and her parents arrived. " She is a pretty and charming girl & Bertie is a lucky fellow," noted the King. Indeed, he took to his first daughter-in-law instantly, falling under the spell of her extraordinary charm and sympathy, appreciating her serenity, quickness of mind and good sense, her spirit and strength of character, and recognising in her one who would be equal to all emergencies and tests which she might be called on to face and would never be diverted from her purpose where she held it right. They got on excellently together, and in letters to his friends his pride and joy in her are revealed.

Early in 1923 he became a grandfather. Princess Mary's first son was born at Chesterfield House shortly before midnight on the 7th February. Before the Court moved to Windsor the King and Queen visited Goldsborough for the child's christening. April, too, was a month in which domestic interests preponderated. At Hawthorn Hill the King again saw the Prince win the Welsh Guards' race. " He rode

[1] Wing-Commander Sir Louis Greig, the Duke's Comptroller 1920–23.

well, but don't like him riding in these races & am going to try & stop him." The 26th was the wedding day of the Duke of York and Lady Elizabeth. It was a dull, rainy morning, " but " (the King noted) " the sun actually came out as the bride entered the Abbey." Indeed, it has never failed to shine on every scene and in all company graced by her presence.

During the first half of May the King and Queen paid a State visit to Italy, in the course of which they had a long conversation with the Pope. On 22nd May Mr. Baldwin succeeded Mr. Bonar Law as Premier.

The Imperial Conference called him South from Balmoral on the 9th October, and on the 11th he gave a dinner to some sixty delegates. On that day he had handed the seals of the Exchequer to Mr. Neville Chamberlain. After a brief visit to Sandringham, he was in London again by the 22nd, when he gave a State banquet to Dr. Masaryk, the President of the Czecho-Slovak Republic, and Dr. Beneš. The Conference delegates were entertained at the Palace once more. On the 30th October Mr. Bonar Law died.

On the 12th November the King wrote:

At 3.30 the Premier [Mr. Baldwin] came to see me & asked me to dissolve Parliament. I deprecated it because of the disturbed state of Europe and because the country is quiet except for the unemployment, but he said he had committed himself & is prepared to stand or fall on Tariff Reform,[1] & so reluctantly I had to give my consent.

In the resultant December election the Government lost its majority, the chief parties showing:

Conservatives .	.	.	258
Labour .	.	.	191
Liberals .	.	.	156

The King commented: "A serious state of affairs & will give me great difficulty to get out of the impasse, as another

---

[1] This issue was regarded as one on which the electorate must give or withhold its mandate.

election is out of the question." On the 10th December he saw the Premier and asked him not to resign but to meet Parliament and await events. To this the Premier, after meeting his Cabinet, agreed.

CHAPTER XX

*First Labour Ministry—Life at Balmoral—Death of
Queen Alexandra—Locarno—The General Strike
1924-26*

[*Mr. MacDonald, Premier; Mr. Baldwin, Premier, November* 1924]

§ 1

THE King opened Parliament on the 15th January in
1924, noting in the galleries the presence of many
friends and supporters of the Labour Party who were
confident that the day, so long anticipated, was
coming at last. There were truculent speeches made all over
the country and hot-heads did not spare the King in warnings
and veiled threats. He remained perfectly cool and very
patient, interviewing leaders of all parties.

One week later the hour struck. The Government was
defeated by seventy-two votes on the 21st January, the Prime
Minister tendered his resignation, and the King sent for Mr.
MacDonald and asked him to form a Government. " I had "
(he wrote) " an hour's talk with him. He impressed me very
much, he wishes to do the right thing. Today 23 years ago
dear Grandmama died, I wonder what she would have
thought of a Labour Government." His comment is worth
quoting, for its light on his own character and as an instance
of a truth more than once stressed in this memoir. Under
democratic sovereignty kingcraft is the adaptation of the
Sovereign's will and character to the ever-changing will of
his people. There is no permanent standard of kingcraft.
A great sovereign of one age might well be an impossibility a
decade beyond his reign.

Mr. MacDonald accepted, and formed his Government,
including in it Mr. Henderson, Mr. Thomas and Mr. Clynes,
with Lords Parmoor, Haldane and Chelmsford, the last-
named a non-political recruit to stiffen the new Government.

In his interviews with his new ministers the King's kindliness stood out. There are many instances of his thoughtfulness, as, for example, in his decision to provide the necessary ceremonial uniform for some of those who took up political Court appointments. He had always judged men as men, he was quite devoid of class-consciousness, he knew exactly how to put strangers and shy persons at their ease as only great gentlemen and the simple-minded know. If a majority of the new Ministry, old Parliamentary hands and men of the world, had no doubts to be resolved and no social anxieties to be banished, it was not so among the Party generally. The King's first contacts with his new Government were closely and jealously watched, and very soon the word went round that the King and Queen had made everything easy and removed all difficulties and suspicions. It was by the light of his nature, not by the exercise of tact, that he welcomed and won the first Labour Ministry.

Mr. MacDonald was very helpful and as anxious as was the King to preserve historic traditions, and to rationalise only what was antiquated. From this date certain Court appointments, very personal to the Sovereign, those of the Great Officers, Lord Chamberlain, Lord Steward and Master of the Horse, acquired greater permanency. Lord Cromer, Lord Shaftesbury and Lord Granard continued in those offices through many changes of the Administration. They were all close personal friends of the King, who fully appreciated and often acknowledged the value of their services. The office of the Lord Chamberlain is no sinecure. As head of the Household, chief executive on all matters of ceremonial, the officer ultimately responsible for the palaces and their inestimable treasures, the chief link between the Sovereign and the House of Lords, in constant and close relationship with the Diplomatic Corps, and the official charged with the control of the theatres and the censorship of stage-plays, his work is varied and vitally important. These delicate and diverse functions were probably never better discharged than by Lord Cromer between 1922 and 1938. By his tact and imperturbability he contrived to offend none and to satisfy all, and he had the confidence and friendship of the King throughout his service. Those rewards came, too, to Lord Shaftesbury and to Lord Granard for their long and valuable service in posts of less constitutional importance. At the same time the King was asked to select three permanent Lords-in-Waiting, and these six offices have since remained non-political.

With tact and understanding on both sides, the new Ministry soon grew familiar with the customary routine work and the doubts and suspicions of the uninformed were set at rest. The Railway Strike, which had begun on 21st January, came to an end, but the King remained in constant touch with his new ministers concerning industrial problems and crises. The dockers were now threatening to increase the paralysis of trade and the shadow of another Miners' Strike loomed close behind.

The Prince had broken his collar-bone while schooling his steeplechasers and the King was again concerned to persuade him to give up riding in races, but he found the Prince not easy to lead. Early in March he gave various entertainments to the new Ministry and their friends, and went to Knowsley for the "National." While there, he held a Council to sanction, if need arose, the use of the Emergency Powers in any transport strike.

Towards the end of April, on St. George's Day, he drove from Windsor to Wembley to open the great Empire Exhibition. The ceremony was carried out in the Stadium before 70,000 people, and the Prince, as President, received the King and read an address. The occasion was made an important landmark in broadcasting. Several royal visits to the Exhibition followed, one such being an item in the State visit of the King and Queen of Italy (in May) and of the King and Queen of Roumania. At the end of July there was an important review of the Fleet at Spithead. The King paid his usual visits to Goodwood and Cowes, enjoyed some racing in the *Britannia,* and got to Bolton Abbey for the 12th on his way to Balmoral. But on the 9th October he was back in London to face one more political crisis.

Mr. MacDonald's Government had in a short time made a signal contribution to world settlement. A conference of creditors in German reparations, convened in London, had smoothed out a mass of complicated obstacles and paved the way for the Dawes Plan. The Labour Government had given Europe a breathing space. But Mr. MacDonald's next stage towards pacification involved the re-establishment of friendly relations with Russia, and for this the bulk of the nation was as yet by no means ready. An Anglo-Russian Treaty, containing conditional provisions for a loan to the Soviet Government, sealed the fate of the first Labour Ministry, though a more trivial cause actually brought about its defeat. On the 9th October, the day of his return to London, the King noted in his diary:

At 10 received the Prime Minister who informed me that the Government had been defeated last night over the Campbell question,[1] & that he must ask me for a dissolution. I gave my consent with regret as it means an immediate General Election & the last one took place only 9 months ago & the Country is tired of these constant elections.

In the result, the Conservatives secured a substantial majority.

After several busy and anxious days the King resumed his holiday at Sandringham. " Our dear Cottage is as comfortable as ever," he wrote. He came in for a very notable partridge year.

Back in London in the first days of November, he wrote in his diary : " *Nov.* 4.—Mr. MacDonald came to see me at 5.30 & placed his resignation in my hands. I like him & have always found him straight. At 7 I received Mr. Baldwin & asked him to form a Government which he agreed to do." After the exchange of seals and interviews with his new ministers, he held a Council to prorogue Parliament until early in December. He opened Parliament on the 9th. " My speech was, I should think, the longest on record. The Crown gave me an awful headache. I could not have borne

---

[1] J. R. Campbell, Editor of a Communist newspaper, had been prosecuted for sedition on instructions from the Home Office. The proceedings were dropped and a debate on the issue resulted in the Government's defeat, the Liberals withdrawing their support. His defeat was neither a surprise nor a disappointment to Mr. MacDonald who in a short time had made a reputation for himself and his Party.

it much longer." No doubt the weight of the Crown in those days bore heavily on him.

§ 2

He was often ill at this time.[1] He was prone to colds and coughs and rheumatic complaints. Soon after his return to London from Sandringham early in February 1925 he caught another cold. Influenza, followed by bronchitis, set in; he had a high temperature and was in great discomfort for several days. But he would not give in, would not forgo the essential duty of the daily " boxes." He worked on in his bed, seeing no one but the Queen (who wrote up his diary), his sons and daughter, and secretaries. On the 4th March he was able to sit up in a chair. He disliked foreign travel, but his doctors insisted on a cruise in the Mediterranean, and on the 19th March the Queen and he left for Genoa, where they went on board the yacht. For a month they cruised between Naples and Sicily, seeing the sights of Pompeii, Messina, Syracuse and Palermo. The King was reading Sir Sidney Lee's life of his father at the time, " very interesting but not always quite accurate." He enjoyed himself in fine weather far more than he had expected, and on the 23rd April " left the dear Yacht sadly " and returned home via Paris.

That summer he carried out many notable ceremonies in addition to the traditional functions. During the Season he went sometimes to the Opera which never failed to give him relief. He had inherited from his mother a real appreciation of music and always commented with shrewdness on operatic performances. Later in August the Queen and he spent a few days with Princess Mary and Lord Lascelles before going to Balmoral.

§ 3

If Sandringham easily held first place in the King's heart among his residences, Balmoral, necessarily more of a holiday

---

[1] On the evidence of his diary. Since his attack of typhoid in 1891, he had grown nervous of minor symptoms, and was inclined to make heavy weather of colds. His accident in France (he often said) permanently cured his indigestion.

home, was always very dear to him. He grew up as a boy to love it, first by tradition as the home planned, made and loved by his grandparents, and next for the experiences and associations of his childhood spent at Abergeldie. In his youth and early middle age he would sometimes go up for the Spring fishing as well as for the customary Autumn holiday. In later life Balmoral saw him only from the last part of August to the first week or so of October. Nevertheless, he found time to examine very thoroughly the current problems and plans of his factor, his farmers, his foresters, stalkers and keepers, to know and regularly visit his neighbours and tenants and employees and their children, and to exercise in the limited time at his disposal all the responsibilities of a Highland landowner and host.

He needed no guide on the hill, he was perfectly competent to stalk alone if he had willed. He knew and loved the high tops, the corries and the woods of Balmoral as well as any of his men. His extraordinary memory for detail enabled him to take up again after a year's absence the points of an argument or proposal left over from the previous Autumn. On his arrival at Ballater, smiling and obviously happy, he would always surprise William Grant, the station-master, by some pertinent remark which showed that he was well informed of recent local events. "Well, Grant, so you weren't washed away by those floods?" He would walk into a cottage and note with approval that missing tiles had been replaced or a luxuriant creeper restrained. So, too, in his walks abroad, when he met the schoolchildren on the roads or paths and entered into conversation with them, as he loved to do, he showed an uncanny memory for their school histories and family details. He loved to talk, and his stalker or keeper or a passing child was as good an audience as any other. He was very fond of children and full of stories of childish humour, liking especially the pawky, Scots type. On returning from the hill one day, he went up to a boy who was herding cows. "How many cows have you there?" he asked. "Dinna ken. Never counted 'em," replied the boy. The King added the story to his repertoire. Sometimes, when he met the schoolchildren, he would take their books and ask them questions about their work and chaff them if their answers were not satisfactory. He often went about quite unattended.

The King would see Abercrombie regularly every morning at eight o'clock to settle the plans for the day's sport for himself, his family and guests. If there was to be shooting, the head keeper was also interviewed, usually the night before. The King was habitually so punctual that you could " set the clock by him," as Abercrombie, who came to Balmoral at the beginning of the century, put it. In earlier days he was a match for anybody on the hill. He seemed always in condition, even in the first days of the Season. He could walk for ever and was as fine a crawler as could be. Out stalking, he would have only the very simplest and plainest of luncheon and drank from a flask of weak whisky and soda. In his prime he preferred stalking to grouse-shooting. During most of his stalking career he used his first rifle, made for him in India, a cordite, hammered rifle.[1] He was as quick and sure with a rifle as with a gun, which is rare. Abercrombie had often seen him bring off marvellous shots, made standing, at moving deer, conditions which King George welcomed. He was never the same man on the hill after his accident in France, which put a stop to his full activities, and towards the end of his life he confined himself to deer drives. In the last stalking years Queen Mary would sometimes give private instructions to Abercrombie to take special care of him and to persuade him to avoid fatigue. And no doubt Archbishop Lang, often his companion on the hill, tried his persuasions also.

The Archbishop has supplied a delightful memory of one such day. He was out on the hill with the King. Grant was the stalker, a real old " candid friend." The King took a fairly easy shot, resting his rifle on Grant's shoulder. He missed and the whole herd galloped away. " Take this damned rifle away. Never let me see it again." " Yer Majesty, dinna waste yer breeth damning the rifle. It was a verra ba-ad shot." The King was as pleased as the Archbishop—in the cool of the evening. There was a day towards

[1] A D.B. Express.

the end of his life when the head stalker reported that two stags had got through the deer fence and were in one of the woods inside the grounds. The King went out, Sir Bryan Godfrey-Faussett with him, to look for them. The wood was driven and the stags broke out together about two hundred yards from the King, affording him right and left galloping shots. He killed both.[1]

To Abercrombie and others at Balmoral he seemed a very religious man. He was deeply interested in the affairs and welfare of Crathie Church, and would often enquire the amount of the collection and concern himself with its objects. His religion was the religion of the old-fashioned country squire. He went to church because it was the " right thing " and to set an example. He loved the hymns and psalms learned in childhood and maintained the habit, acquired at his mother's knee, of reading some verses of the Bible every day. But he had no " inner life " of which others could be aware and was not interested in doctrine, dogma or Church questions. He had his dislikes, of course, and they were the bugbears of the old-school laird. He detested motor-bicycles and their effect on the young men of the countryside, and no doubt the " perpetual motion " and cinema habits came in for his criticism as prime destroyers of the old country life.

He was not only a good landlord but a good neighbour, being very kind-hearted, considerate and generous. He had a deep and abiding affection for the old friends and tyrants of his youth; for Donald Stewart, who taught him to shoot grouse, for Davie Rose, stalker and expert reel dancer to whom kings were but as other men, and for Meysie Anderson, who kept the fishing lodge at the head of Loch Muick and would rule him with a rod of iron if he failed to do justice to the teas which she prepared for him. He knew the children of his tenants by name and had their interests at heart, and he was assiduous in exchanging hospitality with his neighbours. During the Balmoral Season there were usually important guests in the Castle, ministers, ambassadors, dignitaries of Church and State, leaders in business, industry and the sciences. He was a charming host, always anxious to

[1] So Sir Bryan records. The King in his diary claims only one.

find congenial recreation for each and all, always sharing his available leisure between them, always ensuring that life at Balmoral should be no less and no more than the ideal of country-house life. And he supported the local institutions and Season's functions, the games, dog-trials and gatherings, though with these perhaps he entered upon the business in his later years with rather less than the typical laird's enthusiasm.

For Highland life had altered very materially since his youth, and local events on Dee-side had lost some of their charm for him with the coming of the motor-car and char-à-banc. In the old Queen's time the Gathering, small and a strictly local function, was in truth a rally of the Clans. Over the Perthshire hills in those days came the Atholl men, up from Aboyne the Gordons, and from Strathdon the Forbes men, walking tirelessly through the night to meet on the field the Farquharsons and the Duffs and the Balmoral Highlanders. But in King George's reign the Gathering had become a Highland Show widely reported and attracting professionals from a distance and sight-seers from many lands, while Sunday morning service in Crathie Church had become a peep-show. King George was conscious of these changes which may have affected his enthusiasm. But nothing ever changed his deep-seated love of Balmoral and Dee-side or his affection for the simple, kindly, dignified folk who lived there and contributed so much to the pleasure of his Autumn holiday.

§ 4

He was at the Cottage when, on the 19th November, he learned that Queen Alexandra had had a very serious heart attack. He hurried over to the big house and did not leave her until her death next day. So sudden was it that her elder grandsons arrived too late to see her alive. So he said good-bye to the mother whom he had loved from the hour of his first consciousness of her presence and to whom he had never ceased to give the devotion and care of a dutiful son. It is clear from his diary that his own grief was mitigated by the knowledge that for her it was a happy release, peace after long suffering. Her body was brought to the Chapel Royal and buried beside King Edward at Windsor, after lying in state in the Abbey where the funeral service was held. King Albert of the Belgians and King George of Greece and other royal relations attended the ceremonies. No sooner were they over than the King began to concern himself for his beloved sister, Princess Victoria, and for his mother's faithful companion, Miss Knollys. The former soon afterwards settled down at Iver; for Miss Knollys the King bought a charming flat in South Audley Street, and visited her there as soon as she was installed. For many days following, when he had time to spare, the Queen and he, with Princess Victoria, went through the vast accumulations of papers and memorials of his parents at Sandringham and Marlborough House.

The Pact of Locarno—of such happy augury—was achieved that Autumn. This pact, a series of treaties, replaced the Geneva Protocol, which had been approved by the first Labour Government but had not satisfied France. It concerned the Eastern and Western frontiers of Germany. By its terms it " outlawed " war and upheld the principle of arbitration. France, Germany, Belgium, Poland and Czecho-Slovakia, the " Frontier " States, undertook never to go to war with one another, but to invoke arbitration in its place. Britain and Italy joined as guarantors of this procedure in the West, France being the guarantor for Eastern Europe. In effect, Britain, France, Italy, Germany and Belgium guaranteed in the West the *status quo* of the Versailles Treaty, and the ultimate sanctions for infringement (except in a case of flagrant aggression) were left to League machinery.

The Treaty was widely hailed as the end of an era of war. If it bristled with risks and unforeseeable difficulties, it brought Germany back into the concert of European nations and marked a great step forward towards appeasement. Its risks were lost sight of in the dazzle of its swift and unexpected success, which was greatly due to Mr. Austen Chamberlain and Dr. Stresemann,[1] not to mention Mrs. Chamberlain, who

---

[1] M. Briand, who made up the triumvirate, commented: " Nous avons parlé européen. C'est une langue nouvelle qu'il faudra bien que l'on apprenne." But these high hopes were disappointed. The new language

cast a spell of appeasement over the gathering of delegates outside the Council Chamber. The King, in common with scores of his ministers and well-informed subjects, reposed great confidence in its virtues. " I pray," he wrote, " this may mean peace for many years, why not for ever? " On the 1st December he bestowed two signal honours on Mr. Austen Chamberlain; he sent his Lord Chamberlain to the station to meet him on his return to London and later invested him with the Order of the Garter. Soon after he received both Stresemann and Luther, Chancellor and Foreign Minister of Germany.

§ 5

In the early months of 1926 he was busy enough over public and family affairs. Sandringham House was being prepared for him and Marlborough House was being cleared as a possible home for the Prince. He was at Windsor as usual in April, and while there heard of the birth of Princess Elizabeth on the 21st April. Needless to say, the Queen and he instantly drove up to Bruton Street.

There were long discussions with Mr. Baldwin that month on the Coal Crisis which even then seemed to threaten a more general paralysis. At the beginning of May a general strike was practically certain and on the 3rd it was in being. For several days there was an almost total paralysis of the nation's work. Then the Government's strong handling of the challenge brought some sort of order out of chaos, and on the 12th:

At 1 p.m. I got the good news that the T.U.C. had been to the Prime Minister and informed him that the General Strike was forthwith called off unconditionally. . . .
. . . Our old country can well be proud of itself, as during the last 9 days there has been a strike in which 4 million people have been affected, not a shot has been fired & no one killed, it shows what a wonderful people we are.

proved difficult to learn. Germany received a grudging welcome from the League, no general disarmament came about, Stresemann died and Nazism rose to combat Communism and despair in the Reich. In France at least, it must be added, contemporary opinion of Stresemann's constructive statesmanship and appeasement value has since undergone modification.

In these words he reveals himself as the voice of his country, not of a section. In the political and social difficulties of his reign his impartial judgment and his common sense stand out. If it was not in his nature to dig far below the surface, or to attempt seriously to grapple with the intricacies and underlying principles in such problems, always he had the power to apply his common sense and experience to the broad issue in the interest of the country as a whole.

In a letter which he wrote to Mr. Baldwin, acknowledging a great debt of gratitude, he restated those broad principles of constitutional government :

BUCKINGHAM PALACE, 12*th May* 1926.

MY DEAR PRIME MINISTER.—With all my heart I congratulate you and my Government on having terminated the dangerous crisis we have experienced during the past ten days. This success is largely due to your own untiring patience and wise determination to abide by what you believed to be in the best and truest interests of the people by whose suffrages you have been elected to govern. These sentiments will, I feel sure, be shared by the country at large.

I trust you are not feeling the strain too much, after all you have gone through. Believe me, Very sincerely yrs., G.R.I.

The General Strike was over, but the Coal Strike dragged bitterly on until the end of November. The arrival in London of the Dominions Premiers brought him to the Palace early in that month, and among many interviews given by him two receive special mention in his diary. He writes of the intelligence and good sense of Mr. Cosgrave of Ireland and of the great personal charm of Mr. Coates of New Zealand.

CHAPTER XXI

*King George and his Friends—The Rising Generation
—Adherence to Tradition—Love of Animals—
Relations with his Ministers*

§ 1

THERE are many maxims—the essential wisdom of
the ages—which relate to a man and his friends.
To the truth of many of them King George subscribed and testified. No man ever lived who was
more loyal to his friends, more resolute to conserve old friendships. Often he deplored that until he was turned thirty he
had few friends or even close acquaintances outside the Service.
He would sometimes say that, when he became Heir to the
Throne, he " knew nobody," and it was true enough that he
was, for a man in his position, remarkably little known to
politicians [1] and in society. This was in large measure due
to his long absences on Naval service, to a youthful shyness
in general company and to a deficiency in the social arts
which he all his life confessed to but which no guest of his
can ever have suspected.[2] But the gift of friendship was in
him, and he more than made up for the lack of opportunity
in his early youth.

In one thing he was blessed. From the first formation of
a personal Household, he had about him his oldest and his
closest friends.[3] Indeed, a big proportion of the most intimate
companions of his days and the most personal members of his
Staff were the friends of his boyhood or Service days. Sir

[1] Nevertheless, he did not encourage his younger sons to make close
personal contact with politicians, and King George VI on accession found
himself in much the same position in this respect as his father had been.

[2] During his reign at any rate he seemed always to be at the top of his
form in company and never at a loss for the ease-giving remark.

[3] A more comprehensive list of the King's personal friends will be found
on page 221 et seq.

Bryan Godfrey-Faussett, Sir Charles Cust, Sir Derek Keppel,
Sir Harry Stonor, these men had known him intimately in
boyhood, and two of them had constantly served with him
at sea in the freemasonry of the Service. They had watched
his character developing, and observed its reactions under
every kind of test and condition, as only such friends and
companions can do. Lord Stamfordham had known him
in boyhood, and when he was appointed Private Secretary
he became almost immediately an intimate friend, while
younger men, recruited to the Secretariat and Staff, such as
Lord Wigram and Lord Charles Nairne, Lord Claud Hamilton, Sir Reginald Seymour and Sir Alexander Hardinge, soon
enjoyed the same privilege of intimacy. Other friends too,
as old as, or even older than, Sir Charles Cust or Sir Bryan
Godfrey-Faussett, such as Canon Dalton, Admiral Sir Stanley
Colville and Admiral Sir Henry Campbell, were constantly
in contact with him and in his service in various capacities
throughout their lives. So intense indeed was his loyalty to
his oldest friends, so determined was he to see them whenever
he could, that, when his children grew up, there was sometimes little accommodation left for their own contemporaries.

His relations with them were of the happiest possible. His
sense of humour was robust. He was not averse from ragging
which had been a tradition of his childhood. His method of
joking was that " downright to rudeness " method which tried
friends appreciate. He loved a joke, the older the better;
he loved to laugh and had a keen sense of the ridiculous,
gleaning and storing up instances on dull ceremonial occasions. Some of his remembered sayings possessed the point
of wit, as when Mr. Baldwin congratulated him on his looking
fit again after his illness and he replied: " Yes, I'm pretty well
again "; hastily adding, " but not well enough to walk with
the Queen round the British Industries Fair."

Because he set so much store by exact obedience to his orders
and strict observance of arrangements which he had sanc-
tioned, he would often " go up in smoke " when any proof
of deviation came to his notice. These were breezes, never
instances of ill-temper, and, because they were so characteristic of the man they loved and served, his Household always

remembered them with chuckles. They never left behind bitterness or a sense of injustice, for the sun never went down on his wrath nor did night set in before he had in his charming, thoughtful manner, often disguised in rough words, made the *amende* and dismissed the incident with his hearty laugh.[1]

His secretaries were always astonished by his powers of application. They thought, no doubt, that he did too much reading, for he would never be satisfied with marked passages. He read his *Times* from cover to cover. " Where the devil is my *Times* this morning? " was a not infrequent prelude to the day's work. He did not care to be argued with, and when those nearest him sometimes took the liberty of proved friendship to oppose a decision, he was at first deaf to their arguments. " Go on and do it, you obstinate devil," he would say; and then perhaps next day would ask: " Well, have you done it? " " No, Sir, I thought I'd let it cool." " Well, well, perhaps you're right." None of his Staff remembered him ever to have done a stupid action. Often hasty and amazingly free of speech, in all company and on every sort of occasion, he could yet be a well for confidences and seemed to have an uncanny sense of the correct action and the right final decision. Indeed, it sometimes seemed that his words and actions bore less than the normal relation one to the other, except in so far as his pledged word was concerned.

§ 2

Some random notes on King George's character and some memories of a valued friendship covering many years were set down by Sir Walter Lawrence at the end of his narrative of the India tour. His last remarks are as follows:

The last time I saw this great and good man was shortly before his death. I was going out to India and went to wish him good-bye. He gave me most admirable advice as to what I should say to certain of his friends in India. His

[1] " He would call me " (Sir Derek Keppel has said on this subject) " every name under the sun, but always, as I was leaving the room after an ' explosion,' he would call me back and make his peace with, ' Derek, did you ever hear this story . . .? ' "

sister had died two days previously and I said, " These friends of yours in India will be as sorry as the British are about your sad loss." And he replied, "Yes, it was a great loss. Since I became King I have talked to her every day on the telephone, and only yesterday I took up the telephone to speak to her and then remembered she was dead." He had a very loving heart.

I can only testify to this fact, that though I had done very little for him on the Indian tour that any other officer of the Indian Services could not have done equally well, yet he rewarded me for my poor services by a friendship which I esteem more highly than anything in my life. I have had the good fortune to know some great men. Thinking over things very carefully, I am of opinion that the most beautiful character I have ever known was that of King George V.

The King was fond of copying from books or cutting-out from newspapers sentences setting forth the right conduct of life, which struck his fancy. In later years there stood always on his writing-table a copy of " The Good Indian's Prayer." [1] Mrs. Fetherstonhaugh had somewhere come across it and shown it to him. He was immensely pleased with it. It seemed to him to give the essence of his own philosophy of life and to set forth some of the principles of conduct which he strove, not always successfully, to follow.

§ 3

It is impossible to make a satisfactory or complete list of his friends outside the royal circle and Household. To attempt it may be more invidious than profitable. Lord Revelstoke was one of his closest. Others who may be named were the Dukes of Devonshire, Portland and Roxburghe, Lords Derby, Rosebery, Crewe, Durham, Lonsdale, Sefton, Annaly, Chesham, Lovat, Somerleyton; John, Lord Downe, Lord Herbert Vane-Tempest and the Mackintosh of Mackintosh. There were many more, in varying degrees of intimacy. Some—older friends like John, Duke of Buccleuch—have already been mentioned, as have certain friends of his father's.

[1] The well-known lines " I shall journey through this world but once . . . " also took his fancy. He wrote them out at Marlborough House on a card, which long stood on his writing-table. See p. 110.

Of Churchmen, besides Archbishop Lang, there were Archbishop Davidson, Dean H. W. Blackburne of Bristol, Canon Peter Green of Manchester, two vicars of Sandringham, Mr. Grant and Mr. Fuller, Dr. Stirton, the minister at Crathie, Canon Edgar Sheppard, Sub-dean, and Prebendary Percival, Precentor of the Chapels Royal, and Dean Albert Baillie, of St. George's Chapel, Windsor.

From the fighting services, Lords Haig, Jellicoe, Kitchener, Byng, Beatty, Plumer, Sir William Robertson, Sir Horace Smith-Dorrien, Brigadier H. A. Tomkinson,[1] and Admirals Sir Hubert Brand, Sir Henry Buller and Sir Herbert Meade-Fetherstonhaugh, all three of whom commanded the royal yacht at various times. Of business men, Sir Edward Peacock, a partner with Lord Revelstoke in Baring's, did much of the King's private business and was intimate with him. Sir Bernard Halsey-Bircham did his legal business and saw a great deal of him. Lord Hankey and Sir Robert Vansittart were public servants whom he consulted constantly. Among leading Indians, the Maharajah of Jodhpur, Sir Pertab Singh and the Maharajah of Bikanir were true friends. Nor must his boyhood and later friends at Sandringham and Balmoral be forgotten. Messrs. Grant, Abercrombie and Mackintosh at Balmoral, Messrs. Jones, the schoolmaster, and Jackson, Bland, Amos, keepers at Sandringham, must be included in any list of the King's friends.

It was sometimes said that he would have gained much if he had possessed his father's penchant for constant conversation on every variety of topic with women of the world. The remark cannot be accepted without qualification. For one thing, among the Queen's ladies were women of high ability and wide influence, who were always well informed in current thought. They were among his women friends, and it was always his practice, in conversation with women of ability, to draw them out, to get from them the woman's point of view on political or social questions. With them he would never dominate the conversation, as sometimes he did with his ministers. And again, his social gifts have been underrated as his diffidence has been exaggerated. He was critical

[1] Manager of the King's Racing Stable from 1932 onwards.

of women, for his standard was immensely high and he was a shrewd judge of their ability. But he acquired the gift of finding the right conversational gambit and choosing the subject most likely to encourage or draw out his neighbour. To the intellectuals he would listen, prompting them to develop their arguments on subjects of importance. Those of average ability he would draw out on home and literary subjects, and with the shy and tongue-tied he would exert himself with jokes and anecdotes and seldom fail to put them perfectly at ease. Indeed, he was by no means deficient in the social arts.

But no doubt there was something in the criticism. King George occupied much less time than his father did in social converse, was less enthralled by the drama of human life, was much less convinced of his own power to amuse or interest his guests, and for these and other reasons derived less information and drew less inspiration from conversation with women of the world than King Edward did. Outside the Court circle he had no large variety of women friends. He was happiest perhaps in the company of Mme d'Hautpoul, whom he had known from childhood, and Lady Algernon Gordon-Lennox [1]; he was devoted to Lady Mar [2] and to Lady Meux [3] who certainly were able to help him (as later did Mrs. Fetherston-haugh) to assimilate a little of the spirit of the post-war age and to appreciate the claims of youth; but for the most part he derived his impressions of the world of youth outside and of changing fashions of thought from his sister, Princess Victoria, who was not perhaps highly qualified to give a full and impartial picture.

§ 4

Although it is too soon after his death to consider in any detail his relations with his own immediate family, no personal character-study can be regarded as satisfactory or complete which does not examine his attitude to the rising generation

[1] Daughter of Col. The Hon. C. H. Maynard.
[2] Daughter of the 8th Earl of Shaftesbury and wife of the 12th Earl of Mar and (14th of) Kellie.
[3] Daughter of the 1st Lord Alington and widow of Sir Hedworth (Lambton) Meux and of Lord Charles Montagu.

of post-war youth, and seek to find some solution of the paradox revealed in his intercourse with young people after the War.

He himself possessed many of the virtues which make for success in the ideal of family and social relations. He asked nothing better than to enjoy family life in simplicity and peace in his own home. He was acknowledged in the wider circle of his family as an ideal head. His thoughtfulness, his generosity, his practical kindness, are legends. He was devoted to children and, in theory, by no means unsympathetic to the claims and manner of thought of the rising generation. He could instantly banish the shyness of schoolchildren at Balmoral or Sandringham by a kindly word (he lost no opportunity to give it), and liked nothing better than to offer them advice, to joke with them and to retail their sayings. And with the younger members of the royal circle he " got on like a house on fire." Young ladies who showed no fear of him could and did " take liberties " in the exchange of chaff which both pleased him and did him good. He was specially fond of the Queen's niece, the Duchess of Beaufort,[1] and loved to bring out her gifts of banter; and several young men, such as Lord Eldon, Lord Sefton,[2] Lord Airlie and the Dukes of Norfolk and Beaufort, when they began to receive invitations to Sandringham, Windsor or Balmoral, were entirely happy in his company, finding him sympathetic, understanding, even elastic.

When staying with old friends like the Duke and Duchess of Devonshire at Chatsworth or Bolton Abbey, he insisted on being treated as " one of the family." He was the jolliest and least formal of guests, and got on capitally with the Duke's grandchildren. On the moor at Bolton he would often invite two or three of them into his butt, and neighbouring guns would hear them chattering away to him and note him answering, when given a chance to speak, almost while he was letting off his guns. The King was always in happy mood at the beginning of a new shooting season, with his release from London, and he enjoyed all sorts of jokes, even practical.

[1] And her sister, Lady Helena Gibbs.
[2] Son of his friend the 6th Earl of Sefton.

He would in earlier days come down to breakfast and isolate himself at a corner of the table with the Duke's youngest daughter, while she was still a child, and engage her in grave nursery discussions and heated arguments, until one day he was ruefully compelled to admit that he had been " cut out by a young Hamilton of seven or eight years of age who was the owner of a real wooden gun."

In his own children's childhood, he had shown himself very much the family man and loving father. He had " bathed " his babies in turn, weighed them, played with them, taken them for walks, instructed them in country lore, treasured their sayings, delighted in all genuine praise of them, and felt constant pride in the success of their first flights with a gun, a rod or on horseback. In a word, in so far as his nature allowed, he had striven to assure to their youth the blessings which had fallen to his—the happiest of home life. His own marriage was ideally happy, and everything seemed to favour the same relations between himself and the children of that happy union. Yet, even while they remained children, his manner of chaffing them or interrogating them had added to the shyness and tied the tongues of those by nature the most diffident, and the same qualities which gained him the devotion of his Staff and servants and the admiration of his wider family as their ideal head sometimes created a barrier which separated him from his own sons.

Happy memories of his own childhood had a quite un-expected effect on his relations with the post-war generation. Those memories stiffened his resistance to any deviation from the standards and fashions endeared to him by tradition. All his life he regarded the exclusive family life created by his father and mother in his youth as an ideal towards which every succeeding generation should strive. He had not the tolerance nor the easy nature of his father. His code was more rigid, he was closer bound by tradition, he was by nature extremely conservative, and in a broad sense less a man of the world, a cosmopolitan, than was King Edward VII. His conservatism revealed itself in many ways. He once told a friend that he had used for more than fifty years a collar-stud bought in *Bacchante* days, and that, when it showed signs of decay, he had it reinforced with a gold filling; and that he had used the same hairbrushes for half a century with only one re-bristling. He adhered all his life to the dress fashions of the Victorian or early Edwardian age; his gloves, his frock-coats, the side-pressing of his trousers, his curly-brimmed bowler-hats, all recalled the fashions of the first years of his father's reign; he was rigid on the subject of ceremonial dress,[1] and was always beautifully turned-out for every occasion.[2] He distrusted new or foreign fashions in music, dress and dancing. He was quite unable to assimilate, or could only partially make allowance for, the post-war spirit, the revolt of youth against the domination of the elders, a force which was to have so tremendous an effect not only on the social but on the political life of the nations.

It followed that all evidences (and these were inevitably of daily occurrence in social life) that young people were in revolt against the traditions of his own youth genuinely shocked him and evoked his frank criticism. A cigarette lit before some ceremonial occasion, a young man coming out to ride in Jodhpurs and a collared jumper, a girl riding astride, the latest methods of dancing imported from America, painted finger-nails—such innovations distressed, even shocked, him and constantly irritated him. And since he was impetuous by nature, he gave vent to his feelings instantly and without reserve. His trust in the discretion of all his Household, high and humble, moreover, was so complete that he did not stop to mince his words even in the presence of the servants, and his loud and trenchant chaff or criticism would ring out, not sparing the object of his wrath, in a publicity which obviously increased the embarrassment of a youthful victim.

This strong adherence to the traditions of the past increased

[1] As an example: looking from his window, he saw Sir Derek Keppel entering the Palace one day during the London Season, wearing a bowler-hat. He assailed him with that bluff, rough chaff which his Staff appreciated: "You scoundrel, what do you mean by coming in here in that rat-catcher fashion? You never see me dressing like that in London." "Well, Sir, you don't have to go about in buses." "Buses! Nonsense."
[2] He gave the same careful attention to details of his person. His well-shaped, sensitive hands were always beautifully kept. They are finely rendered in Sir William Reid Dick's recumbent effigy in St. George's Chapel.

as the years went on. It was a thousand pities that, with his devotion to Queen Mary and with his immense respect for her character and great ability, he did not consult her more freely about such problems and anxieties.

It must be conceded, too, that in King George's reign the sense of responsibility pertaining to his office had continually increased. The change of thought induced by the War had already radically altered the conception of the Crown and its functions held throughout the Empire, and the pen which was to make operative the Statute of Westminster would add to the weight of the Sovereign's responsibility. Thenceforward the strongest light would beat perpetually on the Throne and reveal to the least detail the conduct of its occupant and his circle. That light had not always shone very brightly on the Court of Victoria; and King Edward had reigned in a laxer, more tolerant age. It was no wonder if to King George the new responsibility which invested his lonely, exalted position seemed to justify his taking the most rigid measures for the discipline of those of the rising generation with whom he came most often in contact. Then, too, if his own youth had been passed under conditions of the warmest and most extravagantly expressed affection, in parental indulgence and general toleration, he had been professionally trained in discipline and rigid obedience. He had the quarter-deck manner and something of the quarter-deck mentality. Training and tradition alike led him to regard young men in general much as a first lieutenant regards the noisy occupants of the gun-room—young nuisances constantly in need of correction.

Yet his difficulty in bringing the rising generation and its claims and aims into a just perspective which would assure easy relations did not, as has been said, prevent him from enjoying the most pleasant intercourse with young women and men who still subscribed to some of his old-fashioned notions or otherwise deferred carefully to his opinions, and it never placed the smallest barrier between him and an understanding sympathy with children. He once remarked sadly to a friend: " I am devoted to children and good with them. But they grow up, and you can only watch them going their own way and can do nothing to stop them. Nowadays young people don't seem to care what they do or what people think." His words give a hint of an almost fatalistic belief in a barrier between generations. He more than once spoke with the same fatalism about the attitude of British sovereigns to their eldest sons in recent centuries. But—and it is an important point to make—in so far as his attitude to the rising generation affected his relations with his own sons, no misunderstandings or loss of sympathy (tragic enough while they existed) continued beyond the dates of their respective marriages. As each of his younger sons found happiness in marriage, he shed his fretting anxiety concerning that son's present doings and future, and the happiest relations were once more established.

§ 5

His gift of friendship extended to all young creatures and to the animal world. He was devoted to his own pets and to his dogs and horses. Jock, his white shooting pony, was a special favourite. Naturally he had not the time to feed and tend his own dogs; that was the duty of his valets. But he possessed a rare magnetic power over them, which his father also showed. It was noticed that the moment King George appeared on the scene, his dogs had no eye for the hand that fed them, but instantly transferred their allegiance and interest to him. He was never without a pet dog, usually a wire-haired terrier, Sealyham or Cairn. His love for his parrot Charlotte was a legend, its privileged existence occasionally a trial to his Household. Charlotte travelled with him whenever it was possible. At Sandringham every morning, punctual to the second, the King came in to breakfast with Charlotte on his finger and she ranged over the breakfast-table, messing things up to her heart's content. He kept budgerigars and retained his interest in his pigeons at Sandringham, leaving them in the care of Mr. and Mrs. Walter Jones. Rare specimens of birds from the Antipodes which were sent him as gifts would be drafted to Mrs. Fetherston-haugh's aviary and not forgotten.

§ 6

The subject has been touched on briefly enough. Stories of the King in his relations with his friends might be multiplied. Some, which illustrate these happy relations, may be read in different parts of this memoir. The verdict needs no weight of evidence, no array of documentation. The judgment of his oldest friends is conclusive enough. There never was such a master to serve, there never was such a friend.

No doubt an enchantment lies over the life of Courts. The graciousness of a prince may be a hollow thing unless a kind heart inspires it, yet the art of charming by graciousness grows with practice and is doubly potent from the exalted position of the bestower. In the palace the elegances of life are ministered to by unseen hands; brilliant uniforms and liveries, beautiful clothes and jewels, an ordered ceremonial and a smooth, unhurried, utterly efficient service play their parts in the enchantment. Such elegances, though taken entirely for granted, yet help to raise the life of Courts above the conscious effort of ordinary existence, and in doing so foster the graces and the arts of social life, by affording leisure for the purpose and by stimulating in all a higher standard of courtesy, goodwill and grace. Yet some of the King's friends were not so held by the enchanter's wand as to be unable to see him through workaday spectacles, to judge him as a man, to see his faults and failings. To one or two, no doubt, he was above criticism; he was their life and their sun, and, when he set, their lives were over. But others, whose loyalty was no less strong, formed their opinions not without critical faculties, and judged him as a man and not as a king. And their testimony is unanimous and too strong to be resisted. He was a prince in friendship. He gained their love by no exercise of social gifts, by no personal magnetism, by no intellectual powers. He was neither a wit nor a brilliant raconteur, neither well read nor well educated, and he made no great contribution to enlightened social converse. He lacked intellectual curiosity and only late in life acquired some measure of artistic taste. But if he lacked ideas, he was none the less sentient and sympathetic, in some ways even sentimental. The tragedies and sorrows of others haunted him. He could not forget his visits to war hospitals; Sir Henry Wilson's murder obsessed his mind for months, as did Lord Herbert Vane-Tempest's death in the Welsh railway disaster of January 1921.

What won and held their admiration was, first and last, his straightness [1] and his loyalty and his thoughtfulness. In him was no variableness, neither shadow of turning. He tolerated no compromise between what was white and what was black, what was right and what might be justified. He won them by his straightness, he held them by his loyalty, he charmed them by his thoughtfulness and generosity.

§ 7

In considering the King's friendships, some reference has been made to his relations with his ministers. In a political biography of a king those relations would demand the fullest examination. The present writer may deal with the subject far more briefly. It is in his relations with his ministers that a constitutional sovereign chiefly reveals his kingcraft. His ministers also are perhaps the best judges of his ability and, observing him often in times of stress and crisis, may be accepted as sound authorities on his character.

Of his chief ministers, it is significant that the first in sheer intellect seems to have thought most highly of King George's ability. Mr. Balfour, when he told Lord Esher that in his view the Prince [2] was " really clever," may have based his verdict on the soundness of King George's expressed views, on his common sense, on his simple and direct approach to the heart of a problem, on his power to see it as it affected the country and ordinary folk as a whole, and on his humility. In a word, Mr. Balfour probably thought that King George had the cleverness which a constitutional king needs. And he was a very constitutional king. He knew to a nicety (and from the start of his reign) what he might and might not do in exerting influence with his ministers or in the exer-

---

[1] " His," said Sir Derek Keppel, " was the straightest Court there ever was and the cleanest, and King George the straightest man I ever knew."
[2] The remark was made in King Edward's reign.

cise of a sovereign's prerogative. That is clearly shown in some of the quoted notes from his diary during political crises.

Mr. Asquith, too, at a time of unprecedented difficulty, came away from his first audience with the new King deeply moved by his modesty and good sense. As a footnote to history the point has already been made that in the House of Lords Crisis of 1910–1911 King George was more mortified by the lack of faith shown towards him by his ministers than by the ill-luck which brought that sharp constitutional testing to an untried, inexperienced king. He felt it as a slight on his constitutional rectitude that his Government should have forced him to announce in advance his decision to exercise his prerogative (in the creation of peers) on an issue which might not arise, and did not in fact arise. No doubt the memory of the more outspoken personal opinions of King Edward on the same crisis influenced the Government in its approch to King George. After years of close contact with him in times of trouble, Mr. Asquith came to appreciate his qualities so highly as to regard the prospect of his death as a national calamity, and he used those words in sober reality and not as a conventional expression.

In character (one of his Prime Ministers told the present writer) King George was typical of the English squire of eighteenth-century literature. He did not care for, understand or trust " the foreigner " generally. He was very vehement and talked much and noisily, expressing his opinions quickly and forcibly and quite regardless of his audience or of the possibility of being overheard.[1] But (as his secretaries found) his decisions and actions were invariably sound and restrained. He did not even pretend to comprehend the intricacies and finesse of foreign politics or diplomacy, though he was deeply interested in foreign policy. Nor was his intellect of a standard to enable him to grasp the finer points

[1] This characteristic was well known to his family and intimates. During a visit with the Queen to Chequers in 1927, he took occasion to consult Mr. Baldwin on a private matter of domestic concern. The Queen and Mrs. Baldwin were walking in the garden and every word which the King spoke floated out clearly through a garden door. With a smile to Mrs. Baldwin the Queen went up and closed it.

or the underlying considerations of any abstruse or complicated question of the day, as for example the Prayer-Book controversy or the technical questions involved in the Statute of Westminster. He was a plain, simple man, and his humility was absolutely genuine. He told Mr. Baldwin that he was really worried over the fuss made in preparation for his Jubilee. When it was over and the nation's tributes to his and the Queen's worth were clear beyond doubt, he was quite as genuinely surprised as he was gratified. Yet he felt no sense of triumph, because of his fear that his successor might not have the chance to hold together what he had built up.

Several writers have considered the influence which, legitimately and within the rights of a constitutional monarch, he may have exercised with his ministers over political events during his reign. Four such events have been named; the first in 1910 at the beginning of his reign, when he himself suggested a conference between Liberal and Conservative leaders in order to reach a compromise on the question of Home Rule for Ireland and on the relations between the two Houses of Parliament. The second in 1914, on the eve of the War, when he summoned a conference at the Palace in the hope of averting a breach between Ulster and Southern Ireland. The third in June 1921, in his carefully prepared speech at the first session of the Northern Ireland Parliament, when he made a very personal appeal for conciliation. The fourth, when, in those critical autumn days of 1931, he encouraged Mr. MacDonald to form a National Government.

A majority of these interventions, if such they may be called, failed of their designed purpose, though they redounded to the King's credit and alleviated the degree of party feeling. Three of them have already been referred to with brief quotations from his journals. One remains to be considered in its place. Apropos of it, an authority, with the best opportunity of knowing the truth, gave it as his opinion, while admitting his ignorance of the exact words which passed between the King and Mr. MacDonald, that the King's initiative in this fourth instance had perhaps been exaggerated. It may fairly be said that to select instances is of little practical utility. The influence of King George's straight and simple character was all his reign being exercised in his relations with his ministers in great events and small, within the compass of his duty as a constitutional monarch, in the light of his increasing experience which, unlike that of his ministers and subjects, was continuous, and in the light of his sound common sense, his intense patriotism and a strictly enforced impartiality.

Of his shrewdness in judging character, most of his ministers were well aware. He sized up a man with uncanny speed. He knew the crooks in politics without any coaching. One high authority, who knew him intimately most of his life, in considering the King's educational standard, gave it as his view that his early teachers did not encourage ideas in the young Princes. At the risk of a charge of repetition, the point must be stressed here. His planned education ended just where and when it should seriously have begun. He was (until he had painfully taken his own education in hand late in life) below the educational and perhaps intellectual standard of the ordinary public-school-educated country squire. He knew it and deplored it, and it gave him, from the time he became heir to the Throne, a deficiency complex which (it has been suggested) was manifested in his growing habit of " doing all the talking," of voicing too frankly and recklessly his opinions on all subjects and personalities, as though he were impelled to show his ministers that he knew something of everything and held concrete views on all the questions of the hour. The restraint and soundness of his decisions removed much if not all the dangers in such a habit.

For indeed he was a man of profound common sense, and he possessed the quality—usually ascribed to women—of going straight to the heart and essence of a problem, not by logical stages of reasoning but by intuition. Those nearest him had many opportunities of hearing him in conversation with his ministers and were constantly struck by that characteristic acumen. They noted, too, that when he spoke to them of his ministers, he never failed to present them in the most favourable light, always stressing their good qualities. Whatever may have been the political direction in which his nature might have pointed him, had he been a private citizen, none knew better than he that a constitutional king could have no politics, and none of his ministers of whatever Party had reason to question his impartiality, to complain of his partisanship, or to deny his constant courtesy, encouragement and thoughtfulness.

He brought his gift of friendship to sweeten and make easy his relations with his ministers. Letters which he wrote to Mr. Bonar Law in March 1921 and in May 1923 must have comforted a great public servant in sickness and disillusionment and have convinced him that, whoever else might misunderstand, his Sovereign had appreciated what he had striven to do, and was grateful for it.

Mr. Baldwin, when he was called to form a Government, was as little known to the King as was Mr. MacDonald. He had as a minister perhaps exchanged a dozen words with him. Yet the King seemed to have summed him up instantly, and was ready not only to trust him to the limit in constitutional matters but to make him free of all the privileges of friendship. "There must be no secrets between you and me, Baldwin. We must trust each other entirely." And so they did; Mr. Baldwin became at once a trusted minister and very soon an intimate friend.

There are several indications in his diaries that his relations with Mr. Lloyd George during the latter's premiership were generally easy and friendly. The King felt the charm of Mr. Lloyd George's personality and responded to it and often paid tribute to his helpfulness. Nor did he underrate his tremendous contribution to the victory of the Allies. A telegram which in the dark days of January 1918 he despatched to Mr. Lloyd George on the latter's birthday (the 17th January) is a tribute to the qualities of both King and Premier: " I wish to send you my hearty congratulations on your birthday and to express my entire confidence in you and am convinced with your help we shall bring this War to a victorious conclusion. . . ."

So, too, he took an instant liking to Mr. MacDonald, swiftly appreciating the most fruitful way in which to ripen his acquaintance with him. He saw that Mr. MacDonald had a scholarly mind, literary tastes and a keener sense of the past than he himself possessed, and he early made a point of conducting him among the treasures of the Library at Windsor. Mr. MacDonald's comments and footnotes, which revealed his wide reading and tastes, both pleased and interested the King and lent ease to their early relations.

With many others of his ministers and high dignitaries of Church and State he was able to employ the same gift, when he came in contact with them for any length of time. He judged men by their characters (and very shrewdly and quickly); he had no other standard of measurement. Political labels and class distinctions had no meaning for him. He was perhaps at his easiest with Mr. Asquith, Mr. Ramsay Mac-Donald, Mr. Baldwin and Mr. Thomas. Sir John Simon had a good deal to do for him in various public and in some private matters, and the King knew him well. With Sir Samuel Hoare, a Norfolk neighbour, he had been on friendly terms for years.

CHAPTER XXII

King George and Racing—His Serious Illness and Slow Recovery. 1927-29

[*Mr. Baldwin, Premier; Mr. MacDonald, Premier, June* 1929]

§ 1

EARLY in January 1927 the King and Queen said good-bye to the Duke and Duchess of York, who were leaving for Australasia in the *Renown*, and next month Princess Elizabeth was a welcome guest at the Palace. " Our sweet little grandchild Elizabeth arrived here [Buckingham Palace] yesterday & came to see us after tea." The King was already devoted to his first granddaughter and never failed to record in his diary his meetings with her and the pleasure which they gave him. From this time forward reference to " sweet little Lilibet " grow more and more frequent. He loved to play with her the games of childhood. Archbishop Lang recalled an occasion when Princess Elizabeth was the groom and the King played the part of horse. The Archbishop saw—a rare but pleasant sight—the King-Emperor shuffling on hands and knees along the floor, while the little Princess led him by his beard.

This year and the next may be reckoned as quiet years for the King. Europe had not ceased to be a danger-zone ever liable to produce problems and crises; industry had not settled down to contentment and hard work. The aftermath of the General and other strikes, despite the absence of victimisation, brought no established peace, but the Trades Unions had learned the lesson that the public would never endure dictation from a section of the nation, and the Government which broke the General Strike settled down to run its natural course. With a stable Government and a Premier whom he perfectly trusted, the King had less anxiety and no abnormally hard work. He suffered most of the technicalities of the Prayer-Book controversy in 1927 to fly over his head, and spilled no ink, at least in his diary, over the "Flappers" or Equal Franchise Bill which was the principal legislation of 1928.

He went, as he often did, to Knowsley in March to see the "National" run. He paid many agreeable calls during his April visit to Windsor, among others on Lord Rosebery at the Durdans, where the old Prime Minister, now eighty years old and paralysed, still charmed him with his conversation. He visited Lord and Lady Derby and he spent several hours one day with Mr. and Mrs. Baldwin at Chequers.

In May a chief event of the London Season was the State visit of President Doumergue, whom the King found "a nice man and easy to get on with." At the end of the month he received young Lindbergh after his first Atlantic flight and was attracted by his modesty. The usual Season's functions were carried out, and soon after meeting the Duke and Duchess of York on their return from the *Renown* tour, the King and Queen went into residence at Holyroodhouse. On their return South the King opened the Gladstone Dock at Liverpool. The Autumn holidays passed exactly as usual, though business brought the King to London from Sandringham more often than formerly.

§ 2

The years which followed brought to the King the chief successes of his career as an owner and breeder, and his interest in racing undoubtedly developed very rapidly now. It is as good a juncture as any briefly to refer to his connection with the Turf.

It has been said that at his accession King George was wounded by the malicious rumour, which perhaps had its origin in a section of Edwardian Society, that he would cut down the royal establishment and would do nothing to encourage racing. The idea implied little knowledge of the new King's character, for if one thing was certain it was that King George would "honour his father's cheques," and would turn his face against nothing worthy of which his father had approved, for which he had striven and from which he had derived pleasure. But King Edward himself had by deliberate policy limited his son's interest in racing and restricted his experience, for he had consistently discouraged him from owning racehorses. Accordingly, when he ascended the Throne and duty and inclination led him to carry on as far as possible as his father had done, King George had no great store of knowledge of the intricate business of breeding and training. Lord Marcus Beresford was manager of the royal stables, and had indeed a good opportunity to stimulate the King's interest and to teach him. But he did not take that opportunity; he was inclined to be uncommunicative and was perhaps too old to alter his ways. It was not until Major Fetherstonhaugh succeeded Lord Marcus after the War that the King's education and interest in racing advanced hand in hand.

In all his hobbies and in all sports which he pursued, it was his wish to be kept constantly informed of progress, plans and hopes, and he always found time to absorb and memorise details and facts. Major Fetherstonhaugh well understood this trait and kept the King regularly posted, and it was not long before his interest was thoroughly aroused. If racing was not among the first three favourites in the sports he pursued, he yet derived great enjoyment and interest from ownership and was never happier than in his rooms at Newmarket or in his morning rides on the Heath or among his yearlings and mares at Sandringham. He came to be a fair judge of the merits of a horse, knew a good deal about form, and was a regular attendant at the chief meetings of the year.

§ 3

1928 was a great year, for King George won his first and alas! only classic race, with Scuttle, a bay filly by Captain Cuttle out of Stained Glass. The excitement and cheering were tremendous when she won the One Thousand Guineas at Newmarket, ridden by Childs. There were great hopes that she might go on and win the Oaks, but she could only get second. Scuttle retired to the Stud in 1930, having won nearly £12,000 in stakes. A useful colt called Limelight was born in 1929, by Pharos out of Vervaine; he won a nice lot of races both as a two-year-old and three-year-old. Limelight and Scuttle were certainly the two best horses Jarvis trained for King George.

In the Summer of 1931 Major Fetherstonhaugh died. He was succeeded in the Spring of 1932 by Brig.-General Tomkinson, who was made manager of the Racing Stable, while Mrs. Fetherstonhaugh was made manager of the Breeding Stud. These appointments lasted till the death of King George in 1936.

King George liked to talk to Childs before he got up to ride a race, and was always much amused at what Childs once said when riding Limelight: " Your Majesty, I hope I shall be well outpaced." As the King said, it was a very funny way to try to win a race, but Childs was right, for Limelight liked to begin slowly and let his field lead him and then come at the end with a burst of speed to win his race.

He was very particular about the naming of his horses and always had them named as foals. He had many disappointments with his racehorses, but he was a good loser, and was always more sorry for the people connected with the horse than for himself. He had his good years, few and far between, but taking his racing career as a whole, it must be admitted that he was not a successful owner. He did not turn his face against betting. He betted in moderation and enjoyed his ventures, devoting such profits as came to him to the purchase of stamps. He liked to think that he was subsidising his favourite hobby by the fruits of his judgment of form. His betting transactions were characteristic of him and sometimes gave much amusement to his Staff. Mrs. Fetherstonhaugh would execute his betting orders and keep his account. He himself kept another in simpler form, and the London office kept a third. He was rather fussy about his betting and not seldom puzzled by its accountancy. His profits, if any, were at first paid to him by cheques drawn to " Cash," to obviate the necessity for endorsement. But he could not understand the procedure and the cheques were therefore made out in his name. Sir Frederick Ponsonby would chaffingly declare that the King was always afraid that the Privy Purse might absorb his hard-earned gains, and a good deal of joking and chaff invested the transactions. Altogether he derived a great deal of pleasure, interest and relaxation from racing, and the verdict of those who served him, here as everywhere else, confirms that he was a master in a thousand, strict and thoughtful, impetuous and generous, just and unswervingly loyal.

§ 4

The Spring and Summer of 1928 held for the King no special functions of first-rate importance.

He remained at Balmoral until the 9th October, stopping at Newcastle and Durham on his way South to perform ceremonial duties and inspections. After a short visit to Sandringham, he returned to London on the 19th November.

On the 21st November he carried out the day's duties, went through his boxes, read his *Times*, received three newly accredited ministers, had a conversation with Sir Ronald Lindsay, and walked with Sir Lionel Earle across the Palace garden to look at the new site of the summer-house recently removed from the " hill." But in the evening he complained of cold and fever and went to bed. Sir Stanley Hewett was sent for, and Lord Dawson joined him in consultation later in the evening.

A part of that day's record in his diary is in his handwriting, the rest in Queen Mary's. Since he began to keep a diary in *Bacchante* days, until this date no single day of his life had lacked its record. In the length of it, perhaps four or five times, another hand, his mother's or Queen Mary's, had taken over the duty for a day or two during his illnesses. Queen Mary was now to assume it for several months, limiting herself to a periodic record of the medical history and progress of the illness.[1]

He had been often ill, once at least very gravely, two or three times seriously; slightly ill constantly. He was susceptible to colds and coughs and shook them off slowly; he

[1] Queen Mary confined herself to a clear and simple statement of details disclosed to her and Her Majesty's account forms the basis of the narrative of the illness. But the whole was subsequently revised by Lord Dawson who, because of the great medical importance of the illness, generously drew upon his private notes of the case and has made possible a commentary sufficiently continuous and technical for the informed and yet not too scientific for the layman to follow. Here and there details by Lord Dawson which seemed out of keeping with the unscientific language of the narrative have been given in footnotes.

had suffered occasionally from rheumatism and sciatica. On the other hand, he was wiry and active in youth and capable of considerable exertion in healthy surroundings. Although he gave the appearance of fitness at the beginning of each shooting season, there was probably too severe a contrast between his manner of life in London and in the country. He was now sixty-three years old and looked his age. After his accident in France during the War, which had resulted in the fracture of his pelvis, those who observed him closely were soon aware that he was not the same man, and latterly they had not failed to observe signs that his physical powers were lessening and that he grew tired more quickly.

It was very clear to the two doctors on the night of the 21st that the King's illness was serious, but they were unable to detect any localised signs and they formed a provisional diagnosis of a blood infection.[1] Four nurses were in attendance, Sisters Purdie, Black, Davies and Gordon, from the Westminster, London, and St. Thomas's Hospitals, representatives of the nursing profession from England, Scotland, Wales and Ireland. As the second week of the illness progressed, the local manifestations were replaced by those of an increasing toxæmia which taxed the King's strength, and Sir Humphry Rolleston, Sir Farquhar Buzzard and Dr. Lionel Whitby joined Lord Dawson and Sir Stanley Hewett in the consultations.[2] At this time the general condition and especially that of the heart showed deterioration and began to cause the King's doctors increasing anxiety. By the 12th December the pleural effusion had increased and following puncture an operation was performed by Sir Hugh Rigby for

[1] A blood culture made the next day by Dr. Lionel Whitby yielded a growth of streptococcus and established this diagnosis. Early on the 23rd November confirmation was obtained by the appearance of the same streptococcus in small clots of blood which were coughed up. During the succeeding days signs of plastic pleurisy appeared over the lower portion of the right lung, chiefly involving its diaphragmatic surface.

[2] It was hoped and expected that the microbic infection would become localised in a pleural effusion, but this was not confirmed by the results of a test made at the beginning of the third week. An X-ray examination by Dr. Graham Hodgson on 8th December showed the focus of localisation to be an abscess cavity situated at the extreme base of the right lung, to the right of the centre of the diaphragm, with scanty effusion in its immediate neighbourhood.

241

the drainage of the right side of the chest, with Sir Francis
Shipway as anæsthetist. During the ensuing weeks there was
a weary struggle to overcome the exhaustion consequent on
so severe an infection, and anxiety persisted. Ray therapy by
Dr. (now Sir Robert) Woods and Dr. Frank Howitt supple-
mented the treatment, and in the last days of December the
opinion of Professor E. C. Dodds was sought on the problem
of nutrition. By the end of the year the prospects of recovery
were considered to be more firmly established.

Meanwhile, as the public was made aware of the seriousness of the King's illness, profound anxiety was shown in the
Press and gradually communicated itself to every house and
cottage in the land and throughout the Empire. Crowds
assembled regularly outside the Palace in the bitter cold, to
wait for and to read and re-read the bulletins, and thousands
would remain silently observing for long hours the comings
and goings of doctors and messengers and watching the lights
in windows which they believed to belong to the King's suite
of rooms. In those dark days of national anxiety strangers
opened their hearts to one another, and forgot their customary
reserve as they recalled and discussed their memories of the
King's constant service and example and his ceaseless interest
in the welfare of humble folk. Current and seasonable topics
and individual objectives faded from interest. Hundreds of
people who rarely went to church joined in the prayers of the
churches, which stood open day and night for intercession.
At the end of the War, the nation had realised unmistakably
that they had found an unexpected treasure in King George.
In these dark days of 1928 the whole Empire realised as clearly
that it could ill afford to lose him.

On the 4th December a Warrant was prepared for the
King's signature appointing six Councillors, any three of
whom should be empowered to execute his essential functions.
In the Warrant were named the Queen, the Prince of Wales,
the Duke of York, the Primate, Lord Hailsham and Mr.
Baldwin. On the same day the Council met in the Audience
Chamber next to the King's bedroom, the communicating
door being left open. The Home Secretary read the Order
Paper in the doorway and the King signed the document with

his own hand. On the 11th, the King was cheered by the coming of the Prince, who had made a breakneck journey home in a cruiser from East Africa in eleven days. He was obviously touched by his son's swift return and presence, and was able to whisper enquiries about the sport the Prince had had on safari. More than once later on he spoke of his kindness in hurrying home. Two more sons returned home from overseas before Christmas Day and saw their father, and by the 29th December Princess Mary felt justified in returning to Goldsborough.

§ 5

With the new year the King showed more definite signs of improvement, but not until the end of January 1929 was he able to leave his bed. In the middle of the month the doctors began to speak of moving him to the seaside. A few days later the place had been chosen. A lease was taken of Sir Arthur du Cros's house, Craigweil, at Aldwick near Bognor. On the last day of January the Queen and Princess Mary drove down to see it and to plan its rearrangement. A week or so later the doctors were satisfied that the King was on the road to recovery.

He had been very near death. All that medical science could bring to bear, all that constant skill and devotion on the part of his doctors and nurses could do, had combined to pull him through[1]; but, for his own part, having lost strength very rapidly at the start of his long illness, he owed his life more to his will to live than to his reserves of bodily strength, though it is not to be denied that, like his father, he had inherited some of the extraordinary stamina of Queen Victoria. Humble as he was at heart, he realised at that time how necessary it was that he should come through to resume his labours and to complete the edifice which stone by stone he

---

[1] Someone in an idle moment once asked Sir Farquhar Buzzard who of those round the King in his crisis had " really saved his life." Sir Farquhar replied instantly, " The Queen." He went on to explain that the Queen's complete faith in and loyalty to the doctors in attendance ensured that they could do their work without fuss, without interference, and without being compelled to consider a mass of well-intentioned advice from outside.

had built up to be the temple and fortress of Empire. A few year later, when illness struck him down again, he was tired out in mind and body, and the lamp of hope was burning with a dimmer and less steady flame; and then he could oppose no such will to enforce his waning powers.

He had come splendidly through the trial. He was by all accounts a wonderful patient. All his qualities and most of his well-known characteristics had played their part in the drama round his bed. He was as brave as his father had been. He had shown patience and philosophy in his own way. That is to say, while he had the strength, he would sometimes explode; would " damn " his doctors and their " nonsensical remedies . . ." and submit obediently to their discipline. He made his jokes even at his weakest, and showed his thought for others, when every mind in the Palace, in the Country and in the Empire was mortgaged to thought for him. He hated to give trouble, he must punctually thank those who ministered to him and show his gratitude to those who came to see him.

In that part of his illness when his mind hovered between consciousness and unconsciousness, he revealed his nature in a way which is worth setting down. Shortly before he fell ill, he had been told by one of his employees (one who was often his companion in sport, one whom he cared for and to whom he spoke freely) that this man's daughter had got into trouble (in the usual way). The father had expressed strongly his shame and grief at the dishonour to his family, and obliquely to his employer; and the King had taken his news to heart. During a period of semi-consciousness he was twice or thrice heard to recur to this conversation. The troubles of one of his own people were heavy on his mind, and he was clearly anxious lest the father should be too hard on the daughter. " —— must show mercy to her," he was heard to say; and again: " Tell —— he must treat the girl gently." That story tells us a lot about the character of a man we never knew. One other story. . . . At a time when his mind was still sometimes clouded by weakness but his strength was returning, the King began to fret at the untidy state of his beard. He much desired to have it trimmed. Lord Dawson had wished to postpone the business a little longer. But one day the King spoke of it to Sir Hugh Rigby during a visit, and Sir Hugh, seeing how much the concession would relieve the King's mind, took the risk and let the barber in, after strictly enjoining him to be silent. Later, Sir Hugh went in again and found the King delighted. " I want to see my photograph," he said (meaning " to look in a looking-glass "). It had obviously cheered him and relieved him to be once more ship-shape and Bristol-fashion.

§ 6

Saturday the 9th February proved suitable for moving him to Bognor. He was carried to an ambulance about 10.30 in the morning, attended by Sister Purdie, with Howlett on the box beside Humfrey, his chauffeur, who drove. Queen Mary saw him off and then motored down separately to meet him on arrival. He covered the sixty-five miles in under three hours. A good many people knew he was coming and there were at intervals groups of sympathetic bystanders along the country roads. Before he reached the outskirts of London, he himself pulled up the blind which hid him from the public gaze and from time to time feebly waved his hand in response to greetings. Near Pulborough, his old shipmate, Commander Hillyard, had come from his house to watch him pass. The King recognised him and later mentioned that he had done so. On arrival he was carried up to his bedroom by the same four bearers of the St. John Ambulance Corps who had carried him down from the Palace. Lady Bertha Dawkins, Sir Derek Keppel, Sir Clive Wigram, Sir Reginald Seymour and Sir Stanley Hewett formed the House-hold-in-Waiting at Craigweil.

The King was still very weak and had lost considerable weight which he could ill spare. Nearly three months had gone by since he fell ill, when on the 12th February he was permitted to smoke his first cigarette. As progress became more firmly established, his family came down and were admitted one by one to see him. By the 26th February the chest wound had healed. By the 4th March he had gained 8 lb. in weight since his arrival and was sufficiently recovered to concern himself over promises[1] newly remembered whose fulfilment had been postponed. On the 5th he performed his first " ceremonial duty," investing Sister Davies with the R.R.C., 2nd Class, before she left him. On the 9th Lord Stamfordham came down to see him. On the 10th he was judged well enough to have five teeth taken out under gas. On the 11th he had his first bath. Soon afterwards, Princess Elizabeth came to cheer him up, and he began to see a wider company, including Lord Balfour, himself an invalid, with whom he held long and cheerful converse, and the Archbishop,[2] " who was so kind and gave me his blessing." Archbishop Lang gave him besides his first Communion after his illness. It was celebrated in the house on Easter Day, the 31st March, and was remembered by King George as one of the most impressive experiences of his life. It was his own special thanksgiving for his recovery.

A military band was sent down to play to him during the Easter holiday, and he listened with pleasure to familiar tunes. When at the end the time came for the National Anthem, he turned to the Archbishop and said: " Now, that's very strange. I used to hear that good old thing almost every day, but I have not heard it now for five months. It is rather moving to hear it once again." Then he began to walk a little and to watch Princess Elizabeth at play; and he was able to see Bland and perhaps to chaff him for his " pessimism." By the end of the month he had resumed some of his constitutional functions; the two Archbishops had done homage, he had seen the Prime Minister and even addressed a few words to a crowd of sight-seers below the Sea Walk—to their unfeigned surprise and delight.

Early in April he was allowed to join the family at tea and soon at luncheon, and during the month several old friends and shipmates came over to see him. At last, on Saturday the 27th April, he was well enough to resume the writing of

---

[1] He had, for example, promised to send Lord Woolavington an album of photographs of sporting pictures and was greatly worried at the delay in despatching it.

[2] On the retirement of Archbishop Randall Davidson in 1928, Archbishop Lang was translated from the See of York to Canterbury, and Bishop William Temple from the See of Manchester to York.

his journal after five months' interval. If proof were needed of how ill he had been and how weak he still was, the change in his handwriting would afford it. It was many weeks before it returned to the normal. The weather was cold and wet early in May, but he continued to make progress, seeing more and more company and driving out to visit in the neighbourhood. One day he saw Rudyard Kipling, on another he paid a surprise visit to his father's pride and care, the Midhurst Sanatorium. There was held in the house on the 10th May a Privy Council which in the circumstances remained in the King's memory as an historic occasion. The members present were Lord Balfour, Lord Southborough, Sir John Gilmour and Sir Arthur Steel-Maitland, who stayed to luncheon after the meeting. It marked a very definite stage forward in his convalescence.

§ 7

At last, on the 15th May, the Court moved to Windsor, where he passed under the immediate care of Dr. (now Sir Henry) Martyn. Two old friends of his had recently died, Lord Revelstoke and Lord Rosebery, and their deaths affected him and perhaps his health. On the 28th May anxiety revived. He became feverish and felt wretched; there was evidence of disturbance at the site of the previous operation and the next day showed no improvement.

The 30th May was General Election Day (the Government of Mr. Baldwin having run its course while he was ill). His temperature was over 102°, and on the 31st a local abscess, caused by bone fragments from the end of a rib at the site of the previous operation, burst with prompt though temporary relief. The Prince came to see him, and gave him the Election results. Again the Socialists returned with the highest figures among Parties,[1] but with the balance of power in the hands of the Liberal remnant. On the 4th June the Prime Minister came down to place his resignation in the King's

[1] During the crisis of the King's illness, someone asked Mr. MacDonald whether he expected the early return to power of the Socialists. He replied: " The nation might recover from the shock of the King's death; it might survive a Socialist success at the Polls. But two such blows falling together . . . No."

hands. " The umpire has given me out and I do not protest,"
Mr. Baldwin said. The King sent for Mr. MacDonald. In
so far as his strength allowed, and with every help from Mr.
MacDonald, he performed his essential functions in the change
of Ministry. It was an anomalous position, which resulted
on the 5th June, when Mr. MacDonald kissed hands on his
appointment as Prime Minister but not as First Lord of the
Treasury. For there was now a Labour Prime Minister with
Conservative Ministers directing the various departments of
State. On the 7th June the outgoing Ministry came down
to surrender their seals, and on the 8th there was another
historic Council following the arrival of Mr. MacDonald's
new Cabinet. The first woman Privy Councillor (Miss
Bondfield) was sworn,[1] while Mr. Sydney Webb, at that time
a member of neither House, took the seals of the Dominions
Office. For seventeen hours the Great Seal, deposited at
Windsor, remained out of the custody of the Lord Chancellor
or his appointed Commissioners—a unique event. At this
Council Lord Dawson was admitted a Privy Councillor in
recognition of his great services during the King's illness.

Owing to the ill chance of the local abscess not having burst
over its site, drainage was incomplete and discharges continued at intervals. This fact, though depressing and a check
to convalescence, did not in itself cause anxiety. It was
decided to keep open the narrow sinus. On the 1st July he
was at last judged to be well enough to return to London.
The King and Queen drove along a restricted route to the
Palace and received a tremendous welcome in the streets.
Many houses were decorated, the route was thronged and the
crowds, forgetting their native reserve, gave rein to their
feelings. " At B.P. [the King noted in his diary] we were met
by Alfonso and all the family. We went out on to the centre
balcony where an enormous crowd cheered us. We had
indeed a wonderful reception after these long, tedious months
of illness."

Careful consideration was given to the date of the Thanks-

---

[1] The King broke the usual silence maintained at this ceremony by
saying to her, " I am pleased to be the one to receive the first woman
minister."

giving Service. The doctors made it clear that the local abscess would require further treatment for its cure, but in the circumstances agreed that the Service could be undertaken at once if reasons of State required it. Accordingly the 7th July was the day fixed for National Thanksgiving Services. As the King and Queen drove that day, between crowds enthusiastically cheering them, to Westminster Abbey, few realised what courage and endurance were called for to enable him to see the ceremony through. He was all the time in discomfort and distress from a still discharging wound, and had a shrewd suspicion that his trials were not yet over. Yet that wonderful manifestation of a people's love and loyalty could hardly have been more clearly expressed if the full truth had been known. He saw the irony and humour of the occasion and remarked to Lord Dawson and Sir Stanley Hewett on his return to the Palace: " Fancy a Thanksgiving Service with an open wound in your back." Nevertheless the Abbey service deeply moved him. That same evening his secretary wrote to the Primate: " The whole ceremony displayed reverence, dignity and ' a beauty of holiness ' which, with the setting of the glorious Abbey, seemed to complete that ' sacrifice of thanksgiving,' offered by the King and his people for ' all the benefits received ' at the hand of God."

In the further treatment of the abscess, it became plain to the King's medical advisers, included among whom was the late Mr. Wilfred Trotter, that for its cure it would be necessary to make an opening immediately over its site, which had been defined by X-ray examination. An operation for this purpose was performed on 15th July. Though his doctors appreciated that for one who had suffered so long any operation was an ordeal, they made it clear that the procedure involved but small risk and would secure the healing of the local abscess. So in the event it proved; the abscess healed steadily and by the 2nd August the King was up and dressed, seeing his family and secretaries daily. And at last, on the 24th, the doctors once more assembled (" I hope for the last time "), and willingly agreed to let him go to Sandringham.

It is touching enough to read of his delight at returning home, his surprise at the warmth of his reception, his pleasure at seeing once more his horses, dogs and birds. He had to be immensely careful, of course. It was not until the 18th September that he was suffered to dine downstairs. Thereafter he began to try his wings in further flights. On the 5th October he got on a pony, Colonel George Paynter walking beside him. On the 21st he went out to try his new 20-bore guns and, though " I did not distinguish myself," managed to kill a dozen pheasants. Gradually he resumed his shooting for an hour or so a day, always keeping an eye on the weather.

In London again on the 4th November, he was well enough to go to the theatre and obviously enjoyed himself. After a few days devoted to essential business, he returned to Sandringham and was there when the year ended, to write in his journal his envoi to 1929. " David sails for S. & E. Africa on Friday. I have had rather a terrible year with my long illness, but I am grateful to God for having spared me." No man can better than he sketch his character with that economy of words and that absence of over-statement which are the secret of literary style. If his illness had set its mark on his body, it had set its mark on his character also. For many years his character had deeply impressed itself on his intimates. Henceforward, during the few years of life which remained to him, its strength, nobility and beauty struck every man who came in contact with him for however short a time.

§ 8

" How little," once wrote Mr. Birrell, " how little is it we know about the character of a dead man we never saw." Probably a majority of those who may read this book will not claim to have seen King George, a very large majority can never have spoken to him. There is room here for another effort to bring him before the reader with greater clearness as the man he was. The broad facets of his character, admittedly, are by no means difficult to comprehend even for those who never saw him. His more personal and intimate traits are best revealed in his private conversations, his personal likes and dislikes, his daily habits and recreations, the books which he read and discussed. There is therefore real value in some memories set down by his librarian, Mr. Owen Morshead, of conversations on various occasions with his master.

The King was a careful reader, taking pains to master what he read. In reading *The World Crisis*, which he greatly admired, he would pause and work out for himself what would have happened had Admiral Sturdee, on receiving a given message at a given time, altered his course by five degrees— a point on which other readers might be content to accept Mr. Churchill's opinion. It was thus a slow process, but pursued with enjoyment over a considerable range of subjects. He was in fact well up in contemporary books.

Opening out of his study at Buckingham Palace was a shelved recess less than a room and more than a cupboard, and here he put the books that he had been reading or hoped to be able to read. From time to time he would send for me and go through them, glad that the best should go to Windsor, content with the residue for his private library at Sandringham. I would find him in his study, facing north and apt to be chilly when the wind was in that quarter; he would be reading in a low armchair, his back to the window. After perhaps some uncomplimentary remarks on the weather he would proceed, more likely than not, to ply me with cheerful banter on a well-worn theme—for he asserted, with more truth than I would concede, that librarians took no exercise. He would ask after the children, not forgetting the one who told him to shut the door, and deplore the expenses of education. " You'll have to do like these hunting men; when they marry they sell a couple of horses, and every time a child comes they sell another."

Presently he would fall to business. " What have we got this time? Well, here's *Trekking On*, by Deneys Reitz, who wrote that capital book *Commando*—did you read that? A fine man, and he tells his story well. Then here's Lloyd George; I read all those and found them very interesting— you see, he's written in them (there's his handwriting), and very kindly, too, I must say. Philip Guedalla; I don't know I'm sure—rather a pity raking out all my Grandmother's letters to old Gladstone I think, but perhaps I'm getting old-fashioned. Anyway there they are, and it's quite interesting.

Then here's Winston's life of his ancestor—no doubt everything he did was right! A bit heavy for me I expect, but I shall take it down to Sandringham and have a try; I daresay I shan't get far. Nice of him to write all that in the beginning —and you see I've stuck his letter in too. Beautiful writer he is, and a wonderful good fellow into the bargain. This is E. F. Benson on my Father; that's Dodo Benson of course— amusing writer, but I didn't find that a very nice book, I'm sorry to say. Still you'd better take it. Here are two more of those Masefields with original illustrations by himself and his daughter—nicely done, aren't they? You've got the others, so you'd better have these; all limited editions, see; it's very good of him. He was a sailor too. Here's a gallant book, *Old Soldiers Never Die*, by that private soldier who went all through the War; I've no doubt what he says is true, that about the pensions and all. Then I thought this quite an interesting one, *Queen Victoria and her Ministers*, by that M.P., Marriott; he takes half a dozen of them, you know—I expect you've read it?"

And so on, until towards the end he would be grouping them in twos and threes to get through them more quickly. Then perhaps he would set off through his rooms to show me his pictures, to which he was much attached. There was Meissonier's little masterpiece *La Rixe*, which he said was given to Prince Albert by Louis Napoleon at the time of the Crimean War; and a fine swaggering French soldier in scarlet uniform—a self-portrait of Détaille in Napoleonic costume. (He described a visit to Détaille's studio in Paris in 1908, relating with pride how Queen Mary had spotted this in a drawer of sketches while he was being conducted round the studio; she had prevailed upon the artist to let her buy it as a birthday present for him.) There were graceful Winterhalters, including the great *Florinda* group, and the cousins, Queen Victoria and her namesake the Duchess of Nemours. One by Luke Fildes of Queen Alexandra in a black dress, sad after the loss of her elder son; and an attractive Cope of King Edward VII in evening dress, genial and intimate, done posthumously at King George's wish—" and the only good one of him I've got." A pair by Partridge of Queen Victoria and the Prince Consort, two or three Landseers, the charming *Margate Sands* by Frith and other Victorian canvases.

Once he observed me eyeing a double-barrelled gun that

stood by his bedside—" not to shoot people with; I like to practise this infernal arm in the morning to try and get it right again. That's what I'm reading in bed now—young Arthur Bryant's *Samuel Pepys*. Didn't you like his life of Charles II? You remember his father, poor old Stamford-ham's secretary—served my father and me for over fifty years; and see what his son's done. Such a nice lad; I remember his being born. I must be getting very old; I think of a boy of forty as hardly grown up—how old are you?" "Forty, Sir." "Good God—then you're only a chicken too! Well, remember me to your wife—and tell her I'll be sure and shut the door next time."

CHAPTER XXIII

Statute of Westminster—The Political Crises—Lord Stamfordham's Death—Life at Windsor. 1930-32

[*Mr. MacDonald, Premier*]

§ 1

THE fateful 'thirties came in. In London the new year was one of important conferences in which the King had a notable part to play. There was the Naval Conference (the Naval Treaty was signed by Britain, the United States and Japan in April), the Press Conference, the Imperial Conference, the India Round Table Conference. Abroad, the eyes of diplomats centred on Germany, watching the stages which led up to the triumph of the Nazis. In March President Hindenburg ratified the Young Plan and Dr. Brüning became Chancellor. In June the Rhineland was completely evacuated by Allied troops. In September in the German elections, the Nazis won more than a hundred seats. All the world over, the first threatenings of the economic blizzard began to be felt.

The King was returning to normal work. He felt so much better (by contrast with the preceding year) that strenuous efforts were required to restrain him. He was watched with infinite care, and Queen Mary saw to it that all who served him in any capacity in his work and in his sport were in a benevolent conspiracy to prevent him from overtaxing his strength. He took no risks in sport, watching the weather and shortening his hours out shooting. He had done with stalking now and spared his legs whenever it was possible.

He came up specially to London on the 20th January to receive the Prime Minister and, shortly afterwards, all the delegates from Britain, France, Italy, Japan and America assembled for the Naval Conference. Next day, in the Royal

Gallery of the House of Lords, he opened the Conference in person. His speech was broadcast all over the world. He realised its importance and took special interest in its composition. There was heavy fog in London and his progress to Westminster was slowed down, increasing a nervousness which he admitted to have felt, and which in the circumstances could cause no surprise. " But," he noted, " I got through it all right."

Back at Sandringham, he fell ill again with a feverish cold at the end of the month, but by the middle of February he was at the Palace and in full work, giving frequent audience to his ministers. In March he entertained the delegates at an afternoon party and remained among them for a full hour, making as many contacts as possible. The Court moved, as usual in April, to Windsor. " I feel," he said, " very different to what I did when I was here in June last." But he knew that he must be careful. He went for his first real ride since his illness on a fine spring morning in Windsor Park, for the most part at walking pace. Towards the end of the month, the Prince, newly returned from his African tour and looking very well, flew over to see him. In May he saw his beloved Heath at Newmarket again, delighted to meet and talk with many old friends. He was present at the first Court of the Season, relieved to note that dresses were worn longer again. But before the month ended he was in intense pain once more, this time from an attack of arthritis centring in the region affected by his accident in France. He soon recovered and there is note on the 1st June of his delight in hearing Toscanini conduct the Philharmonic Orchestra at the Albert Hall.

The assembly of the Imperial Conference, with its important agenda, brought him back to London on the 30th September. Early in October he gave a big dinner-party to the delegates and received the Empire Premiers in turn in private audience. On his return to Sandringham he heard the news of the disaster to the airship, R.101 at Beauvais. On the 28th October he was once more in London to receive the Prime Minister, who was looking desperately tired, and to open Parliament in the presence of the Empire Premiers. Next month one more

Conference opened in London—the India Round Table. The Queen and he received all delegates and their wives, and talked with many of them,[1] and on the 12th November the King, still admitting to great nervousness, opened the proceedings in a broadcast speech. The remainder of the year passed between London and Sandringham.

§ 2

The full force of the economic blizzard was felt all over the world in 1931. Early in the summer a realisation of the plight of the Nation's finances was brought suddenly home to the public,[2] and resulted in the fall of the Government and the formation, under Mr. MacDonald, of a National Government. In the Spring a Spanish Republic was proclaimed under Senor Zamora, and King Alfonso left the country. The first pocket battleship was launched from German slips, and in June President Hoover proposed his moratorium. In July came the French Memorandum on Disarmament and the Seven-Power Conference sat in London. In September occurred the mutiny at Invergordon, and at the end of the month Britain went off the Gold Standard.

In December the conclusions of recent Imperial Conferences were embodied in the Statute of Westminster. If its provisions were the slow and steady evolution of thought[3] over many years and as a result of great experiences, a rationalising of the conception of Empire carried out with goodwill and understanding by all concerned, its imperial and constitutional implications were tremendous and its effect on the Crown and on the King's character and actions and thoughts

[1] He spoke for some time to Mr. Gandhi and begged him to use his influence to put a stop to the terrorist campaign then active.

[2] At the height of the financial crisis the King and Prince gave a lead by surrendering a substantial part of their incomes.

[3] Mr. Balfour's famous passage in the Report of the Imperial Conference of 1926 became the root matter of the Statute of Westminster. "Nothing [it ran] would be gained by attempting to lay down a constitution for the British Empire. . . . The Dominions . . . are autonomous communities within the British Empire, equal in status, in no way subordinate one to another in any aspect of their domestic or external affairs, though united by a common allegiance to the Crown, and freely associated as members of the British Commonwealth. But the principles of equality and similarity appropriate to status do not universally extend to functions."

during the last years of his life cannot be exaggerated.[1] From then onwards all other considerations, public and private, were subordinated in his thoughts and actions to the one supreme task and duty of so maintaining the high conception of constitutional monarchy which he had established, that that sole remaining symbol and link which bound the Empire together as a Commonwealth of free nations should continue to grow in strength and reality and remain unaffected by his death. Long years ago, during the *Ophir* tour, he had come to realise how searching a light played continuously on the occupant of the Throne of Britain and how tremendous was the influence shed by the personal character and integrity of the Sovereign. Henceforward in his view the conduct of the Royal House was of constant and vital concern to the welfare of the Empire.

That year King George lost the friend and counsellor who above all others could have claimed to have trained him in kingcraft and helped him to an understanding of the nature of constitutional monarchy. Since the *Ophir* tour began Arthur Bigge, Lord Stamfordham, had been his guide and stay, chief adviser and close friend, and he lived long enough to know that his life's work was safely accomplished. King George had reason enough to mourn his death, and preserved vivid and constant proofs of his devotion to remind him of what he had lost. Lord Stamfordham's earlier career has been sketched. In the difficult years of the reign he had proved his usefulness to the hilt. A tireless, concentrated worker, he was never in better health and form than in a crisis and he set a rigid standard to his staff. He was as punctual and orderly as his master. Every letter was answered on the day of arrival. Every detail of his conversations was added in résumé to his files. He believed that history was falsified by inaccurate recording, and it was under his direction that the arranging and cataloguing of the Archives were begun. He was always anxious to consult others and had a genius for finding the best source of outside information. Three of his most constant confidants were

---

[1] " The Crown was eliminated from the constitutional machinery; the King was suffered to survive."—Marriott: *This Realm of England.*

Lord Rosebery, Sir George Murray and Archbishop Davidson. He took a vital interest in Church appointments and made it his business to discover special preachers for the Sunday services attended by the King. If ever a man upheld King, Church and State, it was he. Above all, in serving his master he forgot himself. Every good idea which emanated from his experience was the King's, every successful action or decision he took was at the King's instigation, and he never shrank from undertaking an unpleasant duty or endeavouring to smooth out a difficult situation. The Labour Ministry of 1924 has testified in no half-hearted terms to his sympathy and kindness, his breadth and impartiality. No more efficient and faithful secretary ever served a sovereign and, in that devoted service, a country. To the King his death brought a sense of loneliness such as comes to a child (it was the Queen's simile) on parting with a devoted Nanny.

He was succeeded by Sir Clive (now Lord) Wigram, who had been a member of the Household since 1905 and since 1910 Assistant Private Secretary. During those years Sir Clive had gained the full confidence and friendship of the King and Queen and of Lord Stamfordham, and a very complete experience of the duties of his new office, an experience which stood him in good stead in the last troubled years of the reign.

§ 3

The year had opened sadly enough for the King. His sister, the Princess Royal, Duchess of Fife, died on the 4th January and he felt her loss deeply. With all the available members of the Royal Family he attended the funeral service at Windsor, where the body was to rest until its removal to Mar in the Spring. Only a fortnight later Sir Charles Cust, one of his oldest friends, died. " I had known him," wrote the King, " for 54 years." Indeed, Sir Charles was almost the first friend he made when he began his naval career as a cadet.

No doubt these griefs did not help his recovery. It was a cheerless Spring and he had little relief from routine work in London and little in the way of air and exercise save for the daily walks in the Palace garden. He was far from well when he went to Windsor for April, and very soon a severe cold turned to bronchitis, with a hacking cough and a complete loss of appetite. He felt wretched and kept to his bed for some days. He was not allowed out of doors for three full weeks, and the inaction bored him. A nurse was always with him now, Sister Black or Sister Davies, and their turns of duty were no sinecures. It seemed to be a constant struggle which he was waging, to keep illness at bay. His devotion to the two little Princesses of York—for Princess Margaret Rose had now come on the scene—affords gleams of sunshine in a rather grim record.

In the middle of the month he heard of the Spanish Revolution, and of the departure of King Alfonso from Spain. They met at Windsor on the 24th, and the King records his sorrow at King Alfonso's plight and probable poverty, and his admiration for his pluck in adversity. At the end of the month the Prince and Prince George came back from their South American tour.

He spent the months of May and June between London and Windsor, attending the Derby and carrying out the State Ceremonial at Ascot Races. After his usual visit to Newmarket, the Queen and he went into residence at Holyroodhouse early in July and performed many engagements in and near Edinburgh. At the annual garden-party in the Buckingham Palace grounds at the end of the Season many visiting delegates and their wives were present, and the King put in an appearance for an hour or more, talking to many of his guests from overseas, but he was very tired at the end of it. He went on board the yacht and prepared to enjoy his usual fortnight of racing. But an accident in the *Britannia* cost the life of his second mate, a man whom he valued highly, and most of the flavour was taken from his holiday. He returned to face one of the sharpest political crises of his reign.

§ 4

After a brief visit to Sandringham while the expected crisis was imminent, the King left for Balmoral. He was well aware that his holiday would be interrupted, and his journey

North was largely a gesture[1] to allay public anxiety concerning the seriousness of the financial crisis. He had been at Balmoral only for a matter of hours when, on the 22nd August, Sir Clive Wigram telephoned a warning that the Prime Minister would probably ask him to return. The King then and there decided to go back at once to London, and he arrived at the Palace early on Sunday, the 23rd August, to spend two of the busiest and most anxious days of his life.

It is impossible to dismiss this major national and political crisis in a sentence; equally impossible is it to give in a couple of pages even a bare outline of the political undercurrents and financial technicalities which invested it. Controversy must rage round it for years to come, and in that controversy the part played by the King will be examined. Here it is possible to give only the broad outline of the problem as the King saw it and of the chief difficulties which Mr. Mac-Donald saw only too clearly. The finances of the country were on the verge of collapse, and no satisfactory method of balancing the Budget and averting the collapse was yet even approximately acceptable to the Parties. Mr. MacDonald was already tired out and discouraged. He was constantly badgered by experts, from America, from the City, from the Treasury, from Fleet Street, urging upon him the necessity for applying this remedy or that without a day's delay, as the country's gold reserves melted before his eyes. He was in constant communication with the Party leaders. To increase the complications, Mr. Lloyd George was laid up in bed recovering from an operation, and Sir Herbert Samuel took over the leadership of the Liberal Party. At the end of every possible avenue to political compromise stood immovable barriers of Party policy, among which the question of tariffs bulked largest. Mr. MacDonald was torn by loyalties, to his own Party, which now distrusted and cold-shouldered him, to his Government, which had lost the nation's confidence, to his political career, and to his King and country. In a word, he had gone far to losing his nerve and his enthusiasm.

[1] A gesture expensive for his private purse, as he would afterwards ruefully recall. The journeys cost him about £800.

The problem, every whit as grave, presented itself more simply to the King. The country was on the verge of financial collapse, with consequences to civilisation which could not be exaggerated. It was therefore the urgent duty of every patriotic politician to forget Party differences, to forgo Party capital, to serve the State in whatever capacity best suited the nation's needs, and wholeheartedly to embrace whatever measures seemed most likely to avert disaster. He listened every hour of those busy days to the technicalities of financial expedients and to the undercurrents of political policies, but in such a crisis Party politics or personal differences among politicians seemed to him trivial and unimportant in the supreme need of saving the country. The immediate task was very clear in his mind. It was for all hands to rally to the Captain to save the Ship of State from going to pieces on a lee shore. What he had heard of the political deadlock may have suggested to him that the existing Government ought to resign, that a National Government should take its place, and that in the complications of Party differences only Mr. MacDonald could lead that Government. But his own duty was clear, to hear all sides, to compose their differences as best he could, to counsel moderation and compromise to invoke patriotism, and to encourage and re-inspire Mr. MacDonald by every means in his power. To this task he set himself unsparingly.

On that Sunday morning, the 23rd August, he received the Prime Minister at 10.30 a.m. He found him very depressed and gloomy. " He explained to me the situation both financial and political which has arisen in last few days which is a very grave one; the Cabinet is divided & he fears he will have to resign." At 12.30 he saw Sir Herbert Samuel, who made it plain that the proposals, to which the Government were prepared to agree, for balancing the Budget were unacceptable to the Liberals. Sir Herbert impressed the King as being both clear and helpful. After luncheon he received Mr. Baldwin, who expressed his willingness to take office under Mr. MacDonald if by so doing he could best serve the country's needs.

On the 24th (in the King's own words):

At 10.0 I held a conference here in Indian room with the Prime Minister, Baldwin & Samuel, & we discussed the formation of a National Government, composed of all three parties, with Ramsay MacDonald as P.M. as a temporary measure to pass the necessary economy and finance bill through the H. of C., when there would be a dissolution followed by a general election, & this was agreed to. . . .

The Prime Minister came at 4.0 & tendered his resignation, I then invited him to form a National Govt. which he agreed to do.

It was of the essence of the agreement that the General Election to follow (to which the King refers) would not be fought by the Government. There would be no " coupons." Mr. MacDonald's broadcast [1] made that perfectly clear.

After the Conference, and before the Prime Minister's return at four o'clock, a communiqué was issued to the public reporting the Palace meeting and indicating that " the formation of a National Government is under consideration." It was issued not a moment too soon. Mr. MacDonald's acceptance of the invitation implied a lull in the negotiations and the King felt free to rejoin the Queen at Balmoral. He went North again and, needless to say, lost no time in writing a word of encouragement to Mr. MacDonald.

BALMORAL CASTLE, 27th August 1931.

MY DEAR PRIME MINISTER,—After the momentous times through which we have been passing, I should like to assure you how much I appreciate and admire the courage with which you have put aside all personal and party interest in order to stand by the country in this grave national crisis. By this proof of strength of character and devotion to duty, your name will always hold an honoured place among British Statesmen.

I wish you and your colleagues every success in the difficult tasks imposed upon you.

I am happy to feel that I have been able to return to my Highland home without changing my Prime Minister, in whom I have full confidence.

The Queen & I trust you may be able to pay us a short visit here before the House of Commons meets & that you

[1] Reported in *The Times*, the 26th August, 1931.

will very soon be able to get away & have some rest. Believe me, Very sincerely yrs., G.R.I.

The brief details given afford only a faint idea of the complications and anxieties which assailed the King during those two days and give hardly a hint of what Mr. MacDonald had to face.

While at Balmoral the King was in correspondence with the Primate and referred to the crisis:

BALMORAL CASTLE, *2nd September* 1931.

MY DEAR ARCHBISHOP,—I was greatly touched by your kind letter, & I much appreciate what you say about my hurried visit to London. After all, I have only done my duty and when I realized how serious the situation both political & financial had become, I felt that it was necessary for me to be in close touch with my Prime Minister & of course he couldn't come here. Nothing could have been nicer than the leaders of the three parties were, when I suggested the formation immediately of a National Govt. & the other two at once agreed to serve under the P.M. If I had failed there would have been a national disaster in a few hours, as a general election now was out of the question. I must say the P.M. has behaved splendidly, & put his country before his party. I told him so & that I had full confidence in him & his colleagues to balance the budget, I fear they will have a most difficult and unpleasant task & when the H. of Cs. meets I expect there will be some disagreeable scenes. . . Believe me, Your sincere friend, G.R.I.

In another letter of the same period he wrote to the Archbishop: " Thank God, I am an optimist & I believe in the common sense of the people of this country, if only the situation is properly explained to them."

The King returned to London from Scotland on the 29th September, and was once more plunged in the political crisis. Mr. MacDonald was finding insuperable difficulties in persuading all Party leaders to agree to a General Election on a broad-based policy—a " Doctor's mandate "—to restore the financial and economic stability of the country by whatever means (tariffs, if necessary). Once more the King impressed on him the vital duty of saving the country. To that supreme end all patriotic politicians must combine, sinking Party differences. He was ready once more to preside at a conference of national leaders convened in the Palace, if they could come to him agreed on a settled policy. He did what he could to encourage the Prime Minister to make one more great effort.

Mr. MacDonald went away to preside over a succession of stormy Cabinet meetings. He saw the King again on the 3rd October, and once more all the King's efforts were needed to strengthen his determination to find a solution. The deadlock seemed complete. " God knows what can be done. . . . Am much worryed by political situation & I can't see a way out." His consultations with ministers were now frequent, and his interviews with Mr. Baldwin and Sir Herbert Samuel were long. Meanwhile, on the 5th, Mr. MacDonald went down to Churt to see Mr. Lloyd George. That night an important meeting of the Cabinet found the solution. The Prime Minister put to the meeting the proposal that the plan of a General Election should be dropped and that the Government should carry on. This proposal not being generally acceptable, Mr. MacDonald declared for an immediate election on a " Doctor's mandate " to save the country. The Tariff question, the main thorn in the thorny problem, was shelved rather than dropped. Each Party was to issue a separate manifesto, on lines broadly common but unfettered as regarded that question. So it was settled.

" He has," wrote the King of Mr. MacDonald, " worked hard & has shewn great patience." He himself had done no less. The confidential State documents recording his conversations and actions during those days, which future historians will study, will reveal in his words and considered actions nothing outside the functions of a constitutional king. An article by Sir Herbert Samuel on "Democracy and Monarchy" (published in the *News Chronicle* of the 6th May, 1935) may usefully be cited as authoritative evidence of the claim:

. . . It was rumoured, at the time of the financial and political crisis of 1931, that the King had exerted some kind of pressure upon the Ministers and ex-Ministers concerned in order to ensure the formation of a " National Government."

That was not the case. When the Labour Ministry resigned, the outgoing Premier, in accordance with precedent, tendered his advice as to the course to be pursued. That advice was that, in the first place, the leader of the Conservative Party and the acting leader of the Liberal Party should each be brought into consultation and their opinions invited.

His Majesty thereupon took that course. The advice as to the kind of Administration to be formed, which was submitted by both, after consultation with our respective colleagues, coincided; it agreed also with the view expressed by Mr. Ramsay MacDonald. In acting upon these identical representations, and indeed throughout the whole matter, the King pursued a course which was in the strictest accordance with our Parliamentary constitution.

The King went to Sandringham, and was still there when the result of the General Election was made known. The Conservatives had swept the board. On the Government side there were returned 472 Conservatives with 84 Liberal, Labour or Independent supporters. On the Opposition side, there were but 59 of all camps, of whom 4 represented Liberalism. In the overthrow, scores of leaders bit the dust. The King wrote down: " The Prime Minister got a majority of nearly 6,000 at Seaham which is splendid, as he had a very uphill fight, it shows what courage he has." And later on that day he added: " Please God I shall now have a little peace & less worries."

But his anxieties continued for some days. Mr. MacDonald was faced with the greatest difficulty in forming a Cabinet, and the King was constantly consulted and frequently helpful with suggestions. On the 2nd November he received Mr. Baldwin at the Palace, and their interview was protracted. At last, on the 5th November, he was able to approve the submission for the Second National Government. During these troublous days he had found time for several long talks with General Smuts, then in London, on Imperial questions and matters of world interest.

The King had always got on well with Mr. MacDonald, who had led the first Labour Government in 1924, had now been his Prime Minister since the formation of the Labour

Government of June 1929 and was to continue in that position as head of the National Government until almost the end of the King's life, when Mr. Baldwin succeeded him in June 1935.

The exchange of seals took place on the 9th November, the national character of the new Administration being revealed in the names of the principal office-holders. When next day the King said good-bye to Lord Crewe on his resignation as Secretary for War, an office which he had assumed in the September crisis, they talked of the years that were gone and of the political troubles of the reign, and once more the King went back to that conference at the Palace on the 16th November 1910, the memory of which always rankled with him. And to his chaffing attack on the plotters who forced his hand that day, Lord Crewe made the admission that perhaps they had not treated him very well. Parliament was opened on the 10th. On the 11th, the King was dissuaded from attending the Cenotaph Service, as the weather was cold and raw. He was back and forth between London and Sandringham during the rest of the month and half of December, shooting at favourable opportunities and busy with many grave matters. His " usual " cold developed just before Christmas Day and he kept to his rooms or to the house until almost the end of the year, his depression increasing when he heard the guns popping off in the coverts beyond the Norwich gates. " Goodbye, old year, not a very happy one," was his envoi. And indeed he had patiently borne a full ration of afflictions and anxieties.

He picked up again in the New Year, and shot more frequently at the end of the Season. Early in February he came back to London, and his first visit was to the hospital where Mr. MacDonald was recovering from an operation on his eye. The Disarmament Conference had now begun its sessions at Geneva. Easter was early that year and was spent by the Court in London. Before the holiday the King carried out an increasing number of minor functions. At the Castle in April his improvement continued and his activities increased. He made with the Queen a number of private visits in and around Windsor, entertained many of his ministers, and made a very full inspection one day at Aldershot.

§ 5

No doubt King George never grew so fond of Windsor as of his own home at Sandringham or of Balmoral. For one reason, the life he led there was not the kind of life he enjoyed. Windsor implied ceremonial and large-scale entertainment, and he disliked ceremonial and formality. For another thing, he had long ago come to the conclusion when he was first given the house at Frogmore, that the climate did not suit him, and later on the restrictions which Windsor imposed on his walks abroad and casual recreations no doubt helped to confirm his opinion.

Nevertheless, as the years passed, the charm of Windsor and the pride and glory of its storied past exercised over King George the same impelling attraction which almost without exception has captured and held all sovereigns who have lived there. By slow degrees and brief experiments, he began to gain interest in learning and pride in exhibiting the uncountable wealth in treasures of art and historical interest which are contained in the rooms, galleries, library and archives of the Castle. "A half hour in the library," at first an occasional concession to education, soon enough drew out to a full hour, to two hours; such explorations into history, while he was in residence, in time became frequent. Queen Mary of course gradually communicated to him her own deep interest in the wonders of the Castle, and as treasure after treasure was unearthed and properly displayed or documented, the Queen's pride and interest and some crumbs of her knowledge were absorbed by the King, and it was not long before he was finding occasions to take interested guests on personally conducted tours over the Castle, in the course of which his marvellous memory stood him in good stead; he might be heard reeling off information he had received with all the fluency (and some of the automatism) of the museum guide. And sometimes flaming "howlers" crept into the text of his discourse. But the influences of Windsor had done much to improve his taste in art, which was henceforth revealed particularly in his selection of personal gifts for friends.

Of the charm of Windsor there is no dispute. The view in

late Spring over the green country which surrounds it is all England, all poetry, all Shakespeare. It is, within, a city of enchantment, history's fairy-castle. If its gardens are somewhat stark and formal, its parklands are unmatched in beauty and romance. There is a charm, too, about the private apartments, which are lofty and light and indeed remarkably airy. The outlook from the windows is wide and some of them afford the loveliest of the Castle views. Others, the King's among them, looked eastward towards London, and from them the eye travelled across the green lawns and trees of the Home Park to where on a clear day the twin towers of the Crystal Palace could formerly be identified. Beneath his windows lay the semicircular bastion of the East Terrace, enclosing a sunk garden laid out in formal flower-beds, gay indeed but lacking in intimacy and allurement.

Some of the private rooms, in their Regency settings, with their gilded mouldings and wall-hangings of silver-green silk, their well-grouped portraits and beautiful works of art in cupboards and cabinets, are themselves like jewels. Here the Winterhalters contrive to hang " on even terms " with the Gainsboroughs and even cry out for an apology from the shade of Lytton Strachey.

The King's sitting-room was that in which George IV, William IV and the Prince Consort died. As his father left it, so King George insisted on keeping it, the red leather chairs, the stiff sofa, the mahogany bookcase and the varied range of pictures, good and bad. As it was, so it must ever be. What was good enough for his father was good enough for him. He had the most jealous eye for the slightest alteration. He knew the right place for everything. So, when a new housemaid on one occasion " put everything back wrong," the King summoned the housekeeper, Mrs. Rawlings,[1] and, striding up and down in his fury, asked her again and again *why* the girl should have done such a thing. And Mrs. Rawlings who, like everyone else in his service, was devoted to him, even (or perhaps especially) in his tantrums, made answer: " Well, Your Majesty, be sure it never will be wrong again. I'll get the room photographed." The King was startled,

[1] She retired in 1939.

impressed and silenced by the idea. And the photographs were taken.

The King's Audience Chamber, in which Privy Council meetings are held, is a jewel among jewels when dressed for ceremony. It is here that Queen Alexandra, in her superb beauty and youth, looks across at the Empress Elizabeth of Austria over the heads of grave statesmen for ever making history, a pair and peerless in the indescribable charm of their smiles. Treasures of gold and silver, gems of art, are here contained in a setting of old grey stone, the stronghold of English history.

In such a place there can be no informality. Its architecture and vastness do not lend themselves to a stroll before breakfast with the dogs, or to sunning on the terrace. Nevertheless, there were compensations. Walks round the farms and the gardens at Frogmore, those morning rides on warm April days across the park with an old friend like Lord Revelstoke, trips on the river, more frequent in earlier times, shooting days at Flemish Farm or Cranbourne Tower, informal visits to the homes of old friends in and round Windsor, and always, when the weather was unfriendly, walks and talks in the library and galleries. No man ever in a full life exhausted the interests of Windsor Castle. And if the King, who hated change of any kind, saw in Windsor a place above all to be left as it was, it has been urged as a proof of what a good husband he was that, when as often, he came upon the Queen directing a removal or superintending a replacement, he usually accepted the inevitable and afterwards approved the change.

§ 6

Returning to the Palace from Windsor, one of his first acts was once more to visit Mr. MacDonald, in hospital after another eye operation. Another Season began. The day following his sixty-seventh birthday he took the salute at the Trooping ceremony and rejoiced at the splendid discipline of the Guards. It was bitterly cold and he noted that there were fires in many rooms at the Palace. On the 8th June he unveiled the Memorial to his mother on the wall by Marlborough Gate. He enjoyed Ascot more than usual, for on the last day of the races Limelight won him the Jersey Stakes and he was touched by the enthusiasm of the crowd.

At the beginning of July he was shocked by the sudden death of King Manoel to whom he had been a good friend. He received the news at Wimbledon, where with the Queen he was watching Vines beating Austin in the Lawn Tennis Finals, and the next day (as he records) " May and I went down to Fulwell to see poor Mimi, Amélie joined her there this morning. They were both very brave, but it was a terrible shock to them, we stopped about an hour & they gave us tea." On the 8th he heard that agreement had been reached on Reparations at Lausanne, and two days later was able to congratulate the Premier who " looked tired but happy that it was all over." In his journal the King noted down his opinion that the success achieved was in large measure due to Mr. MacDonald's patience, courage and persistence.

The King then joined the yacht and steamed to Weymouth, where he put in three strenuous days with his Fleet. He inspected first the *Nelson*, then the Aircraft-carrier *Courageous*,[1] watching planes rising from and landing on her deck, then the *Hood*. After watching target-practice, he returned to London. The rest of his Season's programme followed, including the opening of Lambeth Bridge with the Queen, and the Palace garden-party which he confessed tired him very much. The same party gathered in the yacht for his Cowes holiday, and he sailed the *Britannia*, now thirty-nine years old, to four more victories. He broke his journey North to stay two nights at Harewood and then settled down for a few weeks at Balmoral. The Premier and Mr. Thomas were among the first of his ministerial guests and he got on famously with them both.

In London again on the 30th September, he heard from the Prime Minister details of the Cabinet crisis which resulted in the resignation of three Free Traders—Lord Snowden, Sir Herbert Samuel and Sir Archibald Sinclair, to whom a day or two later he bade farewell. He passed the next weeks

[1] Sunk by a German submarine, September 1939.

between London and Sandringham, opening Parliament on the 22nd November with a very long speech. A descriptive term, recently coined for application to many of the once most prosperous areas of Britain, was now current—" the Distressed Areas"—and the King had his full share of the anxiety and sorrow implicit in the words. There is a reference in his diary on the 1st December which expresses his warm approval of the terms of the Government's note to America on the War Debt question. It is followed by a brief account of the entertainment at the Palace of M. Doumergue, ex-President of the French Republic, and of Mme Doumergue. " I got on," he said, " pretty well with my French." He ended the year at Sandringham in greater heart and hope than of late. " This has been a difficult year, but God has helped me to overcome some of our troubles. The National Government is a strong one & is backed up by the Country. I am an optimist. Goodbye 1932." In that spirit he had delivered his first Christmas broadcast to the Empire.

CHAPTER XXIV

The Sovereign's Functions—The Christmas Broad-casts—The Troubles of Europe.   1933-34

[*Mr. MacDonald, Premier*]

§ I

IT is fitting that the reader should appreciate the enormous volume of work embracing every sphere of public activity which requires the attention of the Sovereign and can be delegated to no other human being while he remains in the country and well enough to move his fingers.   Ministers come into office and go into retirement, heads of departments take their holidays and forget their cares, but the King goes on working until he is released by death.   His " boxes " follow him, his office is established, whether he be at Balmoral or on a visit to Chatsworth or Newmarket or in the royal yacht.   Before or after he sails a racing yacht or goes up to the butts, there are the day's " boxes " and the day's essential routine to be carried out.

No day passes but there are documents from every one of the departments of Secretaries of State.   There are the minutes to be studied of every Cabinet and of the Committees of Imperial Defence, and résumés of proceedings in Parliament. There is a constant flow of documents emanating from the Dominions and Colonies requiring his close attention.   The Home Office " Miscellanea " range from free pardons to intestate estates vesting ultimately in the Crown.   It is the Sovereign's function to grant charters and warrants, to sanction the wearing of foreign decorations, to implement treaties and trade agreements, to execute any and every document to which the Great Seal is affixed.   No important event affecting his relations with foreign Powers directly or obliquely but he must have instant cognisance of it.   He must digest the principal reports of his diplomatic and consular representatives all over the world, must play an executive part in all appointments and commissions in his fighting services, and make the decisions which appoint his subjects to the higher posts in Church and State. He has duties, not only to his own diplomatic representatives, but to those accredited to his Court by foreign Powers. He directly appoints his last-joined subaltern and must study the character of his newest Army Commander or Minister or Ambassador.

His constitutional functions affecting Parliament and the passing of measures into law are better understood, and his relations with his Governments and the duties required of him when changes in the administration occur have received more notice in this narrative. A British constitutional monarch has in modern times been relieved of the responsibility of governing. He " reigns, but does not govern." In all political matters he is advised by ministers who are responsible to Parliament, which in turn is what it is by the will of the people. But if he be relieved of some, he is by no means relieved of most of the burden of responsibility. If he be not the mechanism of the Clock of State, he is yet its pendulum, and if he does not do his work, the clock stops.[1]

He is the head of the State. Everything that is done in his name is his personal responsibility still. His conscience requires that nothing shall pass which his experience and judgment deem to be unwise (in the interests of the country as a whole) without his first exerting all his influence to secure a reconsideration. It is not that he *may*, but that he must (and every day, in things great and small) exert his influence and employ his experience in the best interests of the country. For the King is above Party, beyond controversy, and these conditions and his continuity of office assure him the opportunity to gain an experience greater and to exercise a judgment cooler than any of his ministers. Within the compass of his abilities, a constitutional King must always influence his ministers and the history of his country; and the more conscientious he is, the more will he try to master the intricacies of the problems which face his Governments, and to

[1] During the King's illness, until the Council of State was in being, the Primate could not draw his salary! A small but illuminating point.

decide for himself if the solutions which they propose are the best and wisest. An effort has been made to show that King George was a very conscientious worker—to a fault, as some of his secretaries thought—and no more need be added to amplify the implications of his phrase, " doing my boxes." They were full enough of important matters this year in which Hitler became German Chancellor, the Reichstag was burned down, Japan and Germany withdrew from the League and the Disarmament Conference broke up in failure.

The use of the King's diary as a basis for the narrative of these years increases the difficulty of presenting fairly every side of his activities. For his journal, constantly growing briefer, deals chiefly with the routine fixtures of ceremonial, with the movements of the Court and with items of sport and family news. And all of these, save the last, were now so ordered and regulated and recur in so precise and punctual a rotation that " one day telleth another," and the very hour and date of a Court move or a covert shoot in a new year can be with practical certainty prophesied by reference to the last. If it be not recognised that wherever the King might be, there was also his office, with its implications of duty to be done and grave decisions to be taken, it might well appear that he moved along smoothly ordered lines from one residence to another to carry out a limited number of exactly planned ceremonies, to attend selected race meetings and sporting and social functions, to dine out and to entertain in reason and to shoot his own and his friends' game.

It remains, after attempting to correct that impression, to remark that no mention has been made of the cares, anxieties and responsibilities of King George in three other aspects of a more private nature: as a great landlord (a job which in these days is often described as a " full-time " one), as the head of a wide and far-flung family, and as the father of his own immediate family. It can be said at once that in these spheres he was as conscientious and as alive to his responsibilities as he was in affairs of State.

§ 2

The early Spring passed with the customary functions. He found time to go to Newbury to see his Limelight win the Spring Cup, and his April visit to Windsor followed its usual lines. His " usual " cold, too, punctually developed and was followed by a sharp attack of neuritis, which remained with him until well into the Season and prevented him from putting on uniform for the first Court. His accession-day came round and caused him a shock of surprise at the swift passage of time. He had reigned twenty-three years already. He saw Hyperion win the Derby and gave his dinner to the Jockey Club, but the Prince took his place at the Trooping of the Colour. Limelight triumphed again at Ascot, and the King was delighted. He returned to London to receive King Feisal of Iraq at Victoria and to entertain him during a State visit, but he was unfit for many of the usual Season's fixtures and put in an appearance only at the fifth and last Court. His summer visit to Newmarket was a very happy one, for the meeting proved a triumph for his stable. With the Queen, he paid a visit to Chatsworth [1] early in July to attend the " Royal " at Derby. But the programme afforded some leisure hours, and he enjoyed his visits to Haddon and Hardwick. His yachting and Autumn holidays followed precisely the lines of the previous year, and he returned to London at the end of September to see Limelight crown the achievements of a glorious year in the Duke of York Handicap at Kempton. He opened Parliament on the 21st November in a speech of abnormal length, which he was thankful to accomplish without a hitch.

§ 3

On Christmas Day of 1932 an innovation had been introduced into his traditional programme. He gave a short broadcast address [2] from Sandringham to the whole Empire.

---

[1] After his illness, King George practically abandoned the habit of visiting the houses of his friends.

[2] It was not, of course, the first time that his voice had been heard on the radio. The first occasion was on the 23rd April, 1924, at Wembley, when he opened the Empire Exhibition.

This message was a feature of the succeeding Christmas Days which he was to see. He referred to it in his characteristic way in his journal: " At 3.35 I broadcasted a short message of 251 words to the whole Empire from Francis' room." [1]

Those " 251 words " had been chosen and arranged with infinite care, and the King himself had weighed and scrutinised every one of them. The homely simplicity and kindliness of his latest addresses to the Country and Empire had been widely appreciated, and had strangely moved all who heard them since the day on which he had returned thanks to the Empire for its sympathy in his illness. He knew himself now to be regarded as the Father of the great Family of Nations which the Statute of Westminster bound only more closely together under his leadership when it severed certain less personal ties. It was as a father of a family and the Father of the larger family of nations that he spoke each year those Christmas messages and he chose ideas, and words to clothe them, which suited the occasion, the conditions and the character of the man who would speak them. The very simplicity of thought and the chosen words gave them the King's authentic signature. He was a simple, natural, frank and friendly man and his favourite words were like himself.

Shortly before the time fixed, he walked along the corridor to a little room which Lord Knollys had once used as an office, tucked away in a corner beside the private stairs and looking on to the front drive. This little ground-floor room, which the King himself never entered in the normal course, best satisfied the requirements of broadcasting. It was furnished simply enough as an office and the King sat before a small walnut table to deliver his message.

. . . . . .

It is not surprising that he appealed in these Christmas broadcasts to so large a proportion of his hearers. He and they had come to know each other, had in the dark and troubled years of his reign been through much together, had

[1] The brief reference is silent about his intense nervousness which practice did not mitigate and which increased as the moment of delivery drew near. He said more than once that the Christmas broadcasts spoilt his Christmas Day.

made common sacrifices, had hoped and feared, toiled and suffered and triumphed at last. Even as they remembered their own individual efforts, their sufferings and sacrifices and anxieties, they recalled that he had shared them, and spent himself and had not been left unmarked.

Some remembered an era when life was easier to live, when the weight of domestic cares was not so heavy, when to keep home and family together was not in itself a life's work. Others in a different walk of life could see in the passage of time from youth to middle age emancipation to a more colourful and perhaps a healthier and happier existence. But whether they looked back across the years to times harsher or happier, all remembered that this man who spoke had made the journey with them, led the march and set the pace, and had come to know very shrewdly where the shoe pinched. He had seen their homes and talked with them of their gains and losses, their problems solved and to solve. He knew a great deal about the difficulties of their lives, wherever they lived and to whatever class they belonged.

The younger generation, too, had come to know his worth. In those four strenuous years of war and war engagements, was there any institution affecting youth or age to which he had not paid the most careful attention? Fighting men had seen him pass, spoken with him, perhaps, on the broken roads of France and Flanders, on one or other of his six visits to the Front. No King of England had ever been so widely travelled in the Empire, so familiar with life in township and outpost, on land and sea. The man who spoke was the Symbol of Empire, the only surviving tie which held its components together. But he was more than that. In the manner of his life of duty and service he was its exemplar. In the simplicity and kindliness of his nature he was indeed the Father of his People. And as he spoke the words of his message, everyone who listened seemed for a moment to be in the room with him in his own home at Sandringham, and to be sharing with him those kindly ceremonies of an English squire's Christmas Day, which our literature and our traditions have hallowed and made dear, all the Empire over.

In the first Christmas broadcast he spoke of the wonders of science which had made possible such an intimate message from his home to every home in his Empire. He spoke of trials past and tests to come and of the work before us to attain peace within our borders, to regain prosperity without self-seeking and to carry with us all whom the burden of past years had overborne.

My life's aim has been to serve as I might towards those ends. Your loyalty, your confidence in me, has been my abundant reward. I speak now from my home and my heart to you all; to men and women so cut off by the snows, the desert or the sea that only voices out of the air can reach them; to those cut off from fuller life by blindness, sickness or infirmity, and to those who are celebrating this day with their children and their grandchildren—to all, to each, I wish a happy Christmas. God bless you.

None who heard it but saw the man who spoke, was with him alone in the little room, and received the final blessing as one given to him personally by his King.

   .   .   .   .   .   .

The broadcasts were interludes in those Christmas ceremonies at Sandringham which have more than once been referred to and yet demand one more note. The regular features of the Christmas days were endeared to King George by tradition and by memories extending back more than sixty years. When Sandringham House had only just been completed, many of them had been planned by his father and mother to give pleasure to him and to Prince Eddy and their young sisters. And now that his own sons were marrying one by one and there were grandchildren to keep alive in their elders the special joys and excitements of the season, the old enchantment of Christmas Day still held him and made of him a central figure radiating kindliness and cheerfulness upon grown-ups and children. Not only for the young Princesses but for the King and Queen, for his sons and for the Duchesses, the Christmas holidays at Sandringham were the most happy and joyous occasions—and memories. So one more year drew to an end at Sandringham and he wrote its epitaph. It had been full enough of worries and anxieties, but he felt much more hopeful about the future than he had been for some time.

§ 4

The year 1934 was another fateful year for Civilisation. Events in Germany outweighed in importance all others. In January came the German-Polish agreement, in February the suppression of the Austrian Socialist Party, in June the meeting in Venice of Hitler and Mussolini, and the " Thirtieth of June," with its mass executions in the Reich. In July the Austrian Putsch and the murder of Dr. Dollfuss, in August the death of Field-Marshal Hindenburg and the emergence of Hitler as Chancellor and Führer. Elsewhere significant events were not wanting. In January came the devaluation of the American dollar, in February there was rioting in Paris streets and the Doumergue-Barthou Cabinet was formed. In the same month died King Albert of the Belgians. In March Pi-Yu was enthroned by the Japanese as Emperor of Manchukuo, and in September the U.S.S.R. was admitted a member of the League. October brought the assassination of King Alexander of Jugo-Slavia and M. Barthou at Marseilles, and December the fighting at Wal Wal and the rejection by Italy of settlement by arbitration of the Abyssinian question. A year full enough of trouble and anxiety for King George and his ministers.

He was able to maintain his ever-growing interest in racing, enjoying his May week at Newmarket, and he entertained Mr. MacDonald in his private stand at Kempton, noting that it was the first visit the Premier had ever paid to a racecourse. He saw Windsor Lad win the Derby on the day on which he learned from Sir John Simon of the failure of the vital conference at Geneva. In the middle of June he received the Belgian mission which came to announce the succession to King Albert. He continued to increase his contacts with all manner of men in many spheres of national life, was photographed at Windsor in a group of Australian Test players, watched a Test Match at Lord's and paid his usual visits to

Wimbledon. One day the Queen and he entertained President Roosevelt's mother, " a charming old lady (79)."

The Queen and he went to Holyroodhouse for the usual week's stay in July and on the return he opened the new Mersey Tunnel and made a tour of Manchester and Liverpool. His yachting holiday followed. The old *Britannia* was forty-one years old now and had carried her record to 231 first prizes and 124 others in 569 starts. With the same party of tried and enthusiastic yachting friends and with glorious sailing, his fortnight at Cowes was still for him the brightest spot and the best restorative in the year. It was fifty-five years since he and Prince Eddy had joined the *Bacchante* from Cowes.

From Balmoral on the 26th September the Queen and he travelled to Glasgow for the launching and christening by the Queen of the great new liner from John Brown's yard at Clydebank. It was an arduous day, carried out in terribly wet weather. They travelled four hundred miles by train and thirty more by road, and though the ceremony went without a hitch and the great vessel, named the *Queen Mary*, slipped into the river Clyde according to plan, the King felt deep sympathy for the drenched crowds which numbered nearly a quarter of a million people.

In London again, he saw the Premier on his return from a holiday in Newfoundland, and one of his first official acts was to preside at a Council called to give his consent to the marriage of Prince George [1] and Princess Marina of Greece. He had warmly welcomed and admired his new daughter-in-law on her first visit to Balmoral. " Marina," he wrote, " is looking very pretty & is charming & will be a great addition to the family." In the months which followed he often spoke of his pride in her beauty and from the first was a tower of strength and comfort to her. The wedding was celebrated in the Abbey on the 29th November, and for some days before it the King and Queen were busy entertaining the guests. It was remarked how cheerful he was on this occasion, and he was obviously delighted at the enthusiasm shown by the London crowds. When it was over, he went off to Sandringham, but he caught a bad cold, a hacking cough developed

[1] Created Duke of Kent in October 1934.

and he missed a week of the shooting to which he had looked forward. Before he left London, he had written to thank the Primate for his share in the success of the wedding ceremonies:

1st Dec. 1934.—. . . I shall never forget the beautiful service in the Abbey, so simple & yet so dignified, which greatly impressed the Foreigners & indeed all that were present. Then the enormous crowds in the streets & especially the one outside the Palace, who showed their love & affection for us & our family, by their enthusiasm, impressed us more than I can say & we deeply appreciated it. I must thank you for all that you did in arranging & carrying out the two services, which we drew up more or less at Balmoral. The Prime Minister and Jim Thomas both came up to me after the breakfast & said, this is a great day for England! . . . You are one of my oldest friends and I always appreciate your kind words. Believe me, always yr sincere old friend, GEORGE R.I.

CHAPTER XXV

The Jubilee—Mr. MacDonald's Resignation—Duke of Gloucester's Marriage—Princess Victoria's Death —Last Days, Illness and Death of King George 1935-36

[*Mr. MacDonald, Premier; Mr. Baldwin, Premier, June* 1935]

§ 1

THE last full year of the King's life came in. Inevitably it is a record of " last times." He recovered from his cold and managed to get out with the guns before the shooting season ended. But he was soon tired and was now clearly unfit for even a short day's covert shooting.

Soon after his return to London in the middle of February, there came another innovation into his ordered routine. The Duke of Devonshire put Compton Place, Eastbourne, at his disposal and the Court moved down there on the 26th. " We all stayed here," he recalled, " in 1892 after Eddy died." He found it very comfortable and remained a full month, paying some visits, making many local expeditions, and seeing a number of old shipmates who lived in the neighbourhood. A remark he made to one of his staff concerning this visit deserves a place here for the light it throws on his character. " We found," he said, " such a fine fellow as parson there. He filled his church to overflowing every Sunday we went to it." No doubt the King never realised the extent to which his presence and the Queen's contributed to that happy state of affairs.

The Silver Jubilee was now drawing near. He was diffident about the immense public interest in the occasion and the scale of the preparations. " All this fuss and expense," he would grumble, " about our Jubilee. What will people think of it, in these hard and anxious times?" During April at Windsor he received and talked with many Empire statesmen and Indian Princes. Then the Court moved back to London for the Jubilee weeks. He went up for the ceremonies in quite good spirits. He had Sir Richard Molyneux as his companion on the drive to London, and, when near Staines they saw the first of the Outer London decorations, " I suppose," he said whimsically, " you think those flags are hung out for you? Let me tell you [with a bow, his hand on his heart] they're all for ME."

It is not improbable that the strain of those continuous ceremonies, although regulated to his strength, hastened his death. Unquestionably the realisation they brought him of the trust and love and veneration which the Nation and Empire felt for him gave him, at a time of deep anxiety and failing health, a brief stimulus and a lasting pride and thankfulness. That realisation, we must believe, came as a surprise to him.

The 6th May dawned fair and warm, glorious as only a May day in England can be.

A never to be forgotten day, when we celebrated our Silver Jubilee. It was a glorious summer's day, 75° in the shade. The greatest number of people in the streets that I have ever seen in my life, the enthusiasm was indeed most touching. May & I drove alone with six greys. . . . The thanksgiving Service in St. Paul's Cathedral was very fine. 4,406 people present. . . . On our return we went out on the centre balcony & were cheered by an enormous crowd. . . . By only one post in the morning, I received 610 letters.

For the rest of the month, and into June, hardly a day passed without its Jubilee functions and ceremonies. There were addresses and congratulations to be received from the Houses of Parliament, the Empire representatives, the Corps Diplomatique and the foreign Courts, from the City of London and other great cities, and from representatives in many fields of national life. And to each and all he was called on for a carefully prepared reply. Most of these ceremonies were moving and memorable. Two stand out. The reception of the Dominion Prime Ministers and other Empire representatives was a unique occasion, a " family party " of tremendous significance, of which the King's speech took ample note. There in London were met together from every part of the Empire chosen representatives to do honour to the King and to the Queen, to the head of the great family of nations. Through the bewildering changes and chances of the last twenty-five years, constitutional, economic and social, all those who now met together had played their worthy parts in the consolidation of that great league of nations. The King and his sons had visited and gained intimate knowledge of every component of the Empire whose members had rallied unreservedly to the flag in times of greatest danger. From great experiences and heavy sacrifices shared, and from difficulties that had seemed insurmountable overcome, had developed close personal friendships and the sympathy and respect which sweeten human intercourse. It was a family party which none who attended it ever forgot—least of all King George.

And—no whit less memorable—that ceremony in Westminster Hall, when the trappings of State were laid aside and the Queen and he listened to the speeches of the Lord Chancellor and the Speaker and to the singing of the National Anthem by a full muster of members representative of both Houses. At that simple, informal meeting he learned the truth, if any of the truth remained hidden from him, and his short speech of ten minutes given in reply was spoken straight from his heart and broken with emotion.[1] " Their cheers moved me very much," he wrote in his diary.

The same clear evidence of his worth in the public mind was given in those famous drives to all parts of London. Each day's progress brought him fresh emotions and fresh surprises. He was astonished by the enthusiasm and the fine display of decorations in the poorer quarters and meaner streets. And night after night there were State dinners, concerts, gala performances. . . . His daily correspondence

---

[1] It was recorded for the gramophone. When, at the end of it, he made a reference to the Queen, the record reveals that his voice failed him. He knew that this would happen, and had said to his secretary when he was preparing the draft of the reply: "Put that paragraph at the very end. I can't trust myself to speak of the Queen when I think of all I owe her."

was an added labour, not fully foreseen. The 610 letters delivered by the first post on the 6th May proved neither a record nor an isolated occurrence. On the next day he received over a thousand such personal congratulations and for weeks to come the daily average seems to have exceeded 300. He was still coping with them when his birthday came round: " My old birthday (70)," and the flood-gates opened again. At his Jockey Club dinner following the Derby, the members presented him with a picture of Limelight, and scores of presents flowed in to add to the rich and varied treasures that filled the Palace and needed acknowledgment.

On the 7th June Mr. MacDonald was received and resigned the Premiership. It was no surprise to the King, for Mr. MacDonald had long been struggling bravely against ill-health. On the same day, he wrote to his retiring Premier:

BUCKINGHAM PALACE, 7th June 1935.

MY DEAR MR. RAMSAY MACDONALD,—It was with feelings of true regret that I accepted your resignation this afternoon. I fully realise, however, the serious demands made upon your health by the strenuous and exacting duties of your high office.

You have been my Prime Minister for seven out of the twenty-five eventful years of my Reign, and I gratefully recognise the sacrifice of old associations and friendships which you faced in 1931 to form a National Administration. During the succeeding four years the National Government, with you at the helm, has been successful in steering the Ship of State into smoother waters.

It has been a relief to me to feel that I had a stable Government under your leadership, and that in times of anxiety I could turn to you with confidence.

I rejoice to think that I shall frequently have an opportunity of seeing you, as Lord President of the Council, and of continuing those happy relations which have existed between us for many years.

It must be a source of pride to feel that your family have the unique record of father and son being Members of the same Cabinet. Believe me, Very sincerely and gratefully yours, GEORGE R.I.

The King later sent for Mr. Baldwin and the exchange of the necessary seals was carried out. He was again suffering from a bad cough and was very tired. After a final State drive through London on the 8th June he got away to Sandringham, convinced at last, proud and happy to know, that his long and faithful service had been appreciated. But he was desperately in need of rest.

It is fitting that some reference should here be made to the dignity and ease with which the King and Queen had long since invested the ceremonial functions of the Sovereign. Their entries and exits in procession, their every movement during ceremonies of great constitutional and of social importance alike, were instinct with a simple dignity which was truly majestic and were carried out with an ease that was less the result of long familiarity than of consciousness of the majesty of their office, a consciousness which perhaps the great Coronation Durbar had first fully awakened. Amid the high officers of State and gorgeous officials, they often appeared to be the only natural figures in a dream-pageant, and yet, to an observer watching them with the strictly professional eye of a pageant-master, the technique apparent in their actions and carriage might well have been judged the perfection of dramatic art. Royal ceremonies in Britain have increasingly impressed foreign observers and are admittedly masterpieces of stage management and performance. But the grace, ease and dignity of the central figures which since the Edwardian age have set the seal on such ceremonies have owed nothing to art and little to practice; much, very much, to the characters and *consciousness* of the individuals who have held the centre of the stage. To King Edward VII ceremonial majesty came easily, pageantry was for him the breath of life. It was otherwise with King George. He was a simple, shy man who disliked ceremony, and the dignity and grace with which he played his part in it had their source in his wholly impersonal consciousness of his great office and in the simplicity of his nature.

§ 2

A chief function on his return to London was the reception of delegates to the Empire Parliamentary Conference, then assembled. His next visit—to the Fleet—was in the nature of a deferred Jubilee item. The royal party drove through dense crowds (nearly half a million) in the streets of Portsmouth and was cheered to the echo. In the royal yacht he steamed between the lines of the Fleet which numbered 160 ships and 40,000 officers and men. It was a tiring day for him, for he was on his legs for long hours and a good deal of entertaining of the senior officers was included in the programme, but he was obviously interested in all he saw during this last contact with the men of his own Service.

Cowes followed. It was in any case to be the *Britannia's* last season. Once more he sailed the old yacht in which he had passed so many happy hours during the course of his life, and those who sailed with him noted how the charm still worked. For a brief time he became more like his old self, lent a hand where he could, and cracked his jokes with the crew. But for once there were no first prizes. The old yacht's day was over and he made the decision to lay her up permanently at the end of the season.

From Cowes to Balmoral, one more long farewell before him. On the 29th August he wrote in his journal: " I have given my consent with great pleasure to Harry being engaged to Alice Scott, John Buccleuch's 3rd daughter. It will appear in the papers tomorrow." On the next day, Lady Alice with the Duchess of Buccleuch arrived at Balmoral. " She seems charming," wrote the King, who then met her for the first time, " and is nice looking." He was delighted once more with his new daughter-in-law, daughter of one of his oldest friends who had made the *Bacchante* cruises with him more than fifty years before and had kept up correspondence with him ever since. The Duke of Buccleuch was very ill, but he wrote a letter which greatly touched and pleased the King who carried it with him for a day or two and would pull it out and consult it when he spoke of his pleasure to old friends. To his great grief the Duke died before the wedding. He went out shooting occasionally during that last holiday and took part in deer-drives. On the 23rd September he killed his last stag and next day used his gun for the last time in Scotland, taking part in a scratch day in search of black game.

He was at Sandringham on the 11th October, with another

cold which kept him indoors for several days, but he was well enough to pay one more visit to Newmarket on the 16th to see the Cesarewitch run, and he talked with many old friends on the course. He returned soon afterwards to London and at the end of October was shocked by the sudden death of Lord Sysonby (Sir Frederick Ponsonby), who had since 1914 been Keeper of the Privy Purse. It was the breaking of a very old tie. Lord Sysonby's experience at the time of his death was unique, for his service at Court dated back to 1894. If his character was contradictory, his gifts were great. On all social problems and matters of etiquette he was the court of first instance and final court of appeal. His knowledge of Germany was invaluable. His resource, his conversational gifts, his wit, his faultless manners, adorned and sweetened life in the royal circle.

The 6th November was the wedding-day of the Duke of Gloucester. It was celebrated in the private chapel of the Palace, and owing to the Duke of Buccleuch's death was a very simple ceremony. " Now," wrote the King, after a brief account of the wedding and the departure of the bride and bridegroom to Boughton, " now, all the children are married but David."

§ 3

On the 11th November he went back to Sandringham without attending the Cenotaph ceremony. The 14th November gives the last record of his going out shooting. It was the Grimston Carr beat and the bag was satisfactory. It was the day of the General Election which confirmed the National Government again by a substantial majority. On the 15th he felt giddy and thought it best to stay at home, but he managed to get through a good deal of business.

On the 18th he returned to London, and spent many hours with his ministers. There had been matters enough to claim his attention all the year through, and now the invasion of Abyssinia by Italy was in progress. Then on the 20th another old friend of fifty years, Lord Jellicoe, died. Blow followed blow and loss succeeded loss in these last days of his life, and it is small wonder if important political events occupy less space in his ever-briefer diary entries. Towards the end of November he was in intense anxiety for his sister, Princess Victoria, and she died on the 3rd December. Her death hastened his own. The blow which struck him was physical as well as spiritual. " How I shall miss her & our daily talks on the telephone.[1] No one had a sister like her." The funeral at Windsor was a terrible ordeal for him. It is to be noted that from the day of her death his handwriting underwent an obvious change. Henceforth he found writing difficult.

He went back to his work, and on the 20th December the Prime Minister came to see him before his departure to Sandringham. They spoke of the resignation of Sir Samuel Hoare and of the political situation at home and abroad, and turned then to discuss private matters. At the end they spoke for a moment of the Christmas holiday. Both were to be at home with their children and grandchildren, and they agreed that that was the happiest way to spend it. Mr. Baldwin of late had seen the King worried by public and private matters, tired and constantly anxious about the future. At this last interview in London it seemed to him that a new serenity had replaced the fretting cares of past months. The King appeared to him like a man who had seen the end of his life's work for better or worse, and was now prepared to leave the future of his Empire to Providence and the past to the judgment of God and man. Perhaps he had worried too much, trusted of late too little in the great destiny of his peoples and derived less than his usual support from his simple religious faith. Like Prospero in the last scenes of the *Tempest*, he saw perhaps the limits of man's power to direct events or avert disasters, and in calmness and faith waited for his own life to be rounded by the sleep he was in sore need of.

[1] There is a charming story which he more than once told with zest concerning these daily talks. It illustrates very well his relations with his sister and his own sense of humour. " Every morning," he would relate, " I ring up my sister at half-past nine, just to have a chat. Of course, we're not always too polite. One morning her telephone bell rang at the usual time and she took up the receiver and said, ' Hullo, you old fool.' And the voice of the operator broke in, ' Beg pardon, Your Royal Highness, His Majesty is not yet on the line.' "

Before leaving for Sandringham next day, he took leave of Sir Samuel Hoare, an old friend. Certainly he went home for the last time a very sick man. The world was slipping from him. Recently so many of his oldest friends had gone. The last stage of his journey had been measured with stones of remembrance.

§ 4

With the Queen and his granddaughters he arrived home in icy weather. There was no question now of his going out shooting. He had fired his last cartridge. He was well enough to take part in the time-honoured ceremonies of the season. He went to church on the Sundays and on Christmas Day and stayed for the Communion Service. Some ministers arrived to receive their seals. On Christmas Day he gave his presents and broadcast the last of his Christmas messages to the Empire. It was perhaps the most moving of all which he gave, for his voice was weaker and an abundant kindliness and humanity warmed his last blessing to his far-flung family. *Ave atque vale.* Many thousands who heard him that afternoon must have taken his blessing for a long farewell.[1]

In the days that remained to him he would drive out with the Queen and ride a little when the weather was favourable. Some of his guests would walk beside his pony as he visited parts of his estate. If he walked at all, he was compelled to stop for breath every hundred yards. In the evenings he

[1] In letters which he wrote under various dates between 1932 and 1935 to the Primate, the King revealed his opinions about the Christmas broadcasts.

Writing at the end of December 1932, he said: " I am glad you approved my message which I broadcasted to the Empire on Xmas Day, it was not easy to find some simple words which everyone could understand, spoken in 1½ minutes; anyhow they came from my heart & if they were appreciated I am happy."

For the remainder of the Christmas broadcasts the Archbishop helped the King in the choice of the words, and this the King acknowledged in a letter at the end of December 1935. " From the bottom of my heart I thank you for all the trouble you took about the Christmas Day message. Everyone said it was the best I have done yet. What more could be said in its praise? I suppose it does give pleasure, but it is rather an effort for me. No doubt it brings me into close touch with my peoples all over the world, & that of course I am very keen about."

played with his granddaughters and saw his " Kent grandson [1] in his bath," and he attended films in the evening, though they always seemed to him now to last too long. At the end, indeed, he would fall asleep at meals and force himself awake again with obvious distress.

§ 5

He had carried on to the limit of his physical powers and when death came he was at the end of his road. Although he made a remarkable recovery from his long illness in 1928, there remained a damaged heart, and an increasing liability to bronchial attacks and to rheumatism, the latter in part at least a legacy from his serious accident in France during the War. As he himself said, " I have not been the same." Yet during those last seven years—anxious, even critical, years crowded with events—the Empire had the advantage of his constant labour and counsel and enjoyed constitutional sovereignty at its best.

It may be asked how in the circumstances were those labours accomplished. First, by the unremitting care of the Queen and the devotion to duty of Sister Black and his personal attendants. His life was so planned as to enable him to do his work, to keep contact with people and things and to enjoy his outdoor pursuits within the limits of his strength. His interests never flagged; he became at no time an invalid. The celebration of the Jubilee with its revelation of his people's gratitude and admiration brought him happiness and therefore strength; his realisation that a great purpose had been fulfilled helped to maintain his vitality during those last months of his life. The rest which he had at Sandringham during Ascot week helped to spare his body from undue fatigue, so that when he paid his last visit to the Navy before Cowes regatta he looked indeed fitter and happier than in some previous years. But above all the triumph of those years and those last months of duty was a triumph of character. Right down to the final official act of his life, his

---

[1] He was immensely proud of the baby's health, strength and beauty, and delighted in watching him put to bed, offering expert advice to the nurse.

spirit sustained him when his bodily powers were failing him.

It was almost his last shoot at Sandringham that he had shared with his old friend, George Brereton. They had been out together and finished up before luncheon at Parson's Clump. The King was obviously tired. " Well, Mr. Brereton," he said, " I think I must go home." " Yes, go, Sir, we've had a nice morning's sport." And so the two old friends parted.

§ 6

On the 15th January the King went early to bed and on the 16th remained in his room, attended by Sir Stanley Hewett and Sir Frederic Willans. Sister Davies came to share duty with Sister Black. He wrote up his diary that day and tried to do so on the next, the 17th. But the last words he wrote in that punctually and faithfully kept record of his years from boyhood are barely decipherable. There is some reference to snow and to the wind, and the words: " Dawson arrived this evening, I saw him & feel rotten." The next word, the last he wrote in his diary, is but half formed. He had completed the final page of one more leather-bound volume, and there is a note in Queen Mary's hand [1] explaining how much distressed he had been at the bad writing and how he had asked her, as once or twice before in illness, to write his journal for him next day.

§ 7

The last hours of the King's life will need no recalling to scores of thousands of men and women. He died, as he had lived, close to the people of his Empire, and it seemed that his death-bed was brought within reach of every home in the Commonwealth. While they waited for the inevitable hour, very many of them went back in memory over the history of that troubled reign and recaptured their impressions of the

---

[1] " My dearest husband King Geo V. was much distressed at the bad handwriting above & begged me to write his diary for him the next day. He passed away on January 20th at 5 minutes before midnight.
" MARY R.
"Feb. 14. 1936."

King they had learned to prize so highly. They had doubted him, for he was little known to the public when his dazzling father died. They had doubted while they sympathised with an untried man launched, before he was equipped, into a stormy sea of trouble. And they recalled how very soon evidence of character emerged, how before the First Great War came the new King and Queen had " struck out a line of their own," and how in a series of notable visits to many great industrial centres they had shown a determination to learn and to understand the problems of industry and the difficulties and aspirations of working men and women. They recalled the War years, reminded one another of the King's war service, the everlasting round of visits to troops and hospitals, industrial and social centres, the visits to France and to the Fleets and to the Air Force, the constant investitures, the innumerable speeches, the ceaseless work, the broadening and beneficent influence of his example in duty, courage, patience and simplicity of living; of his faith in God and in his Empire. It had been no mere impulse of relief that had led them on many occasions since that distant Armistice Day to cheer him to the echo from the railings of the Palace and in the streets of London.

There had sat on the throne of England sovereigns more brilliant, more able, more romantic. None who, reigning during an era of hitherto unparalleled danger and ceaseless anxiety, had carried out his functions with a sense of duty so constant, with ideals so high, patriotism so strong, straightness so rigid, impartiality so absolute. No sovereign in our history had proved himself more honourable, more selfless, more approachable. None had ever gained a greater knowledge of the Empire and of the lives of all sorts and conditions of men within it. He was the first to be called the Father of his People and his Empire, the first to establish an unquestionably democratic sovereignty, the first to stand as the sole link which bound together the commonwealth of nations called the British Empire by a personal tie of which the strength was nothing but the character and integrity of one man.

He was a simple, honest, good man who had loved his country and his peoples with an abounding pride and sympathy. He had worn as heavy a crown as any of his predecessors, and now in a few more hours he would lay it aside and find the peace he needed and earn the crown of a life most nobly lived and of duty greatly done.

§ 8

The sad record of those last days is fresh in the memories of those of the Family and Household who, still in mourning for Princess Victoria, watched and waited in Sandringham House. On Saturday, the 18th January, the first bulletin was given out and the nation was made aware of the grave anxiety. There was no change on Sunday the 19th. It was a day of intense frost, nearly 30 degrees. The Prince went up to London in order to see the Premier. The Duke of Kent and the Primate arrived. The Queen's calmness and courage impressed everyone.

On the Monday the news was much graver and the Council arrived. The members, the Archbishop of Canterbury, Lord Hailsham (Lord Chancellor), Mr. MacDonald (Lord President), Lord Dawson of Penn (Physician-in-Ordinary), Lord Wigram (Private Secretary) and Sir John Simon (Home Secretary), with Sir Maurice Hankey as Clerk of the Council, went up to the King's room. Small, cheerful and as simply furnished as a cabin in a big yacht, it contained the fittings specially built for his father's voyage in the *Serapis* and was filled with memorials of his travels in many lands, pictures of ships he had sailed in and of scenes he had loved. They found him sitting in a chair in his dressing-gown, with a table before him. He greeted them with a nod and his familiar smile. The formal business was swiftly done; the Lord President read the proceedings and in a firm voice the King said, " I approve." But by now his right hand had lost power, and he could not sign the order.[1] Lord Dawson, who was kneeling beside him, whispered to him that he should try to use his left hand. He said, with a return of his characteristically vigorous humour: " Why? Do you wish me to sign with both hands? " Several minutes elapsed while he strove with either hand to shape the letters and the pen turned between

[1] Setting up the necessary Council of State.

his fingers. And as he strove, looking up at the Council he said: " I am sorry to keep you waiting, Gentlemen, but I find it difficult to concentrate." He would not give up nor allow a subject to guide his hand, and at last he achieved two barely recognisable marks. When he had dismissed them with his charming smile and they came out, it was noted that some of them were in tears.

Earlier that morning, Lord Wigram had seen him for a few moments. He had heard the King whisper very feebly to him and caught the word " Empire? " and he had answered: " It is all absolutely right, Sir," and the King had smiled and slept again. The Archbishop, too, had seen him before the Council and had recalled the long years of their friendship. " More than forty years, Sir," he said, and the King had replied, " Yes, yes, a long time; more than forty years." The Archbishop asked if he might give him his blessing. And the King had answered, " Yes, do please give me your blessing," and thereafter had tried to repeat the Lord's Prayer, but sleep closed down on his mind again.

The Prince and the Duke of York came back and the Duchess of Kent arrived, and that night the Royal Family dined alone. During the Household dinner they sent in to Lord Dawson for the wording of the nine o'clock bulletin. Lord Dawson consulted Lord Wigram who sat next to him and said to the company: " I think the time is past for details." Then it was that he wrote on the back of a menu-card, which Lord Wigram handed him, the doctors' last and beautifully worded message: " The King's life is moving peacefully towards its close."

The message was heard at regular intervals during that dark and bitter night all over Britain and the Empire, solemn, inexorable, peaceful, as the tolling of a passing bell. In the King's room the Queen and his children kept vigil round his bed and, as he drew his last breaths, the Archbishop offered up the commendatory prayers. Five minutes before midnight on that Monday, the 20th January, 1936, George the Fifth of England died.

INDEX